LITTLE GIANT® ENCYCLOPEDIA

SPELLS & MAGIC

LITTLE GIANT® ENCYCLOPEDIA

SPELLS & MAGIC

THE DIAGRAM GROUP

Sterling Publishing Co., Inc.
New York

Compiled by Jane Johnson
Edited by Nancy Bailey
Designed by Lee Lawrence
Artwork by Kyri Kyriacou

Library of Congress Cataloging-in-Publication Data Available

10 9 8 7 6 5 4 3 2 1

Published by Sterling Publishing Company, Inc.
387 Park Avenue South, New York, N.Y. 10016
A Diagram Book first created by Diagram Visual Information
Limited of 195 Kentish Town Road, London NW5 2JU, England
© 1999 by Diagram Visual Information Limited
Distributed in Canada by Sterling Publishing
c/o Canadian Manda Group, 165 Dufferin Street,
Toronto, Ontario, Canada M6K 3H6
Distributed in the United Kingdom by GMC Distribution Services,
Castle Place, 166 High Street, Lewes, East Sussex, England BN7 1XU
Distributed in Australia by Capricorn Link (Australia) Pty Ltd.
P.O. Box 704, Windsor, NSW 2756, Australia

Manufactured in China

Sterling ISBN-13: 978-1-4027-4732-8
          ISBN-10: 1-4027-4732-2

FOREWORD

The *Little Giant Encyclopedia of Spells and Magic* is a
fully illustrated, comprehensive guide to magic people,
magic beings, magic rituals, magic tools, magic signs
and symbols, magic and numbers, magic and astrology,
magic and divination, alchemy and spells.

Section one provides an overview of the kinds of
people involved in magic practices and spell casting,
including witches, magicians, sorcerers, shamans, witch
doctors, voodoo priests and priestesses, and santeros,
as well as people believed to have the power of
divination, such as gypsy wise women, druids, augurs
and oracles.

The section on magic beings provides comprehensive
lists of those spirits commonly called upon by witches
and magicians to help them carry out their art. Such
beings included demons (such as the 72 spirits of
Solomon), angels, spirits and magic animals.

Many of the rituals inherent to magic and witchcraft are
included, with instructions to illustrate witch initiation
ceremonies, coven rituals, how a magic circle was cast,
a pentagram was used, and spirits conjured . Aspects of
the Black Mass, pacts with the Devil and performing
exorcisms are described.

There is an A–Z of magic tools, with descriptions of
how the Book of Spells, candles, a cauldron, a censer, a
chalice, ritual cords, drums and rattles, the magic knife,
lamp, pentacle and wand were used.

A complete range of magic signs and symbols are
provided, including astrological symbols, alphabets,

magic shapes, alchemists symbols, and most
importantly, the sigils used for invoking spirits.

Two of the most important ways numbers and magic
were used—magic squares and the use of letter and
number equivalents—are explained.

For centuries, magicians related all things to all other
things, especially the planets, the elements, the signs of
the zodiac, numbers, colors, and hours of the day.
Complete tables of correspondences are provided with
information on how these are used in modern magic
making.

The relevance of the planets and signs of the zodiac is
revealed in the section on magic and astrology.

The section on alchemy explains what alchemists do,
their equipment, symbols, concepts and processes.

Having read through these sections the readers is then
introduced to the many examples of spell-casting which
are provided. These include love spells, spells for
protection, flying spells, spells for invisibility, spells as
cures, spells for the prevention of illness, spells for
empowerment, and two short sections: evil spells and
death spells. All the spells included in this encyclopedia
are for interest only, and it is not recommended that
anyone try working these spells for themselves.

There are two glossaries: a glossary of magic and a
glossary of the spirits described throughout the book.

CONTENTS

Section 1: Magic people

Section 2: Magic beings

Section 3: Magic rituals

Section 4: Magic tools

Section 5: Magic signs and symbols

Section 6: Magic and numbers

Section 7: Correspondences

CONTENTS

Section 1
MAGIC PEOPLE

Over the centuries many people have been accused of practicing magic, witchcraft and sorcery. Perhaps the best known of these are witches, commonly portrayed as evil old women mixing potions in their big black cauldrons using unpleasant substances including bits of animals such as bats and spiders. Men, too, were accused of meddling with evil forces and were often labelled as magicians or sorcerers. Even today those who are superstitious believe that some people have magic powers (such as the seventh son of a seventh son) and stereotypes survive.

1

This section provides information about all kinds of people associated with magic, including both medieval and modern witches, magicians, sorcerers, shamans, gypsy wise women, witch doctors druids, augurs, oracles, voodoo priests and priestesses, santeros and monarchs.

WITCHES

When asked to illustrate a witch, many children draw an old woman with a hooked nose, wearing a pointed black hat and riding a broomstick, perhaps with a black cat at her side and a black cape billowing behind her. Witches are generally thought to be evil people who cast spells and mix potions in big black cauldrons, who use strange ingredients such as spiders and bats' blood, cackling and chanting as they meddle in the art of black magic. However, modern witches are far removed from this early stereotype and practice what they themselves describe as white magic, using a variety of special tools and rituals. This section describes both the popular image of the witch (developed in medieval times), as well as the modern white witches of today.

MEDIEVAL WITCHES AND WITCHCRAFT

What do witches look like?

During medieval times a witch was "...an old, weather-beaten crone, having the chin and her knees meeting for age, walking like a bow, leaning on a staff; hollow-eyed, untoothed, furrowed on her face, having her limbs trembling with the palsy, going mumbling in the streets..." (Samuel Harsnett, writing in 1599). Although men were later accused of witchcraft, too, initially witches were popularly believed to be women because women were thought to be inferior beings and therefore more susceptible to sin than men. It was also believed that, being male, the Devil would prefer female assistants.

How to identify a witch

- they are usually female
- they are ugly
- they are old
- they usually dress in black
- they often wear a conical hat
- they have a "witch's mark," a spot or teat on their body from which their familiar is permitted to draw blood

Kinds of witches

Having such terrible magic powers, it was necessary to try and classify different types of witch in order that they could be more easily identified and persecuted. Two such classifications are given here, those of William West (1594) and John Gaule (1646).

Almost anyone claiming to be able to divine the future was considered to be a witch, no matter what was used for prophesying. If you used water (hydromancy), fire (pyromancy), air (aeromancy), or the entrails of animals (haruspicy) you risked being accused of witchcraft.

Types of witch according to William West

1 Divinators, anyone who can locate lost or stolen things.
2 Enchanters and charmers, those using words, images, or herbs to bring about their own ends.
3 Jugglers, and anyone capable of curing disease quickly by adorning the body with words in the form of charms and spells.
4 Magicians, people who meddle with things outside nature (such as attempting to conjure ghosts).
5 Soothsaying wizards, anyone who can foretell the future and raise evil spirits using devices such as crystal stones or rings.
6 Witches, women in league with the Devil who act for their own evil purposes and who conform to the stereotypical notion of a witch (such as riding on a broomstick).

Types of witch according to John Gaule

1 Diviners, also known as gypsies or fortune-telling witches.
2 Astrologers, witches who engage in star-gazing and prognosticating.
3 Calculating witches, also known as chanting or canting witches, who use signs and numbers.
4 Witches who poison.
5 Witches who are exorcists and conjurers.
6 Witches who use gastromancy.
7 Witches with special scientific, artistic or speculative powers.
8 Necromancers.

Names for witches

Medieval synonyms for witch included:

Synonym	meaning
bacularia	riding on a stick
fascinatrix	use of the evil eye
femina	wise woman
incantator	worker of charms
lamia	bloodsucking night monster
magus	wise man
maleficius	worker of evil against men, beasts and property
maliarda	working evil
pixidaria	using magic ointment
strix	nocturnal bird
veneficia	poisoner
vir sortilegi	magician

What magic powers do witches have?

Witches were believed to have a host of magic powers, including the following:

- they have the ability to fly by riding on a broomstick, cleft stick, demon, or simply by themselves (**a**)
- they are able to cast evil spells, charms and hexes
- they know the recipe for love potions (**b**)
- they can turn themselves into wolves or hares
- they can damage a person's house or property (**c**)
- by stirring their own urine, a small hole filled with water or a pond they can call up foul weather (**d**), strong enough to wreck ships at sea or destroy crops
- they can wreck marriages
- they can cause impotence and sterility in men
- they can cause barrenness or stillbirths in women
- they can conjure demons or the Devil himself
- they can bring disease, insanity, accidents and death on anyone, perhaps using a wax effigy of the person
- they can injure cattle or cause their milk to dry up
- they have the ability to fascinate (give people the "evil eye")
- they can leave a room by way of the chimney or a keyhole
- they can turn people into beasts
- they can make themselves invisible

What other things do witches do?

- they use animal parts to concoct lotions and potions (**a**)
- they eat babies
- they disinter buried bodies in order to use them for death-spells
- they dance and sing bawdy songs (**b**)
- they are generally members of the local community and meet regularly in a local group known as a coven
- novice witches undergo an initiation ceremony
- they repudiate the Christian faith (**c**)

In what way do witches repudiate the Christian faith?

- they worship the Devil
- they sell their souls to the Devil by making a pact with him
- they serve the Devil's purposes and are human emissaries of hell (in the same way that the clergy are human emissaries of heaven)
- they copulate with the Devil
- they trample on crosses (**d**)
- they spit at the time of elevation
- they break fast on fasting days
- they fast on Sundays
- they go to sabbats to meet other witches, demons and the Devil himself

Witches and flying

It was once popularly believed that witches had the ability to fly, either by themselves or with the aid of a broomstick (also called a besom). One of the reasons it was believed that witches killed babies was that infant flesh was thought to have magical powers and that it was the principle ingredient of "Devil's grease," (also known as unguentum sabbati or witches' salve) a black- or repulsive green-colored ointment used by witches to enable them to fly. The ointment was smeared on the witch's broomstick or body, a ritual commonly performed before setting out for the sabbat.

Some of the ingredients believed to have been used in making Devil's grease

- aconite
- baby's fat
- bat's blood
- belladonna
- hashish
- lizards
- opium
- soot
- spiders
- toads

Today, aconite is known to cause excessive excitement and belladonna to produce delirium. The use of such drugs may have caused some people to believe they had actually been able to fly.

Medieval white witches

During medieval times some people offered a variety of services to the local community and were consulted on medical matters when traditional methods of cure failed. Such people were believed to be "white" witches, practicing "good" magic.

Magical services offered by medieval white witches

- divination of the future
- creation of love potions (**a**)
- tracing lost or stolen property
- detection of thieves
- treatments for sick animals (**b**)
- remedies for common complaints such as headaches, warts, rheumatism and impotence
- protection of households from lightning
- conjuring rain in order to promote the growth of crops (**c**)
- promise of fair winds to sailors
- counter-measures to spells cast by other witches.

Magic methods used by medieval white witches

Many methods were used by white witches to relieve common ailments, including the following:

- Wax figures (**a**) were sometimes made of the sufferer and used as part of the healing treatment.
- An ailment might be "transferred" from a client to an animal or a tree (**b**).
- An ailment might be linked to a piece of food (**c**) so that when the food rotted, so too did the ailment.
- Small animals were ritualistically sacrificed (**d**) to placate the spirits causing an ailment.
- Knots were tied in bits of thread (**e**) and these buried in cemeteries, another method of relieving bodily ills.
- Patients might be sung back to health (**f**).

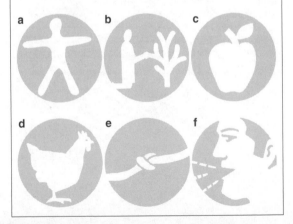

a   b   c

d   e   f

Warlocks

In medieval times male witches were often referred to
as warlocks and many people still use the term in this
way. However, modern practitioners of witchcraft do
not use the term, preferring to call themselves witches
whether they are male or female.

Although the majority of witches were once thought to
be women, warlocks were believed to have the same
powers and were therefore considered just as
dangerous.

A warlock going to sabbat

MODERN WITCHES AND WITCHCRAFT

In modern witchcraft there are many different sects, and it is therefore difficult to provide a global definition of a modern witch's beliefs and practices. Witches live all over the world, some by themselves, practicing alone (hedgewitches), others joining together in covens — some belonging to the religious and magical system known as Wicca. Some covens do not accept men; in America there is a 'radical faerie' group comprising gay males, and in Australia Wymyn's' Wicca is for lesbians. Overall, they claim to use their abilities to do good and are therefore often termed "white" witches.

What do modern witches look like?

- They can be male or female and conform to no particular stereotype.
- They may be young or old.
- They may be beautiful or ugly.
- They do not wear special clothes.

What do modern witches do?

- They despise evil.
- They practice their craft for the good of mankind
- they worship nature.
- Many worship the Earth Mother (also known as the Great Mother) and the Horned God, a fertility god usually known by the Roman name Dianus or Janu. They deny there is any link between the Horned God and the Devil.
- Some claim to be inheritors of an ancient religious tradition.
- They may have a close affinity with animals but refute the notion that their pets are "familiars."
- They use rituals in order to help raise their magical powers.
- They cast spells.
- They rely on their powers of instinct.
- Many believe in reincarnation.
- Most celebrate the eight seasonal festivals, or "sabbats."
- Many undertake a heirarchical initiation procedure.
- Some conduct their ceremonies naked ("sky-clad").
- They use magic tools.
- They may use amulets and charms.
- Most use chants.
- Some use divination and some claim to be clairvoyant.
- Some use astral projection.
- Many use visualization techniques.

MAGICIANS

The typical image of a magician is someone characterized by the figure of Merlin, a wizened old man in flowing robes, wearing a pointed hat covered in stars; someone who can work magic by casting spells, with a knowledge of things greater than the rest of us, someone who may wave a magic wand and work miracles.

Although many of us imagine the wise old magician to be essentially good — and perhaps a little eccentric — in medieval times, anyone fitting this description would probably have been labelled a witch or sorcerer and suffered the consequences.

Today, a man who practices magic for the good of mankind may be thought of as a white witch or white magician, whereas a man who practices magic with evil intent may be considered a black magician, more properly called a sorcerer.

One of the distinctions sometimes made between a witch and a magician was that magicians studied the Kabbalah (also known as the Cabala, Kabala or

Qabalah), an ancient Hebrew mystical doctrine, whereas witches did not. In practice, many witches may today draw on aspects of the Kabbalah for use in their own lives.

Characteristics of a magician

Listed here some traits that may characterize a white magician.

- Traditionally they had to be someone of pure character and unblemished morals who would abstain from animal food and women, and who must never touch dead bodies.
- Their underlying purpose is one of spiritual development.
- They work alone, without the aid of other magicians and do not need to join a group in the way some witches join covens.
- They study the Kabbalah.
- Their magic involves much ceremony and planning.
- They are particularly scholarly, and understand the universal laws of nature.
- They use different methods of divination.
- They can evoke magical entities.
- They perform exorcisms.
- They may undertake healing practices.
- They do not flaunt their magical powers.
- They use special tools.
- They are opposed to sorcerers.

SORCERERS

Most people picture a sorcerer as being male, an evil person, such as a black witch or black magician, who dresses in black and practices black magic.

In medieval times, a sorcerer could be almost anyone — a gypsy, a necromancer (someone who calls up the dead), an intellectual or learned man, anyone who practiced science or set up a laboratory. Sorcerers were believed to be the priests of Satan and were assumed to attend sabbats along with witches in order to worship their evil god.

Today sorcerers (sometimes called black witches or black magicians) are believed to be people who work magic for the purpose of harming others, and may use wax dolls to inflict pain, or evoke deities or spirits in order to ask their assistance in evil matters.

Characteristics of a sorcerer

- They use magic for evil purposes.
- They generally work alone.
- They often evoke demons.
- They use magic tools.
- They may worship the Devil.
- They are generally male.

SHAMANS

The Eskimos, Maoris, Mongolians, Polynesians, and American Indians believe in the abilities of shamans, people who have magic powers resulting from contact with the supernatural, often through dreams and trances. Because of their ability to cure the sick, shamans are also sometimes called medicine men and

A Samoyed shaman traveling to the world of the dead on the back of a bear, beating a magic drum

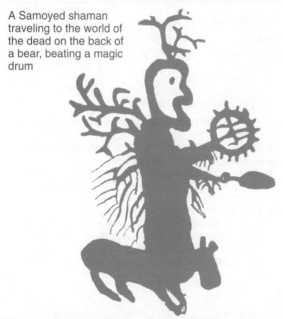

are usually—but not exclusively—male. Their powers
are often believed to be hereditary and their assistants
ancestral spirits. Many have to undergo initiation
ceremonies before fully realizing their powers.
Members of the societies in which shamans operate
believe that the human soul can leave its body and that
this results in illness. Shamans alone can enter the spirit
world and recapture the soul, returning it to the sick
individuals, thereby restoring health.

Functions of a shaman

- to protect individuals from hostile supernatural
  influences
- to heal
- to divine the future

Magic abilities of a shaman

- to function in both the ordinary world and the spirit
  world
- to exorcise evil spirits (and therefore cure illness)
- to evoke the help of good spirits
- while in the spirit world, to see the future, to see
  spirits, to identify disease and metamorphose into
  a spirit and fly through the air
- to mediate with birds, animals and trees
- to implant a spirit in an object (known as a fetish)
  and give it to his patient for additional protection
- to devise protective amulets which are given to
  patients to wear to prevent further attacks by evil
  spirits

Non-magic abilities of the shaman

- to prepare and use herbal remedies
- to set broken bones

What else might a shaman do?

- blow tobacco smoke over a sick person, as tobacco is believed to have magical properties
- suck on the body of a sick person to locate the object causing the illness, then spitting it out
- perform sacrifices
- take part in frantic dancing and drumming in order to induce a trance state
- some take hallucinogens to help induce the trance state
- sometimes they join together to form an organization known as a curing society, such as the False Face Society of the Iroquois

The shaman must obtain a guardian spirit (also known as a power animal, tutelary spirit, totemic animal or familiar). This may be done by the vision quest, an all-night vigil outdoors at night. The guardian spirit—which may appear as an animal or human—is invited to enter the shaman's body and protects him from illness and the unfriendly forces in the lowerworld. These spirits change over time as the needs of the shaman change.

GYPSY WISE WOMEN

Gypsies are Romany peoples, travelers often portrayed
as living in caravans and wandering from place to
place, stopping to earn money whenever a fair or circus
was in town. Many of us hold the image of a veiled
woman calling herself Madam Za Za or the like, who,
crouched over a crystal ball in a darkened tent, would
divine our future providing we crossed her palm with
silver. Romany people call fortune telling *dukkerin* or
dukkering, and a crystal ball was certainly used by
them, handed down from generation to generation.
One of the reasons gypsy women may have been
credited with having magic powers was their rich
knowledge of herbalism. To Romany people, the
drabarni were the herb or wise women of the clan.
Another reason why gypsy women may have been
credited with magic powers is that the dancing bears
which often accompanied circus troupes were believed
by some to be familiars.

Magic abilities of gypsy wise women

- wart charming
- the preparation of herbal potions
- the ability to heal horses by magic means
- the preparation of aphrodisiacs
- divination by
  - palmistry
  - crystal gazing
  - tasseography (reading tea leaves)
  - second sight

WITCH DOCTORS

Also called jujumen, obeahmen, root doctors, conjure men and leaf doctors, the witch doctor is a priest and physician called upon by African tribal members and followers of religions such as vodoun, Santería and macumba. General witch-doctor practitioners are known as ngangas and use their power only for good. Their job is to protect people from witch-induced sickness.

Magic abilities of a witch doctor

- to divine the witch responsible for causing a person's sickness
- to send a ngozi (grudge-bearing spirit) to an evil witch
- to cure patients by casting counter spells
- to divine the future by casting the hakata, bones, dice, seeds or shells which are scattered and the patterns then interpreted
- the use of animal sacrifices, chants and charms

Non-magic abilities of the witch doctor

- the use of poisons
- the preparation of herbal remedies

DRUIDS

Druids were once portrayed as a group of people with powers to divine the future and perform magic. They were in fact a class of Celts, peoples of ancient Europe, who acted as judges, lawmakers and priests. Their attempts to divine the future involved using the remains of sacrificed animals and the flights of birds. They were wise men who acted as soothsayers and undertook many ritual acts. Druids today are active in the British Isles and claim to practice ancient Druidism. They use the Ogam (Ogham) script as a means of divination, an ancient alphabet, described in detail by Robert Graves in *The White Goddess*. They stress the importance of self-development.

AUGURS AND ORACLES

Augurs were aristocrats living in ancient Rome who interpreted natural signs for government officials. They dressed in a white robe with scarlet stripes and a purple border (known as a trabea) and their advice was sought on all important matters. They carried a lituus, a staff bent at the top and free from knots. Originally there were only three augurs, but by the time of Julius Caesar there were sixteen.

Oracles were priests or priestesses of ancient Greece, the most important of whom was the Pythia, the priestess of Delphi. The Greeks believed that Apollo spoke through the Pythia when she sometimes went into a trance and spoke hysterically.

Methods of divination used by augurs

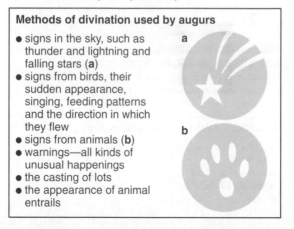

- signs in the sky, such as thunder and lightning and falling stars (**a**)
- signs from birds, their sudden appearance, singing, feeding patterns and the direction in which they flew
- signs from animals (**b**)
- warnings—all kinds of unusual happenings
- the casting of lots
- the appearance of animal entrails

VOODOO PRIESTS AND PRIESTESSES

Vodoun (also known as voodoo) is an African religion practiced by many millions of people, developed in Haiti but also practiced in other West Indian countries, Brazil and the United States. Voodooists believe that the world is populated by gods, demons and spirits of the dead, and that gods communicate with devotees through spirit possession during special ceremonies. Voodooists themselves cast spells and wear magic charms to protect them from evil spirits; sometimes they use a doll into which they stick pins which they believe will bring harm to the person in whose image the doll has been made. Sometimes followers require the assistance of a priest or priestess.

A voodoo priest is known as houngan (papa or papa-loa) and the priestess as mambo (manman or mam). They act as intermediaries to summon the loa, one of many Vodoun gods, using an asson, a ritual rattle made from a type of squash, inside of which are dried stones and serpent vertebrae. A houngan involved in black magic is known as a bakor or boko, "one who serves the loa with both hands."

Function of the houngan and mambo

- to divine the future
- to heal
- to be a spiritual leader
- to play music
- to act as a psychologist

SANTEROS

Santeros are priests and priestesses belonging to a religion similar to vodoun, known as Santería. Babalawo, the highest order of priest, has power to divine the future, punish the unjust and heal the sick. All babalawos are male and have almost endless powers, as they are believed to be superior magicians. Many sacrifice animals and black magician babalawos are said to use cats and dogs as ingredients of their magic spells.

One of the methods of divination used by babalawos is reading the seashells. Priests who specialize in this form of divination are known as italeros.

Some functions of the santeros

- to divine the future
- to heal
- to punish the unjust
- to cast counter spells (known as ebbos)
- to prescribe a protective talisman (known as a resguardo)
- to reveal a new-born infant's magic plant, birthstone and animal
- to smoke out evil spirits by burning garlic skins

Santeros who practice black magic are known as myomberos, or "black witches." They specialize in necromancy, revenge, and the destruction of human life in general. Myomberos undergo an initiation rite and must make their own nganga, a cauldron which holds all their magical powers and potions.

MONARCHS

In the Middle Ages, tubercular disorders were commonplace and showed up especially in the glands of the neck (an illness known as scrofula). For centuries, European monarchs were believed to possess special healing powers and undertook the ritual of touching the sick on the head in order to cure them. The disease became known as King's Evil and the ritual was called "touching for King's Evil."

The first English monarch to perform this task was Edward the Confessor, said to have received the ability to heal through touch as a divine gift which he passed on to subsequent rulers. On Easter Sunday, 1686, Louis XIV of France touched 1,600 sufferers, and during his reign Charles II is believed to have touched a total of 92,107 people.

The last monarch to touch sufferers was Queen Anne, who reigned until 1714.

OTHER MAGIC PEOPLE

According to Western superstition, many ordinary people are believed to have magical powers. Some of the more common are listed here.

Ordinary people with magic abilities

- The seventh son of a seventh son is believed to have great healing powers.
- Blacksmiths were traditionally believed to possess the "horseman's word," a secret word used to calm horses. Children were often held over the blackmith's anvil (believed to be particularly magic) in order to cure them of illness.
- Women whose maiden names and married names are the same (e.g., a woman called Jenny Smith marrying a man called Tom Smith). Such women are believed by some to have special healing powers, and to be able to cure ailments such as whooping cough.
- Women who marry two husbands each with the same surname.
- People with significant names (e.g., a married couple called Joseph and Mary). They, too, are believed to have special healing powers.
- For those who are superstitious, chimney sweeps, sailors, hunchbacks, dwarves and prostitutes may be particularly lucky.

Section 2
MAGIC BEINGS

There are so many magic beings that it is impossible to cover them all in a book of this size. Included here are those most commonly associated with magic and the occult, such as spirits. Witches and magicians called upon spirits when they needed assistance with their work. They did this by conjuration (see the section on Magic Rituals). Some spirits were good and benevolent, others were evil and malevolent. Which kinds of spirits you call on depended on the kind of magic you were performing. This section includes information about both kinds of spirits—the bad (commonly known as demons) and the good (such as

2

angels). Also included is information about other kinds of magic beings, such as animals, and an A–Z of creatures that may or may not be spirits but which are associated with magic in various parts of the world. Readers interested in finding out more about magic creatures in general are advised to consult some of the many books on religion and folklore. Many beings are actual deities or creatures of myth and legend which may have special powers, but which are not necessarily associated with spells and magic.

DEMONS

Just as a white magician may wish to call upon good
spirits, a black magician may wish to call on evil ones.
In Western occultism the demons from Hell are
counterparts to the angels of Heaven and are sometimes
referred to as infernal spirits. All are believed to be
God-haters, and some are more evil than others. Some
people believe demons are human souls who lived evil
incarnations on earth, others suggest they are fallen
angels.

Demons may appear to magicians and sorcerers in a
variety of guises, the most popular being human or
half-human. They may also appear as animals,
particularly cats, owls, dragons and goats.

What do demons do?

- specific demons may attack specific parts of the body, including the mind
- they cause nightmares
- they cause unpleasant things to happen
- they cause men and women to behave unnaturally
- they cause men and women to undertake evil acts
- they play wicked jokes on people
- they may possess a person
- they may obsess a person
- some are helpful

Identifying a demon
- they may be black and repulsive
- they may be shapeless but may borrow the form of other beings
- they may be present in thousands or even billions
- they inhabit the earth and atmosphere

Demonic possession

During the Middle Ages it was commonly believed that almost anyone could be possessed by a demon and that this resulted in strange behavior (listed here) and blasphemy. Such possession was facilitated by witchcraft and yet treated by exorcism—those possessed were not treated as witches as they were believed believed to be victims rather than true perpetrators of evil. Only the very virtuous were immune from such possession. Today it is thought that the behavior of people believed to be characteristic of demonic possession was, in fact, evidence of mental disturbance such as hysteria and schizophrenia, or even epilepsy.

Stages of demonic possession

Persons who are being overcome by a demon might respond in the following way:
1 their face and body may begin to contort
2 their expression may become fiendish
3 their voice may become gruff
4 they are likely to shriek invective against God
5 they are equally likely to speak absolute gibberish

In certain cults (such as voodoo), possession is regarded as a favorable condition and is deliberately induced by drumming and dancing. Self-induced possession represents a willingness to form a link with the spirit world, characteristic of shamanism.

Characteristics of a possessed person

In addition to displaying blasphemous and obscene speech and actions, a possessed person might:
- foam at the mouth
- make animal noises
- perform feats of superhuman strength
- vomit strange objects such as hair, bark, stones, pottery, needles

---

Demonic obsession
This occurs when a person is harassed by the Devil and his agents without the demons actually entering the person's body. Saint Anthony suffered from such a complaint, although it is today thought that the demons he believed to be trying to tempt him were hallucinations brought about by self-infliction or even from eating bread infected with the fungus *Claviceps purpurea,* which contains lysergic acid from which the hallucinatory drug LSD is made.

Numbers of demons
The Egyptian Book of the Dead claims there are 4,601,200 demons. According to Jean Weir, a sixteenth-century physician, there were 7,409,127 infernal spirits commanded by 79 princes. Others have suggested that

there are 1,758,064,176 demons organized into six legions, each legion having 66 cohorts, each cohort with 666 companies, each company comprising 6666 individuals.

The number of demons inhabiting the universe also varies according to different cultures. For example, Eskimos believe that every single thing in nature has a guardian spirit, each of which is malignant. The Koreans believe there are thousands of billions of demons who fill every corner of the globe; they are in all parts of the house, in the air, and everywhere.

Incubi and succubi

These are demons that are half human, half animal in appearance, sent by the Devil to seduce men and women, the most susceptible of whom are those who lead lives of celibacy. During the medieval period, if you were found guilty of having had intercourse with

Girl and an
incubus

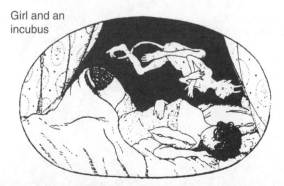

one of these creatures, you had committed the sin of bestiality and were doomed to eternity in Hell. An incubus is a demon that mates with sleeping women; a succubus is a demon that mates with sleeping men. Princess Nahemal (Lilith) is believed to be head of the succubi.

Merlin was rumored to be the product of a coupling between a woman and an incubus, as was the Roman King, Servius Tullius. It was believed that the same demon could act as either an incubus or succubus and that witches were sent such creatures by the Devil. Incubi and succubi were also sent to people who were not witches, to try and conscript their souls for the Devil.

Satan

Of all demons, Satan is believed to be the worst. He was believed to be worshipped by medieval witches and appeared at their sabbats, often portrayed with the taloned feet of a bird of prey, the claws of an alligator and a second face where his genitals would be. He was also depicted with three horns, one of them sometimes twisted into a curl. His methods of gaining control over an individual include

THE SIX SUPERIOR SPIRITS OF HELL

Name	Rank	Functions
Lucifuge	Prime Minister	• Has power over all treasures on earth.
Satanachia	Commanding-general	• Has power over all women and girls.
Fleuretty	Lieutenant-General	• Can perform any deed during the night.
Sargatanas	Brigadier	• Confers invisibility. • Transports anything anywhere. • Opens all locks. • Teaches lovemaking.
Nebiros	Field-Marshal and Inspector-General	A necromancer. • Teaches the properties of metals, minerals, vegetables, animals. • Can do evil to anyone. • Discerns the location of the Hand of Glory.
Agaliarept	General	• Discerns secrets. • Unveils mysteries.

demonic possession, sending an incubi or succubi, or getting a person to make a pact with him.

The six superior spirits of Hell

Although there is no agreed heirarchy for the demons of Hell, it has been suggested that there are six superior spirits (see box, p. 47) who between them command many thousands of demons.

The 72 spirits of Solomon

According to legend, King Solomon of Israel shut up 72 rebellious kings into a brass vessel, throwing it into a deep lake. In an attempt to locate great treasure, the Babylonians broke open the vessel, allowing the demons to escape. The Babylonians then worshiped Belial, believed to be the most powerful demon.

In *Lemegeton*, a text incorrectly attributed to King Solomon, each demon is presented by a sigil seal (see the section on Magic Signs and Symbols for these) that can be used to evoke the demon (described in the section on Magic Rituals) and request its help.

Using the tables showing the spirits of Solomon

On the pages that follow you will find a table listing the spirits of Solomon in alphabetical order, detailing the form in which they appear and their principal functions. This information can be used for evoking demons. To do this, read the general rules for evocation in the section on Magic Rituals. Next, look through the tables that follow and find those demons that might be appropriate to your needs. For example, you may require the powers of invisibility— in which case you might pick Asmoday, Baal, Balam, etc. Or, perhaps you need to locate hidden treasure, so may prefer to summon Amy, Andromalius, Asmoday or Cimeries, etc.

Read also about the appearance of the demons. If you have a weak constitution you may prefer to evoke only those demons who appear in human form, such as Agares, Andromalius, Berithor or Cimeries. Remember, however, some demons can be asked to appear in human form — such as Amsuscias, Amy, Andrealphus and Caim — but usually manifest themselves as something else first.

WHERE A DEMON IS PARTICULARLY DANGEROUS, WARNINGS ARE GIVEN IN CAPITALS UNDER THE "FUNCTION" COLUMN.

THE 72 SPIRITS OF SOLOMON
(Alternative names given in brackets)

Name	Appearance
Agares	Appears as an old man riding a crocodile with a hawk on his wrist.
Aini (Aym) (Haborym)	Appears as a handsome man with three heads: one serpent, one a man with two stars on his forehead, and one a cat. He rides a viper and carries a lighted torch.
Allocen (Alloien) (Allocer)	Appears as a soldier with a redenned lion's face with flaming eyes. Riding a horse, he has a loud, hoarse voice.
Amduscias	Appears as a unicorn but can assume human form on request.

Functions	**Image**
• teaches all languages • causes earthquakes • brings back runaways • destroys dignities	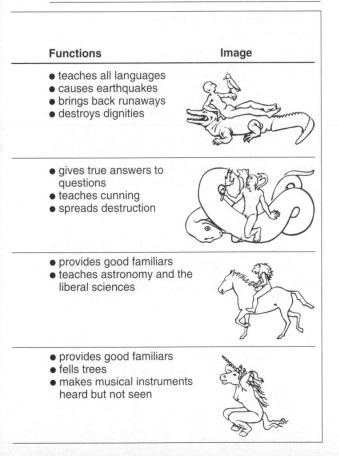
• gives true answers to questions • teaches cunning • spreads destruction	
• provides good familiars • teaches astronomy and the liberal sciences	
• provides good familiars • fells trees • makes musical instruments heard but not seen	

THE 72 SPIRITS OF SOLOMON
(continued)

Name	Appearance
Amon	Appears as a wolf with a serpent's head, or as a human with dog's teeth, or as a human with a raven's head. Vomits flame.
Amy	Appears first as a flaming fire, then as a man.
Andras	Appears as an angel with a raven's head, riding a black wolf and carrying a sharp, bright sword.
Andrealphus	Appears first as a loud peacock, then in human form.

Functions	Image
• discerns the past • foretells the future • reconciles friends and foes • procures love	
• provides good familiars • teaches astronomy and the liberal sciences • can discern treasures hidden by spirits	
A HIGHLY DANGEROUS DEMON WHO CAN KILL THE MAGICIAN AND HIS ASSISTANTS	
• teaches astronomy and geometry and everything concerning measurement • can transform men into birds	

THE 72 SPIRITS OF SOLOMON
(continued)

Name	Appearance
Andromalius	Appears as a man holding a serpent.
Asmoday (Sydonay)	Appears with three heads (a bull, a man and a ram), with a serpent's tail and goose's feet. Appears riding a dragon and carrying a lance and banner. Vomits fire.
Astaroth	Appears an angel riding a dragon, holding a viper in his right hand. Has stinking breath.
Baal	Appears with human head or the head of a toad or the head of a cat or with three heads: one human, one of a cat, and one of a toad. Speaks with a hoarse voice.

Functions	image
• locates hidden treasure • reveals thieves • returns stolen goods • discovers all wickedness	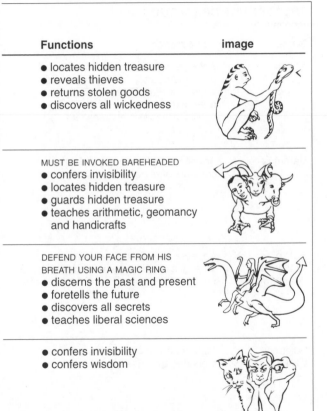
MUST BE INVOKED BAREHEADED • confers invisibility • locates hidden treasure • guards hidden treasure • teaches arithmetic, geomancy and handicrafts	
DEFEND YOUR FACE FROM HIS BREATH USING A MAGIC RING • discerns the past and present • foretells the future • discovers all secrets • teaches liberal sciences	
• confers invisibility • confers wisdom	

THE 72 SPIRITS OF SOLOMON
(continued)

Name	Appearance
Balam	Appears with three heads (a bull, a man and a ram), flaming eyes, and a serpent's tail. Rides an angry bear and carries a hawk on his wrist. Speaks in a hoarse voice.
Barbatos	Appears with four kings and three companies of troops.
Bathin (Bathym) (Marthim)	Appears as a strong man with a serpent's tail, riding a pale horse.
Beleth (Byleth)	Appears riding a pale horse preceded by musicians.

Functions	**Image**
• discerns the past and present • foretells the future • confers invisibility • teaches wit	
• discerns the past • foretells the future • reveals treasure hidden by enchantment • reconciles friends • teaches all sciences	
• reveals the value of herbs • reveals the value of precious stones • can transport men between countries	
FURIOUS WHEN FIRST SUMMONED. COMMAND INTO A TRIANGLE OR CIRCLE USING A HAZEL WAND POINTED TO THE SOUTHEAST. WEAR A SILVER RING ON THE MIDDLE FINGER OF YOUR LEFT HAND. • procures love	

THE 72 SPIRITS OF SOLOMON
(continued)

Name	Appearance
Belial	Appears as an angel on a chariot of fire and speaks with a pleasant voice.
Berith (Beal) (Berith) (Bofi) (Bolfry)	Appears as a soldier dressed in red, wearing a red crown and riding a red horse. Has a clear and persuasive voice.
Bifrons	Appears as a monster but if requested can assume human form.
Botis	Appears as a viper carrying a sharp sword but if requested will assume human form (with large teeth and horns).

Functions	Image
MUST BE MADE OFFERINGS AND SACRIFICES • provides good familiars • causes favors of friends and foes	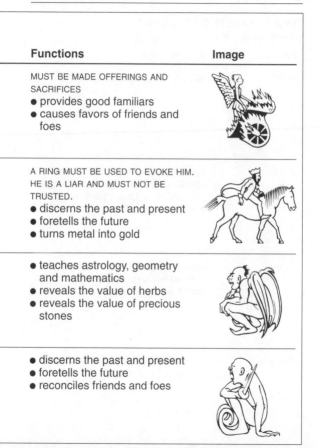
A RING MUST BE USED TO EVOKE HIM. HE IS A LIAR AND MUST NOT BE TRUSTED. • discerns the past and present • foretells the future • turns metal into gold	
• teaches astrology, geometry and mathematics • reveals the value of herbs • reveals the value of precious stones	
• discerns the past and present • foretells the future • reconciles friends and foes	

THE 72 SPIRITS OF SOLOMON
(continued)

Name	Appearance
Buer	Appears as five-legged starfish
Bune	Appears as a dragon with three heads: one of a dog, one of a griffin and one of a man. Has a pleasant voice.
Caim	Appears as a thrush or blackbird then later assumes the form of a man holding a sharp sword.
Cimeries	Appears as a soldier on a black horse.

Functions	Image
APPEARS WHEN THE SUN IS IN SAGITTARIUS • provides good familiars • heals all diseases • teaches philosophy and logic • reveals the value of herbs	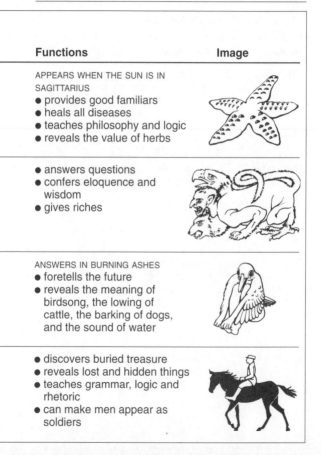
• answers questions • confers eloquence and wisdom • gives riches	
ANSWERS IN BURNING ASHES • foretells the future • reveals the meaning of birdsong, the lowing of cattle, the barking of dogs, and the sound of water	
• discovers buried treasure • reveals lost and hidden things • teaches grammar, logic and rhetoric • can make men appear as soldiers	

THE 72 SPIRITS OF SOLOMON
(continued)

Name	Appearance
Dantalian	Appears as a man with many faces (of men and women), and holds a book in his right hand.
Decarabia	Appears as a star in a pentacle but on request can assume human form.
Eligor	Appears as a knight carrying a lance, banner and scepter.
Flauros	Appears as a leopard but on request can assume the form of a man (with fiery eyes).

Functions	**Image**
• knows all human thoughts and can change them at will • procures love • teaches all arts and sciences	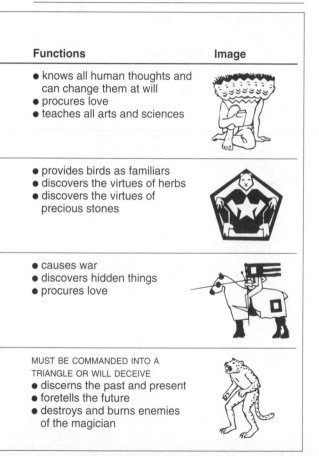
• provides birds as familiars • discovers the virtues of herbs • discovers the virtues of precious stones	
• causes war • discovers hidden things • procures love	
MUST BE COMMANDED INTO A TRIANGLE OR WILL DECEIVE • discerns the past and present • foretells the future • destroys and burns enemies of the magician	

THE 72 SPIRITS OF SOLOMON
(continued)

Name	Appearance
Focalor	Appears as a man with the wings of a griffin.
Foras (Forcas)	Appears as a strong man.
Forneus	Appears as a sea monster.
Furcas	Appears as a cruel old man with hoary hair and a long beard, riding a horse and carrying a spear.

Functions	Image
<ul><li>has power over the winds and sea</li><li>drowns men</li><li>sinks warships</li></ul>	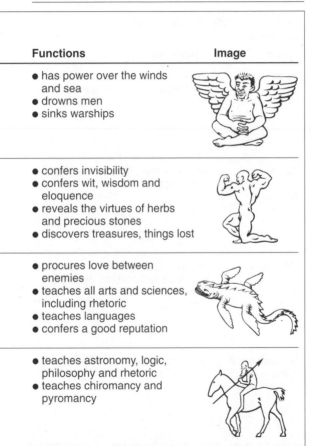
<ul><li>confers invisibility</li><li>confers wit, wisdom and eloquence</li><li>reveals the virtues of herbs and precious stones</li><li>discovers treasures, things lost</li></ul>	
<ul><li>procures love between enemies</li><li>teaches all arts and sciences, including rhetoric</li><li>teaches languages</li><li>confer a good reputation</li></ul>	
<ul><li>teaches astronomy, logic, philosophy and rhetoric</li><li>teaches chiromancy and pyromancy</li></ul>	

THE 72 SPIRITS OF SOLOMON
(continued)

Name	Appearance
Furfur	Appears first as a stag with a fiery tail then as an angel. Speaks with a hoarse voice.
Gaap (Tap) (Goap)	Appears as a human preceded by four kings.
Gamygyn	Appears first as a small horse or ass, then as a human. Speaks hoarsely.
Glasyalabolas (Caacrinolaas) (Caassimola)	Appears as a dog with the wings of a griffin.

Functions	Image
WILL NOT OPEN HIS MOUTH UNTIL WITHIN THE TRIANGLE • raises thunder, lightning and wind • procures love between a man and wife	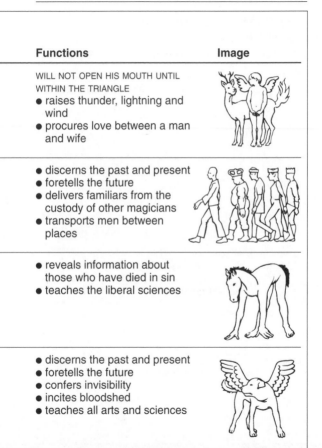
• discerns the past and present • foretells the future • delivers familiars from the custody of other magicians • transports men between places	
• reveals information about those who have died in sin • teaches the liberal sciences	
• discerns the past and present • foretells the future • confers invisibility • incites bloodshed • teaches all arts and sciences	

THE 72 SPIRITS OF SOLOMON
(continued)

Name	Appearance
Gomory	Appears as a beautiful woman with a crown, sometimes riding a camel.
Gusion (Gusayn)	Appears as a cynocephalus.
Hagenti	Appears as a bull with the wings of a griffin but on request can assume human form.
Halpas	Appears as a stockdove, speaking with a hoarse voice.

Functions	Image
• discerns the past and present • foretells the future • discovers hidden treasure • procures the love of women, especially girls	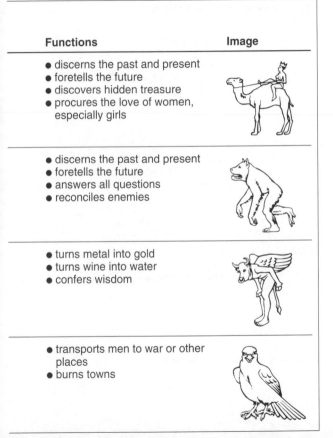
• discerns the past and present • foretells the future • answers all questions • reconciles enemies	
• turns metal into gold • turns wine into water • confers wisdom	
• transports men to war or other places • burns towns	

THE 72 SPIRITS OF SOLOMON
(continued)

Name	Appearance
Ipos (Ipes) (Ayporos) (Aypeos)	Appears as an angel with a lion's head, a hare's tail, and the feet of a goose.
Lerajie	Appears as an archer, wearing green, and carrying a bow and quiver.
Malpas	Appears as a a crow, but will appear in human form on request. Has a hoarse voice.
Marbas (Barbas)	Appears first as a lion, and then as a human.

Functions	**Image**
• discerns the past • foretells the future • confers wit and courage	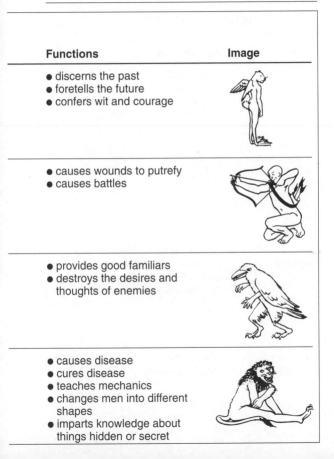
• causes wounds to putrefy • causes battles	
• provides good familiars • destroys the desires and thoughts of enemies	
• causes disease • cures disease • teaches mechanics • changes men into different shapes • imparts knowledge about things hidden or secret	

THE 72 SPIRITS OF SOLOMON
(continued)

Name	Appearance
Marchosias	Appears as a wolf, with the wings of a griffin and and the tail of a dragon. On request, will assume human form. Breathes fire.
Morax (Foraii) (Forfax)	Appears as a bull with a human head.
Murmur	Appears as a soldier wearing a crown, riding a griffin, preceded by two monsters sounding trumpets.
Naberius (Cerberus)	Appears as a crowing cock, and speaks hoarsely.

Functions	Image
• gives true answers to all questions	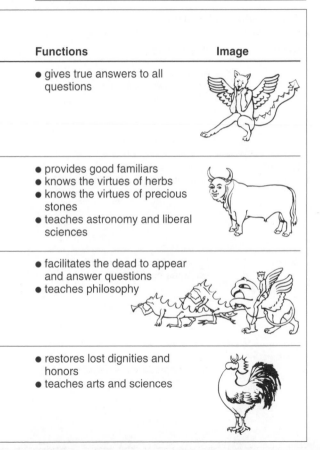
• provides good familiars • knows the virtues of herbs • knows the virtues of precious stones • teaches astronomy and liberal sciences	
• facilitates the dead to appear and answer questions • teaches philosophy	
• restores lost dignities and honors • teaches arts and sciences	

THE 72 SPIRITS OF SOLOMON
(continued)

Name	Appearance
Orias	Appears as a lion bestride a horse, carrying two huge hissing snakes in his right hand.
Orobas	Appears as a horse, but will assume human form on request.
Ose	Appears first as a leopard, then assumes human form.
Paimon	Appears wearing a crown, seated on a dromedary preceded by musicians. Has a roaring voice.

Functions	Image
• transforms men • teaches about the planets	
• discerns the past and present • foretells the future • protects against temptation from other spirits	
• changes men into any shape • makes men insane for about an hour • teaches liberal sciences • gives true answers to questions.	
• provides good familiars • gives the magician power over other men • teaches arts and sciences	

THE 72 SPIRITS OF SOLOMON
(continued)

Name	Appearance
Phoenix	Appears as a phoenix, but will assume human shape on request. Sings in a child's voice.
Procel (Pucel)	Appears as an angel.
Purson (Curson)	Appears as man with a lion's head, riding a bear and holding a viper, preceded by many trumpeters.
Raum	Appears as a crow, but will assume human form on request.

Functions	Image
• an excellent poet • understands all sciences	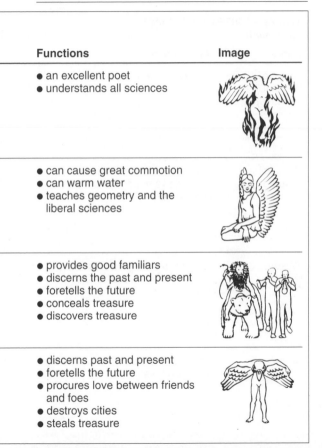
• can cause great commotion • can warm water • teaches geometry and the liberal sciences	
• provides good familiars • discerns the past and present • foretells the future • conceals treasure • discovers treasure	
• discerns past and present • foretells the future • procures love between friends and foes • destroys cities • steals treasure	

THE 72 SPIRITS OF SOLOMON
(continued)

Name	Appearance
Ronobe (Roneve) (Ronove)	Appears as a monster.
Sabnack (Saburac)	Appears as an armed soldier with a lion's head, riding a pale-colored horse.
Saleos (Zaleos)	Appears as a soldier wearing a crown and riding a crocodile.
Seere	Appears as a beautiful man riding a winged horse.

Functions	**Image**
• teaches the arts and rhetoric • teaches languages	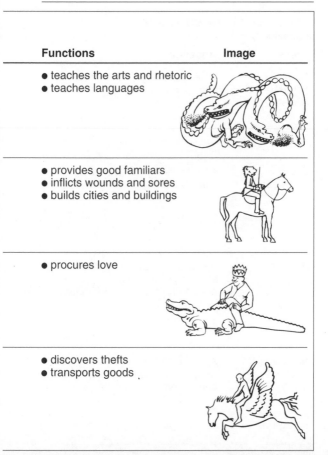
• provides good familiars • inflicts wounds and sores • builds cities and buildings	
• procures love	
• discovers thefts • transports goods	

THE 72 SPIRITS OF SOLOMON
(continued)

Name	Appearance
Shax (Chax) (Scox)	Appears as a stockdove or stork, and speaks with a hoarse voice.
Solas (Stomas)	Appears first as a raven, and then as a man.
Sytry	Appears with a leopard's head and the wings of a griffin, but will assume human form on request.
Valac	Appears as a small boy with the wings of an angel, riding a two-headed dragon.

Functions	Image
MUST BE TRANSPORTED INTO THE TRIANGLE OR WILL BE DECEPTIVE • provides good familiars • discovers hidden things • steals money • will transport anything	
• teaches astronomy • teaches the virtues of herbs • teaches the value of stones	
• procures love • causes women to reveal themselves naked	
• reveals hidden treasure • delivers serpents to the magician	

THE 72 SPIRITS OF SOLOMON
(continued)

Name	Appearance
Valefor (Malaphar)	Appears as a lion with many heads.
Vapula	Appears as a lion with griffin's wings.
Vassago	Unknown
Vepar (Separ)	Appears as a mermaid.

Functions	Image
• is a thief	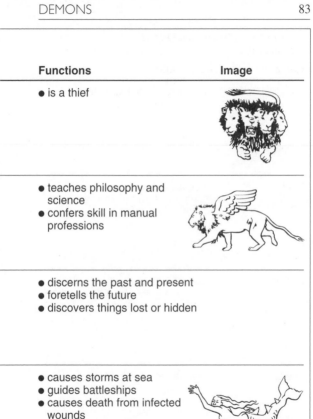
• teaches philosophy and science • confers skill in manual professions	
• discerns the past and present • foretells the future • discovers things lost or hidden	
• causes storms at sea • guides battleships • causes death from infected wounds	

THE 72 SPIRITS OF SOLOMON
(continued)

Name	Appearance
Vine	Appears as a monster, but will assume human form on request.
Vual	Appears as a dromedary, but will assume human form on request. Speaks in Egyptian.
Zagan	Appears first as a bull with the wings of a griffin, then as a human.
Zepar	Wearing red, is armed like a soldier

Functions	Image
<ul><li>discerns the past and present</li><li>foretells the future</li><li>reveals witches</li><li>discerns hidden things</li><li>destroys walls</li><li>builds towers</li></ul>	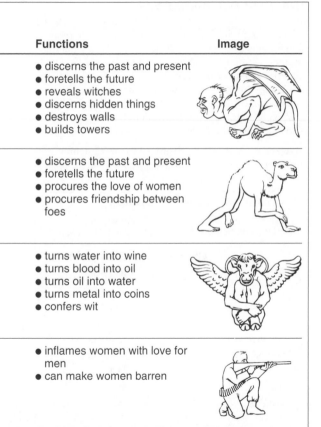
<ul><li>discerns the past and present</li><li>foretells the future</li><li>procures the love of women</li><li>procures friendship between foes</li></ul>	
<ul><li>turns water into wine</li><li>turns blood into oil</li><li>turns oil into water</li><li>turns metal into coins</li><li>confers wit</li></ul>	
<ul><li>inflames women with love for men</li><li>can make women barren</li></ul>	

THE INFERNAL HIERARCHY

Just as there is a hierarchy of archangels and angels in Heaven, so might there also be a hierarchy of demons in Hell. However, there is no agreement as to what the infernal hierarchy might be, only that Satan is God's Adversary and is what we call the Devil. Some people call Satan "Lucifer", the name he was given before he was thrown out of Heaven for opposing God. Lucifer was a celestial seraphim. Beelzebub, Lord of the Flies, is second in command to Satan.

Given here are the ranks attributed to the 72 demon spirits of Solomon. Note, some spirits hold more than one rank.

Hierarchy of the 72 spirits of Solomon

Shown here are the spirits of Solomon with their alternative names and hierarchical position in Hell.

Spirit	Alternative name(s)	Hierarchical position
1 Baal		King
2 Agares		Duke
3 Vassago		Prince
4 Gamygyn		Marquis
5 Marbas	Barbas	President
6 Valefor	Malaphar	Duke
7 Amon		Marquis
8 Barbatos		Count and Duke
9 Paimon		King

Hierarchy of the 72 spirits of Solomon (continued)

Spirit	Alternative name(s)	Hierarchical position
10 Buer		President
11 Gusion	Gusayn	Duke
12 Sytry		Prince
13 Beleth	Byleth	King
14 Lerajie		Marquis
15 Eligor		Duke
16 Zepar		Duke
17 Botis		President and Earl
18 Bathin	Bathym Marthim	Duke
19 Saleos	Zaleos	Duke
20 Purson	Curson	King
21 Morax	Foraii, Forfax	Earl and President
22 Ipos	Ipes, Ayporos, Aypeos	Earl and Prince
23 Aini	Aym, Haborym	Duke
24 Naberius	Cerberus	Marquis
25 Glasyalabolas	Caacrinolaas Caassimola	President
26 Bune		Duke
27 Ronobe	Roneve, Ronove	Marquis and Earl

continued

Hierarchy of the 72 spirits of Solomon (continued)

Spirit	Alternative name(s)	Hierarchical position
28 Berith	Beal, Berith, Bofi, Bolfry	Duke
29 Astaroth		Duke
30 Forneus		Marquis
31 Foras	Forcas	President
32 Asmoday	Sydonay	King
33 Gaap	Tap, Goap	President and Prince
34 Furfur		Earl
35 Marchosias		Marquis
36 Solas	Stolas	Prince
37 Phoenix		Marquis
38 Halpas		Earl
39 Malpas		President
40 Raum		Earl
41 Focalor		Duke
42 Sabnack	Saburac	Marquis
43 Vepar	Separ	Duke
44 Shax	Chax, Scox	Marquis
45 Vine		King
46 Bifrons		Earl
47 Vual		Duke
48 Hagenti		President
49 Procel	Pucel	Duke

Spirit	Alternative name(s)	Hierarchical position
50 Furcas		Duke
51 Balam		King
52 Allocen	Alloien, Allocer	Duke
53 Caim		President
54 Murmur		Duke and Earl
55 Orobas		Prince
56 Gomory		Duke
57 Ose		President
58 Amy		President
59 Orias		Marquis
60 Vapula		Duke
61 Zagan		King and President
62 Valac		President
63 Andras		Marquis
64 Flauros		Duke
65 Andrealphus		Marquis
66 Cimeries		Marquis
67 Amduscias		Duke
68 Belial		King
69 Decarabia		Marquis
70 Seere		Prince
71 Dantalian		Duke
72 Andromalius		Duke and Earl

MAGIC ANIMALS

Certain animals are believed to be magical, perhaps
because they were once believed to be witches'
familiars. Sometimes a demon appears as an animal;
sometimes a witch transforms into an animal;
sometimes an animal is used as part of a magic spell, to
carry out an evil deed. Although there are superstitions
surrounding almost all animals, perhaps the most
mysterious and magical are bats, cats, black dogs,
goats, hares, snakes, toads and wolves. They are listed
here along with some of the popular superstitions
concerning magical cures made from their flesh, blood
and bones.

Bats

Perhaps because of their nocturnal habits and the ability
to navigate in the dark, or perhaps because they seem
both animal and bird, bats have been linked with

Magical uses of bats

- Wash your face in bat's blood to enable you to see
  in the dark.
- Keep the right eye of a bat in your pocket to make
  you invisible.
- Keep a bat bone in your clothes to ensure good
  luck.
- Carry a powdered bat heart to staunch bleeding or
  stop a bullet.
- Put bat's blood into someone's drink to make them
  more passionate.

---

supernatural forces in many parts of the world. It was assumed that witches used the blood of bats as one of the ingredients in their flying ointment and in magic charms and love potions. In the Ivory Coast, bats are believed to be the spirits of the dead, and in Madagascar, they are believed to be the souls of criminals, sorcerers and the unburied dead. Certain groups in South America believe the Devil appears in bat form.

Cats
Legend has it that cats were invented accidentally by the Devil. These animals—particularly black ones—were once believed to be transformed witches or devils incarnate. Perhaps this notion derives from their nocturnal behavior, independent ways, and the fact that their eyes dilate and contract rather ominously, glowing in the dark. Or from the fact that cats always land on

Witches carrying a cat on a litter

their feet. Throughout Europe thousands of cats were burned because of their connection with witchcraft, and there persist today many superstitious beliefs about these creatures and their magical properties.

Magical uses of cats

- To cure a wart, rub the tail of a tortoiseshell cat on it during the month of May, or smear it with cat's blood.
- Hold a dried catskin over your face to cure toothache.
- Swallow nine hairs from the tail of a black cat to alleviate whooping cough.
- Eat gravy made from stewed black cat to cure consumption.

Dogs

The Devil is assumed to take the form of a dog and a fear of black dogs was once common in the British Isles. Black dogs (like many other black animals) were feared as witches' familiars. Almost all kinds of howling by dogs is said to be a death omen.

Magical uses of dogs

- Wear a dried dog's tongue around your neck to cure scrofula.
- Let a dog lick sores on your skin in order to cure them.
- Apply a poultice made from dog's head and wine to cure jaundice.
- Rub in melted dog fat to cure rheumatism.

Goats

The goat is commonly associated with the Devil, perhaps because the satyrs and fauns of pagan times were depicted as half human, with the legs and feet of a goat.Superstition holds that every twenty-four hours the animal visits the Devil to have its beard combed, and that one drop of goat's blood will smash a diamond.

Hares

These creatures were commonly associated with witchcraft, perhaps because of their strange, human-like cry and their ability to sit upright. Many believed they were witches in disguise because of their swift and darting movements which enabled them to escape their pursuers. Anne Boleyn was believed to haunt her

parish church in the form of a hare, having been
accused of bewitching Henry VIII. Carrying a hare's
foot is still believed to bring good luck, and that it will
protect against rheumatism and cramp.

Snakes
Snakes were widely used in medieval potions, as they
were believed to be particularly curative.

A fifteenth-century physician preparing lotions using
snakes

Magical uses of snakes

- Eat snakes' flesh broth to cure tuberculosis.
- Cure diseases of the spleen by eating powdered snakeskin.
- Carry a snake tooth to ward off fever.
- Prevent a headache by wearing the cast-off skin of a snake under your hat.
- Wear a cast-off snakeskin around your leg to cure rheumatism.
- Lay a snakeskin against your body to draw out thorns and prickles.

Toads

Witches were said to be able to transform into toads and commonly used them as familiars. They are associated with the supernatural because demons— identified by two tiny horns on their forehead—often take this form when sitting on the left shoulder of a

Magical uses of toads

- Wear a dried toad in a silk bag to cure a nosebleed.
- Carry a dried toad's tongue to make you more popular with the opposite sex.
- Swallow a toad's heart to cure epilepsy.
- Wear the ashes of a dead toad to cure rheumatism, plague and dropsy.
- Wear the hind leg of a toad to cure warts, skin diseases, swellings and tumors.
- Rub a live toad on the skin to cure breast cancer.

witch. The secretion of venomous fluid from the skin may be one reason why toads were believed by some to be able to spit fire.

Toads dancing at a witches' sabbat

Wolves

In Germany, the Devil was said to sit between the eyes of the wolf, and it was said that witches could transform themselves into wolves and commonly used them for riding to sabbat. They are perhaps the most common type of lycanthrope—creatures that are half-human, half-animal.

Magical uses of wolves

- Eat wolf meat to prevent your seeing ghosts.
- Sleep with a wolf's head under the pillow to prevent nightmares.
- Rub wolves' teeth against the gums of children to relieve them of toothache.
- Wrap an epileptic in wolfskin to cure him of fits.
- Wear a wolf's tooth to protect you from evil.
- Apply wolf dung to limbs to cure colic.

WITCHES' FAMILIARS

All medieval witches were believed to have a familiar, a low-ranking demon in the form of an animal, given to them by the Devil for the purpose of strengthening the witch's own power. Common European familiars were believed to be cats, dogs, rabbits, toads and insects. Japanese familiars were dogs and foxes, and in Africa it was believed witches relied on the assistance of baboons, hyenas and owls.

The familiar—often only visible to the witch herself— would be rewarded for its services by being allowed to suck some of the witch's own blood from a teat or spot on her body known as a "witch's mark" (note, this is different from the "Devil's mark" given to witches during their initiation).

Common European familiars

1 Cats	**4** Toads
2 Dogs	**5** Insects
3 Rabbits	

The frontispiece (right) of one of the most famous accounts of familiars, Matthew Hopkins' *Discovery of Witches* (1647) in which the author describes the five familiars said to assist the witch Elizabeth Clark.

1 Holt, a white kitten
2 Jamara, a fat spaniel
3 Vinegar Tom, a long-legged greyhound
4 Sack and Sugar, a black rabbit
5 News, a polecat

THE SEVEN OLYMPIC SPIRITS

These spirits can be evoced (see the section on Magic Rituals) in much the same way as demons.

Seven Olympic spirits

Name	Ruling planet	Functions
ARATRON	Saturn	• Confers invisibility • Bestows long life • Converts anything to stone • Provides familiars • Teaches alchemy, magic and medicine • Transforms treasure into coal • Transforms coal into treasure
BETHOR	Jupiter	• Obtains treasures • Prolongs life to 700 years • Reconciles other spirits so that they will transport precious stones and provide medicines
HAGITH	Venus	• Converts gold into copper • Converts copper into gold • Provides other spirits

Name	Ruling planet	Functions
OCH	Sun	• Converts anything into gold or precious stones • Provides 600 years of perfect health • Bestows wisdom • Provides other spirits • Teaches medicine • Provides gold
OPHIEL	Mercury	• Provides spirits • Teaches all arts and alchemy
PHALEG	Mars	• Confers great honor in warfare
PHUL	Moon	• Prolongs life to 300 years • Converts all metals into silver • Provides spirits • Heals dropsy

ANGELS

These angels can be evoked (see the section on Magic
Rituals) in much the same way as demons.

The Angels governing days of the week

Angel	Ruling day	Functions
MICHAEL	Sunday	• Procures gold, gems and wealth in general • Makes people the recipients of favors • Confers honors
GABRIEL	Monday	• Transports things • Procures silver • Discloses secrets
SAMAEL	Tuesday	• Causes infirmity, death, war and combustion
RAPHAEL	Wednesday	• Reveals the past, present and future • Pacifies judges. • Gives victory in war • Teaches experiments • Opens all locks

Angel	Ruling day	Functions
SACHIEL	Thursday	• Procures the love of women • Makes people joyful • Pacifies arguments • Heals the sick
ANAEL	Friday	• Instills a passion for luxury • Procures love • Cures disease • Provides silver
CASSIEL	Saturday	• Procures hatred and deceit • Procures arguments and attacks • Causes evil thoughts

Section 3
MAGIC RITUALS

All forms of magic involved some kind of ritual or ceremony, many very elaborate, with instructions for what kind of clothes to wear, what color candles to burn, talismans to make and words to recite. Early magicians were convinced that their magic would only work if they adhered to very specific rules about when and where to practice it, and tables and charts were produced detailing times of the day or night believed to be of particular importance.

3

This chapter explains some of the more well-known rituals and includes descriptions of earlier witch initiation ceremonies (medieval, modern and tribal), how a magic circle was cast or a pentagram used, aspects of the Black Mass and how a pact with the Devil might have been made, how spirits were conjured, and how exorcisms were performed. All witches and magicians had their own system of rituals, and it is recommended that interested readers consult specialist books for further information.

WITCH INITIATION CEREMONIES

Medieval witch initiation ceremonies
These were believed to take place during the sabbat,
communal celebrations involving the Devil and other
demons. Although there is little evidence of medieval
sabbat practices, they were generally believed to
involve ritualistic ceremonies (see box, *right*) during
which the Devil appeared as a huge black-bearded man,
a black goat with a light shining from his horns, a
gigantic feathered toad, a crow, a raven, or a black cat.
He sat on an ebony throne or stood on an altar. (At
lesser sabbats a demon or witch masked as the Devil
could preside.)

Before the sabbat, a witch was believed to undress and anoint herself and her broomstick with Devil's grease (unless she had been given a flying goat, ram or dog), and then to leave via the chimney, perhaps transforming into an animal as she passed under the chimney mantle.

Proceedings at the medieval sabbat

1 The Devil reads a roll call.

2 Any novice witches are brought forward and initiated (see box on next page).

3 Delinquent witches are punished, usually by whipping.

4 Everyone present pays homage to the Devil, presenting him with black cakes (made of black millet mixed with the flesh of unbaptized infants), black candles and black fowls.

5 Everyone kisses the Devil's buttocks (a practice known as the *osculum infame*, the "kiss of shame" or the "obscene kiss").

6 The witches gorge themselves but remain hungry. The meat (which is carrion, the flesh of those who've been hanged or the hearts of unbaptized children) tastes like rotten wood and the wine like manure juice. There is no salt, no olives and no oil.

7 There is dancing, *widdershins* (counterclockwise) in a ring around the Devil or some phallic object.

8 The sabbat concludes with a sexual orgy in which the Devil copulates with everyone present. The Devil was said to have a freezing touch, making sex highly painful.

9 The sabbat ends with the crowing of a cock before dawn.

The medieval witch initiation ceremony
It was believed that novice witches underwent an
initiation ceremony that took place during one of the
sabbats. Although the ceremonies differed, they were
generally believed to be obscene and sacrilegious in
nature and to embody all or some of the following
elements:

1 At the sabbat the new recruit is presented to the
  Devil or one or his representatives by an existing
  member of the coven. The novice witch swears an
  oath of allegiance to the Devil. This may involve
  promising not to divulge the secrets of the coven to
  others, to recruit further members to the coven and
  to agree to carry out deeds for the Devil.
2 The Devil brands the novice by drawing blood from
  her ear or marking her skin, making a mark known
  as the "Devil's mark" (later used by persecutors to
  identify witches).

3 A black cockerel is sacrificed and the novice witch is asked to sign a pact using blood, agreeing to sell her soul to the Devil in return for wealth on Earth. The novice may be given a new name.

4 The novice kisses the Devil's buttocks (a practice known as the *osculum infame*, the "kiss of shame" or the "obscene kiss").

5 The novice and Devil copulate with each other.

6 After copulation the novice witch is presented with the tools of her trade: flying ointment, a broomstick or a familiar.

7 The name of the new witch is entered in a Black Book or Roll kept by the Master of the coven.

8 The initiation ceremony over, other witches join together to work spells; there is feasting, dancing and orgiastic sex.

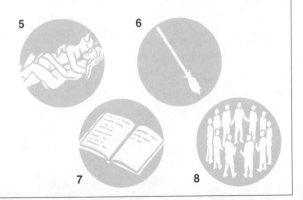

5

6

7

8

Modern witch initiation ceremonies
Initiation (sometimes called dedication) take many
different forms, with different covens following
different procedures. At its most simple level, new
members may swear an oath of loyalty and secrecy, and
may have parts of their bodies blessed, perhaps by being
washed with oil or wine while standing within a magic
circle. Other witches may dance around the circle. The
new witches may be introduced to the eight tools of the
craft: the athame, the white-handled knife, the censer,
the sword, the cauldron, the scourge, the wand, and the
cord. They may then be presented to other members of

WICCA INITIATION CEREMONIES

First degree initiation
The purpose of this initiation was to bring initiates to
the doorway of spiritual awakening and to help them
link with the collective mind of the coven and the
family of wicca.

1 Unclothed, the initiates are taken round the
  guardians of the circle.
2 They are blindfolded and tied with three cords, at
  the wrist, neck, knee and ankle.
3 The passwords "love" and "trust" are given to them.
4 The magic circle is cast.

1   **2**   **3**

the coven and a closing ceremony undertaking during which everyone enjoys cakes and wine.

Initiation ceremonies are often performed with the initiate naked, as are many personal rituals, as some witches believe that clothes hinder the witch's ability to release and direct energy.

Wicca ceremonies

There are three levels of wicca initiation ceremony. A novice would not usually undergo the first initiation before training for about a year, learning about the craft and its methods.

5 The Bagahi rune is recited and a charge to invoke the deities.
6 A gap is made in the circle and a broomstick placed across the threshold of the circle. The initiator holds the athame against the candidate's breast and asks if he or she has the courage to step across the threshold. When the candidate says "yes," the athame is laid across the broomstick and the initiate is spun into the circle with a kiss of greeting and presented to the four quarters beginning in the east and moving clockwise (deosil) around to the north.

continued

4

5

6

Wicca initiation ceremonies (continued)

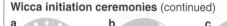

a   b   c

7 The coven dances in a circle (**a**) and chants and a
bell is rung.

8 The initiator kneels before the initiate (**b**) and
offers a fivefold kiss (on the feet, genitals, breast
and lips). This symbolizes the sacred nature of the
body and activates the chakras (some initiations
involve a sevenfold or even ninefold kiss).

9 The initiates ankles are loosely tied with a cord
and the initiate lightly scourged (**c**).

10 The initiate takes the oath of occult allegiance to
wicca.

11 The initiate is consecrated three times and the
blindfold removed.

12 the initiate is presented with the eight symbolic
tools of power and led once more to the four
guardian watchtowers of the circle.

Second degree initiation

After the second degree initiation the initiate became
a full priest or priestess. This time the initiation
involved a rite known as the Legend of the Goddess,
an oath more binding than that of the first degree
ceremony.

- The initiate may be naked (**d**) and tethered, but not blindfolded.
- The ceremony may involve the transfer of a ring (**e**), worn on the third finger of the right hand, a personal gift from the initiator to initiate. This ring symbolizes the transference of powers.
- The initiate is offered wine (**f**) and receives the fivefold kiss.
- Any bonds are removed. The initiate is presented with the eight working tools and asked to put them to use.
- They are also presented with ritual cords and a scourge.
- They are given the teaching of the Three Fold Law.
- The Legend of the Goddess may be enacted by the coven.

Third degree initiation

This allowed individuals to form their own covens and to initiate other witches at second and third degree levels. The initiate rite centred on the Sacred Marriage through which the *animus* (male spirituality) or *anima* (female spirituality) of the initiate becomes one with his or her opposite. The ceremony was performed either symbolically or as actual intercourse between a priest and priestess.

LONE INITIATION

Many witches did not belong to covens and undertook their own private form of initiation. One such example is set out here.

1 Contemplation

- Spend a year and one day thinking about the practice of modern witchcraft (**a**), studying its techniques, considering the different deities, healing practices and whatever else they could learn about modern witches and their way of life. Meditate each day and choose a new name for themselves.

2 Purification.

- Collect together an old garment, a new robe, some salt and some oil.
- Take a leisurely bath (**b**) with either the salt or some of the oil (scented if desired) and put on old garment.
- Collect together magic tools (athame, incense, oil, candle, chalice, pentagram (**c**)), some wine and some bread.
- Spend some time out of doors, in a quiet, deserted place.
- Begin ritual after sundown.

a   b   c

3 The ritual

- Cast a magic circle (**d**).
- Burn incense.
- Offer themselves to the north, east, south and west, holding up their arms.
- Facing north, ask to be accepted, using their new name.
- Fold their arms across your chest and ask to be protected and filled with energy.
- Pass the oil through the incense and candle flame and over the chalice. Then trace a pentagram over it, using the athame.
- Annoint themselves between the eyes, on the heart and on the genitals.
- Standing in the circle, facing north, ask the gods to accept them.
- Sit down and feel themselves become fashioned as a witch (**e**).
- Put the wine into the chalice, trace a pentagram over it. Drink it and eat the bread to celebrate their new life.
- Shred their old garment and put on their new robe (**f**). Thank the gods for accepting them.

d   e   f

Mayombero initiation

Mayomberos were voodoo priests who practiced black magic. They are sometimes known as "black witches" and, like other witches, underwent a special initiation ceremony, after which they could go about their business of necromancy, revenge, and the destruction of human life. The section on Magic Tools explains how mayomberos made a *nganga*, their magic cauldron.

Mayombero initiation

- The initiate sleeps under a ceiba tree for seven nights.
- At the end of the week the initiate takes some of his clothes and buries them in a grave in the local cemetary.
- The initiate takes several purifying herbal baths.
- The initiate digs up his clothes after 21 days, or three successive Fridays.
- He puts on his clothes and returns to the ceiba tree.
- He is joined by other mayomberos and together they invoke the spirits of the dead and that of the cebia tree.
- The initiate is crowned with cebia leaves.
- A lighted candle is placed in a white dish which the initiate holds.
- He is given a scepter (known as *kisengue*), a human tibia bone wrapped in black cloth.
- He may now practice as a mayombero.

COVEN RITUALS

Different witch covens have their own forms of ceremony and ritual. Outlined here are some of the items likely to form part of any witch meeting, although the order that they are undertaken is likely to vary between different covens.

The work of a coven
This may include:
- appointing someone to keep a record of the evening's work
- performing initiation ceremonies
- performing healing work (for individual members or non-witches who are not present)
- dealing with personal problems (whether personal or professional)
- divination (such as scrying)
- consecration of objects, such as presents

Usually,
- A magic circle is cast.
- The Drawing Down the Moon ceremony may be performed. This ceremony calls the Goddess to descend into the High Priestess (if there is one) who represents the Goddess until the circle is banished.
- Together members raise the power. This means chanting and dancing in order to heighten everyone's awareness. It is sometimes called the "cone of power" and is visualized rising from the center of the magic circle.

CASTING A MAGIC CIRCLE

Perhaps the most important of all magic rituals is the casting of a magic circle, the purpose of which is to both concentrate the user's powers and to protect against psychic entities. A witches' circle, also known as the Circle of Being, allows users to move in and out of it (although it may be symbolically "opened" and "closed"). The circle used by magicians is essential for protection and once closed tends to remain so until the

The magician Dr Faustus standing within a magic circle with a demon he has invoked.

end of the ritual. Circles used by witches and magicians are constructed differently. An example of each is presented here.

THE WITCHES' CIRCLE

The circle used by witches might be of any size. Outdoor gatherings might have circles as large as 50 feet across, whereas a witch working within the confines of an apartment would have to make do with making the circle as large as an apartment room would allow. Some witches believe that the circle should be 9ft in diameter, as this represents the nine orders of the angels and invokes the power of Mars.

Anyone might cast the circle, although some covens believe that it should be cast by the High Priestess, if there is one. The act of creating the circle is known as Drawing down the Moon.

Equipment

To cast a witches' circle the following tools would be needed, all of which would have been consecrated beforehand:
- four candles
- a sword or athame
- a pentacle
- a small bowl of water
- a censer with incense

(For more information, see the section on Magic Tools)

To cast a witches' circle

1 Light four candles just outside the circumference of the circle. These represent the four compass points, north, east, south and west (which themselves correspond to the elements Earth, Air, Fire and Water, respectively). Some witches believe that it does not matter if these are not "true" compass points, so long as the altar is at North.

2 Turn off any artificial lights.

3 Light the incense.

4 Place all the witches tools on the altar, including the incense.

5 Begin at the north. Pointing the athame down to indicate the circumference of the circle, walk clockwise (deosil) until you reach north again. As you walk, say something like, *"Oh Circle of Power, I conjure thee that thou may serve as a boundary between this world and the world of the Mighty, that you shall preserve the power I raise in thee, and serve to as a guardian and protector."*

6 Walking deosil again, from north to north, sprinkle water around the circle.

7 Carry the burning censer around the circle.

8 Take up the north candle, and carry it round the circle, then replace it on the altar.

9 Holding the athame, face east and say something like, *"Lords of the East, I summon thee to guard this circle and witness my rites."* As you say this, draw a five-pointed star in the air using the athame, following the directions set out in the section Using a Pentagram.

10 Repeat the procedure facing south (Fire), west (Water), and last, north (Earth), each time following the ritual for using the invoking pentagram. The magic circle is now complete.

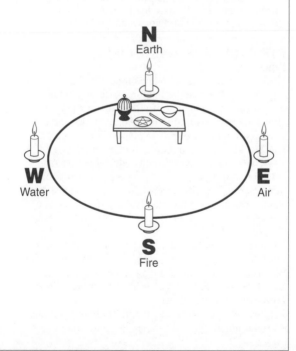

N
Earth

W
Water

E
Air

S
Fire

Banishing a magic circle

Once a magic ritual is over it is necessary to banish the magic circle. Do this starting at the East and say something like, *"Lords of the East, thank you for attending and protecting, farewell."* As you say this, trace the banishing pentagram for the east (Air) using the athame. Repeat the procedure for south (Fire), west (Water) and finally, north (Earth).

THE MAGICIANS' MAGIC CIRCLE
Types
There are three types of magic circle used by magicians: those that are imaginary (drawn in the air using a finger or magic tool), those that are portable (drawn on paper or embroidered onto cloth), and those marked out on the floor (using chalk, for example). This last kind was commonly used by practicing magicians, and often encompassed a large area of ground that was blessed and consecrated with holy words, sprinkled with holy water (which had also been blessed by the magician) and had the Holy Names of God (see the section on Magic Things) written about it.
Purpose of the circle
The circle was believed to have the power to expel evil spirits who might otherwise try to molest the magician and his assistant. The magician sometimes went to great lengths to protect the circle itself from pollution.
Times for making circles
The best time to construct a magic circle is when there is bright moonlight or during a raging storm.

Places for making circles

It was believed that the best places for making circles were those that were dark and lonely. (See box)

Places for making magic circles

- in a large parlor hung with black, with a black floor and wax candles
- in a churchyard
- in a churchyard vault
- in an abbey
- in a castle
- in a monastery
- in a desert
- where three roads meet
- on the seashore by moonlight
- if the circle is being used as part of necromancy, choose a wood (especially if it is where someone was killed or has committed suicide)

To summon subterranean spirits
- the circle should be constructed in a cave or cellar

To summon spirits of water
- the circle should be made on a ship or sea rock

To summon fairies, nymphs and satyrs
- the circle should be constructed in the woods or mountains

For airy spirits
- choose the tops of turrets for your circle

Constructing a magicians' magic circle

1 Make a circle in black, nine feet in diameter, perhaps with your altar in the center.
2 Inside this make another circle, six inches smaller, with six inches of both ends open. The purpose of this gap is to enable you or an assistant to enter.
3 Between the two circles write down all the Holy Names of God, interspersed with a cross or triangle.
4 At one side of the circle, make a triangle. This is to hold any malevolent spirits you conjure up.
5 At the corners of the triangle write the names of the trinity—JEHOWA RUAH (**a**), KADESH (**b**), IMMANUAL (**c**)—in small circles.
6 Bless the circle by sprinkling it with holy water.

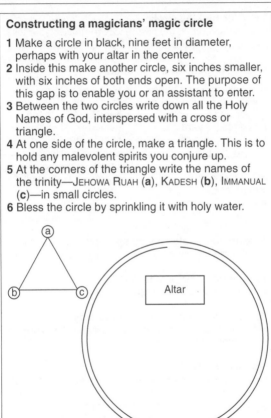

An imaginary magic circle

Wear a black garment reaching to your knees.
Beneath this wear a white linen robe falling to your
ankles. You will also need a pair of consecrated
shoes and a magic wand.

1 Stand in the exact center of the place that will be
   the imaginary circle.
2 Throw your old shoes about a yard away.
3 Put on your consecrated shoes made of leather,
   with a cross cut or marked on the top of each toe.
4 Using a magic wand made from a hazel stick, two
   yards in length, stretch out your arm to all four
   winds three times, turning round at every wind,
   and repeat this verse:

*I am the servant of the all-highest, do by the virtue of
His Holy Name Immanuel, sanctify unto myself the
circumference of nine foot about me.*

From the east, west, north and south.

*Which ground I take for my proper defense from all
malignant spirits; that they may have no power over
my soul or body, nor come beyond these limitations;
but answer truly summoned, without daring to
transgress their bounds.*

USING A PENTAGRAM

INVOKING PENTAGRAMS

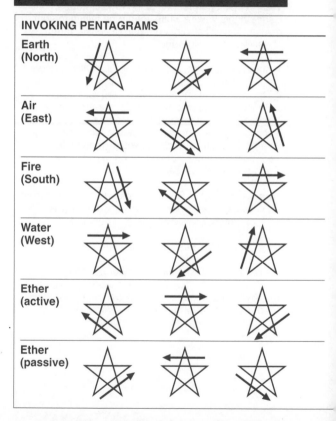

The pentagram is used for both invoking and banishing spirits. Each element has an invoking and banishing

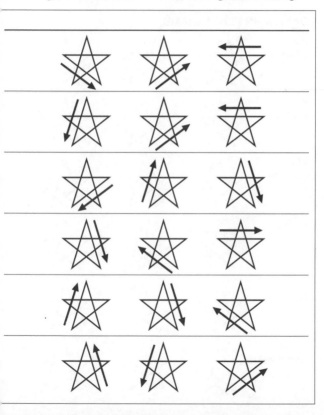

pentagram, formed by six strokes. Each element also corresponds to one of the four compass points and

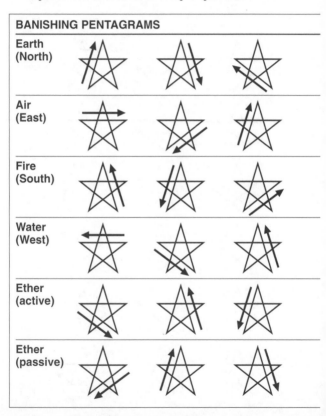

BANISHING PENTAGRAMS

Earth (North)

Air (East)

Fire (South)

Water (West)

Ether (active)

Ether (passive)

associated pentagrams can therefore be used when
casting and banishing the magic circle.

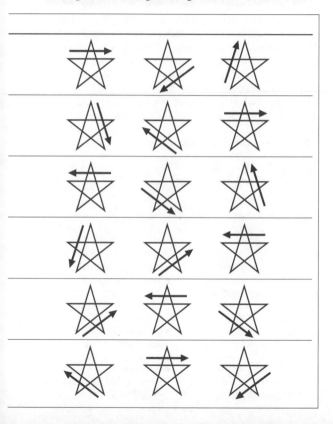

ATTENTING BLACK MASS

The term Black Mass was first used in English in 1896 to describe ceremonies practiced as part of Black Magic. There is little evidence of the Mass having been performed by witches, although it is known to have been practiced in modern times by some Satanists. One early account described how the marquise de Montespan (who was maid of honor to Queen Marie Thérèse and mistress of Louis XIV) had a Black Mass

Aspects of the Black Mass

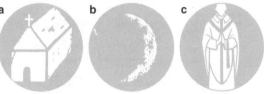

a   b   c

- The location was usually an old, ruined chapel, adorned with obscene pictures (**a**).
- Mass was held in the dead of night (**b**).
- A defrocked priest was required to preside over the ceremony (**c**).
- A crucifix was inverted and placed between

black candles (**d**).
- The congregation would stand, dressed in black, with their backs to the altar.
- Consecrated wine was sprinkled on the congregation (**e**).
- After recital of the Mass there would be praise of Satan (**f**).

said in order to oust the existing queen and her rival
(the duchesse de la Vallière) and to win the king's love.
When the marquise's schemes came to nothing she had
it said against the king to bring about his death.

The Black Mass was said to be a perversion of the
Roman Catholic Mass—the same ceremony was used,
but was said backwards. It was not necessary to have
demonic presence for this ceremony (unlike the sabbat,
where the Devil usually presided).

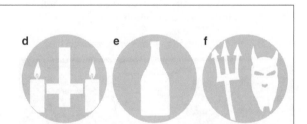

- A sign of the cross was made on the floor, perhaps using the left foot.
- A Host was drenched in black pigment or blood
- The crucifix would be defiled. It might be replaced with a turnip stained black.

- Some say an unbaptized infant was either drowned in water (which was then drunk by the congregation) or its skin and body parts used in an orgy.
- The congregation engaged in wild behavior.

PACTS WITH THE DEVIL

During the thirteenth century it was popular for
members of the Inquisition to accuse witches of having
made a pact with the Devil. How such pacts were made
varied between centuries and regions. They could be
made in front of a sabbat congregation, or privately,
with the Devil himself. Some witches claimed to have
made a pact through another witch. The overall
outcome of such a pact was that, by agreeing to serve
the Devil, he would help you to increase your wealth or
power, or to further some ambition.

The Devil forcing a pact on those who invoked him.

Previous ways of making a pact with the Devil

a b c

d e

- Renouncing the Christian faith
- Paying homage to Satan (**a**)
- Kissing Satan on the buttocks
- Having his or her head scratched by Satan to remove previous Christian baptism
- Having a permanent mark put on their bodies by Satan
- Having sexual intercourse with Satan
- Giving Satan a piece of clothing (**b**)
- Drinking the blood of murdered children
- Trampling a cross underfoot (**c**)
- Having their names written in a Book of Death (**d**)
- Being renamed
- Agreeing never to use holy water or candles (**e**)
- Promising to regularly sacrifice young children to the Devil
- Agreeing to ensure secrecy in all dealings with the Devil
- Handing Satan the pact, written on paper, using blood drawn from the left hand

Making a pact according to *Le Dragon rouge*

1 Say:

"Emperor Lucifer, master of all the rebellious spirits,
I beseech thee be favorable to me in the calling
which I make upon they great minister LUCIFUGE ROFOCALE,
having desire to make a pact with him;
I pray thee also, Prince Beelzebub, to protect me in my undertaking.
O Count Ashtoreth! be propitious to me,
and cause that this night the great LUCIFUGE
appear unto me in human form and without any evil smell,
and that he grant me, by means of the pact which I shall deliver to
him, all the riches of which I have need.
O great Lucifugé, I beseech thee leave thy dwelling,
in whatever part of the world it may be,
to come and speak with me; if not,
I will thereto compel thee by the power of the mighty words of the
great Clavicule of Solomon, whereof he made use to force the
rebellious spirits to accept his pact.
Appear, then, instantly, or I will continually torment thee by the
mighty words of the Clavicule!"

2 The spirit replies:

"I cannot grant thy demand but on condition thou give me thyself at
the end of twenty years, so that I do with thee, body and soul, what
shall please me."

3 Show the Devil the pact you have written using your own blood. It should say:

I promise great LUCIFUGE to repay him in twenty years for all he shall give me. In witness whereof I have signed

In 1634, Urbain Grandier was convicted of magic, witchcraft, and causing possession. He was burned alive. The pact he made with the Devil survives in the Bibliothèque Nationale and is written in his own blood.

Pact of Urbain Grandier

*My Lord and Master, I won you for my God;
I promise to serve you while I live,
and from this hour I renounce all other gods and Jesus Christ and
Mary and all the Saints of heaven and the Catholic, Apostolic,
and Roman Church, and all the goodwill thereof and
the prayers which might have been made for me.
I promise to adore you and do you homage at least three times a
day and to do the most evil that I can
and to lead into evil as many persons as shall be possible to me,
and heartily I renounce the Chrism, Baptism,
and all the merits of Jesus Christ;
and, in case I should desire to change,
I give you my body and soul,
and my life as holding it from you,
having dedicated it for ever without any will to repent.*

TO CONJURE SPIRITS

In magic and witchcraft, it was sometimes necessary to conjure spirits. There were many different ways to do this, some highly complex. Set out here is a brief example of the general procedure for invocation.

1 Decide on the exact purpose for which the spirit is required. To help you, look down the list of demons and spirits and angels in the section on Magic Beings, and identify those that may be useful to you.

2 Using the information in the section on Magic Signs and Symbols, locate the sigil necessary for evoking the spirit of your choice.

3 Prepare yourself and your environment. Choose colors, scents and patterns appropriate to the spirit you hope to invoke. Collect together your magic tools.

4 Create a magic circle. Note that for the invocation of some demons it is essential to create a magic triangle also.

5 Recite the necessary invocation. (An example of how to invoke Olympian spirits is given top right.)

6 If the spirit appears and you complete your magic, it is necessary to give the spirit license to depart. (An example of how to banish an Olympian spirit is given right.)

Example of an invocation

O eternal and all-powerful Lord,
who has caused the whole creation to praise and honor thee,
and for the salvation of mankind,
I entreat thee to send thy spirit (name the spirit you require),
of the (name the planet) creation,
so that he may teach me those things which I desire to ask him.
Not my will, but thine, through Jesus Christ,
Thine only begotton Son, our Lord.
Amen.

Example of a licence to depart

Since thou hast come, and answered my questions,
and come in peace, and with gentleness,
I render thanks unto God,
in whose Name thou camest.
Thou may now depart to thine own sphere,
in peace; but thou shalt return again unto me,
upon my calling upon thee by name,
or by thy order, or by thy office;
all of which have been given to thee by thy Creator.
Amen.

USING THE KABBALA

The mystical body of knowledge known as the kabbala was used by many early magicians as part of their magic rituals and ceremonies, often involving

---

USING THE KABBALA

Begining the ritual

- The room is prepared, the altar arranged, with candles and perhaps a gong.
- The magic circle is cast. This will protect the magician throughout the ritual.
- To the east of the circle the magic triangle is drawn. This is used to confine any demons that are invoked.
- Before entering the circle, all lights are turned off so that only the altar candles remain buring.
- Once inside the circle, the magician makes the sign of the cabalistic cross. This drives away any undesirable forces.
- The magician visualizes a cloud of light above his head, the light of Kether. The magician uses his right hand to draw some of this light to his forehead, solar plexus, right shoulder and left shoulder. As he does this he says "Malkuth", "Din," and "Hesed."
- The magician traces pentagrams in the air, using his ritual sword.
- He greets the archangels Raphael, Gabriel, Michael, and Uriel.
- He imagines a six-pointed star above his head.

visualization of the Tree of Life.

An example of how the kabbala might have been used is outlined below.

Making the journey

- The magician now travels from Malkhuth, the earth, to Yesod, the gateway to the astral world. He travels along path 22, the Path of Saturn.
- At the gate to Yesod he is given entry in the name of Gabriel.
- He explains which sefirs he wishes to work with and travels to his destination. On his journey, it is necessary for the magician to envisage all those things he is likely to meet on any one particular path.
- He conjures the required sefirothic form into the triangle, and also conjures the planetary form associated with the chosen sefira.
- The magician must induce in himself a state of great force. He visualizes being taken over by a god or goddess and at the same time visualizes that which he hopes to accomplish.

Returning

- Using the same path, the magician returns to Malkhuth, thanking the sefiroth and archangels for their help.
- He forms the cabalistic cross to make sure any mischievous spirits cannot leave their domain.

Voodoo method for conjuring spirits

- A magic circle is drawn.
- Using corn gruel or ashes, an occult signature known as a *vévé* is drawn round a decorated central post. Just like the sigils used for the invocation of demons, the *vévé* is an earthly representation of the god (*loa*) to be summoned.
- Candles are lit and the ground sprinkled with water.
- Drumming and dancing begin.
- The *loa* is begged to descend.
- The *loa* slips down the post to its *vévé* and may be heard through the body of a medium who goes into a trance. (This trance may last several days.)
- A blood sacrifice is offered, such as a chicken or a goat.
- Throughout the ceremony, priests and priestesses chant to keep out unwanted spirits.
- If the *loa* is summoned, it is essential that the summoner gains possession over the demon, who would otherwise create havoc. The demon is told what is expected of it and must be made to comply.
- During the dancing the *vévé* is destroyed.
- After the ceremony the demon must be banished. This is believed to be the hardest part of the black magic ritual, as in voodoo demons are known to be dangerous and will resist being banished at any cost.

Examples of *vévé*
a Agwé (god of the sea)
b Erzulie (goddess of tragic love)
c Avizan (goddess of spirit protection)

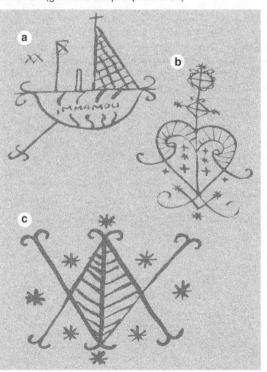

PERFORMING EXORCISMS

Exorcisms were performed to expel evil spirits, thought to enter and depart from people by the natural openings in the body. In the Catholic Church today, they can only be performed with special permission from a bishop. In medieval times, persons possessed of an evil spirit might be given holy water to drink, using a church bell as a cup, or they might have the relic of a saint forced into their mouth. To prevent the accidental swallowing of a demon, a cross was often made over food. Many talismanic devices were used, such as the sign of the cross, holy water, rosaries and scapulars. People got into the habit of putting their hand over their mouth when they yawned to prevent a demon from entering.

Example of an exorcism

I exorcise thee, impure spirit,
in the name of Jesus Christ.
Tremble, O Demon,
enemy of the Faith, enemy of mankind,
who has caused death to come to the world,
has taken life from men, and rebelled against justice:
seducer of man, source of avarice,
root of evil, discord and envy.

Demons were believed to be persistent and had to be dislodged using prayers and even fumigations. When being exorcised of a demon, people were believed to vomit strange substances (manifestations of the demon) such as coal, dung, bats, spiders, reptiles or steam.

Types of exorcism

Exorcisms were performed against demonic possession of a whole range of things, including:

baths
beds
clothes (**a**)
flocks
food (**b**)
herbs
herds (**c**)
houses (**d**)
incense
medicines
people (**e**)
perfumes (**f**)
potions
roses
salt
salves
ships (**g**)
sulphur
vines
water
wine (**h**)

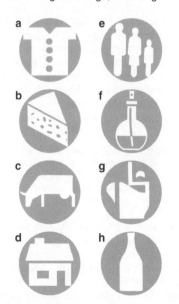

Section 4
MAGIC TOOLS

This section provides information about the wide variety of tools used by witches and magicians. Perhaps the most familiar of these is the magic wand, a tool magicians and fairies are often depicted as waving when they cast magic spells. Another popular tool was the cauldron, a large metal pot believed to be used by witches to brew potions using strange ingredients (often comprising animal parts) and to cast spells.

Also called the Instruments of the Art, each tool had its own purpose. Many were used to aid concentration and visualization and were consecrated before being used.

This might involve:
- immersing it in or sprinkling it with salted water
- passing it through or over a flame
- passing it through incense smoke
- touching it with a disk of earth or baked clay or plunging it into the earth

Some tools were inscribed with runes, sigils and symbols, and many were handmade (which was believed to help to imbue them with the witch's or magician's personal power). Most were used in ceremonial magic (such as the consecration of magic circles) and might be characteristically "masculine" or

4

"feminine". In modern witchcraft, Fire and Air tools are masculine; Earth and Water tools are feminine.

Provided in this section is information about the altar, magic books, the broomstick, candles, the cauldron, the censer, the chalice, clothing, cords, crystals and stones, magic drums and rattles, the magic knife, the magic lamp, the use of special pens, ink and paper, the pentacle, and the wand.

Information is provided about the characteristics and uses of each item, although it is recommended that readers consult the grimoires and other specialist books for fuller information on the design and consecration of these instruments, which would vary according to whether the tool was used by a witch or by a magician, and whether it was used for black or white magic.

ALTAR

Although not strictly a "tool," the altar is central to most magic practices, and in modern witchcraft may be dedicated to a particular deity. It is usually covered in a sacred cloth—white for white magic and black for black magic. These cloths are preferably made from

Characteristics of the altar

- It can be made from anything—such as a table, mantlepiece or windowsill.
- It should fit inside a magic circle.
- It should be placed facing north (the direction from which power flows: from darkness to light); although some people prefer to have them facing east, to honor the rising sun.
- Modern witches often place symbols of the four elements on the altar (a stone, for example, symbolizing Earth; a magic knife or incense for Air; a wand and candles for Fire; and the chalice and cauldron for Water).
- It is usually decorated with talismans, herbs, flowers, crystals, etc.
- It faces east for benevolent ceremonies, west for malevolent ones.

Uses of the altar

- It holds the tools used in magic.
- It provides a focal point for meditation.

silk and stored in a white silk bag when not in use.
They should never be used for any purpose other than
to cover the altar. Sometimes a range of cloths in
different colors are used, corresponding to different
planets. These help increase the intensity of the magic
when it is necessary to evoke a particular spirit (as all
spirits have governing planets).

ALTAR CLOTH COLORS

To evoke a spirit whose planet is:	Use cloth color:
Saturn	Black
Jupiter	Blue
Mars	Red
Sun	Yellow (or gold)
Venus	Green
Mercury	Multicolored
Moon	White (or silver)

BOOK OF SPELLS

Modern witches and magicians use a book for writing out magic spells, instructions, invocations, incantations, prayers, recipes and diagrams associated with the magic they practice. Such a book is known as a Book of Spells or a Book of Shadows. Some people recommend keeping the book in a safe place and only writing in it using blue ink (see also paper, pens and inks later in this section).

Grimoires

Also called Black Books, these are handbooks of magic (many examples of which are very ancient) in which the names of demons are often set out, with instructions for their evocation and exorcism. They are often very detailed, with laborious instructions for rituals and rites, the creation of magic circles, the uses of amulets and talismans, and the working of spells. They may also include instructions on what to wear, which magic tools to use (how to make and consecrate them), prayers and incantations to say, and details of astrological times and dates relevant to the working of magic.

Such books were commonly used during the thirteenth century by magicians, sorcerers and those who needed magical help (including physicians). They were particularly popular during the seventeenth to early nineteenth centuries and contained information about both black and white magic.

Being illegal, they were often distributed in manuscript form, although some were eventually printed as books.

SOME FAMOUS GRIMOIRES

Grand Grimoire A French grimoire perhaps written in the seventeenth century with details for evoking the Devil and other spirits, making diabolic pacts, necromancy, and ritual poisoning.

Grimoire of Honorius Attributed to Pope Honorius, and published in Rome between 1629 and 1670.

Grimorium Verum Written in French and based on *The Key of Solomon*, but perhaps translated from Hebrew by a Dominican priest and published by "Alibeck the Egyptian" in 1517.

The *Key of Solomon*, and the ***Lesser Key of Solomon*** (also known as the ***Lemegeton***) grimoire believed by some to have been written by King Solomon.

Red Dragon Almost identical to the *Grand Grimoire*, this was published in 1822, but may have been written in 1522.

The Black Pullet (also published as ***Treasure of the Old Man of the Pyramids*** and ***Black Screech Owl***) Perhaps written in the late eighteenth century in Rome, emphasizing magic talismans and rings.

The Book of Black Magic and of Pacts Written in 1898 by Arthur Edward Waite.

The Book of Sacred Magic of Abra-Melin in the Mage Attributed to a Jewish mage of Würzburg known as Abramelin the mage in 1458, but perhaps written in the eighteenth century.

The Magus by Francis Barrett, published in 1801.

BROOMSTICK

Also known as a besom, this is a tool
traditionally associated with witches. It
was once believed that left out of doors
at night, a broomstick would take itself
off to the witches' sabbat and that
witches sometimes left one in their beds
to trick their husbands while they
attended a secret witches' coven.
Once commonly believed to be a means
of transport, many pictures of witches
"flying" show a broomstick or forked
branch being "ridden."
They were used during pagan wedding
ceremonies when couples "jumped the
besom" to symbolize their union. Today
they are more likely to be used by
modern witches to ritually cleanse the
working area.

Characteristics of a broomstick

- The staff was originally made from
  the broom shrub and sold to ward
  off evil.
- The staff is today often made from
  ash (for protection) and the brush
  from birch twigs (for protection and
  exorcism), bound with a branch
  from willow (for protection, healing
  and love).

CANDLES

Candles made from human fat were once used by
magicians to locate hidden treasure. They were taken to
where the treasure was believed to be located and lit. If
the treasure was in the near vicinity the candle flashed
noisily, spitting the nearer the operator got to the
treasure and going out at the point the treasure could be
located. They are today used in religious ceremonies, as
they have been for centuries, and represent knowledge
and spiritual illumination. Modern witches use them to
represent the element of Fire and to help focus the mind
and thought. They are also connected to the south.
Altar candles are usually placed either side of the altar:
white for good magic, black for bad.

Characteristics

- They come in different colors and
  shapes and are used for different
  purposes.
- They may be scored with runic
  symbols or special patterns.
- They should be lit using matches
  rather than a lighter.
- Once lit, candles should not be
  touched.
- Candles used in magic rituals
  need to burn down completely.
- Candles used for lighting or
  decoration are not re-lit for use
  with magic spells.

Zodiac candles

If you are using candles in part of a ritual involving a person whose zodiac sign is known, you might want to enhance your magic by using the color candle associated with that particular zodiac sign and to

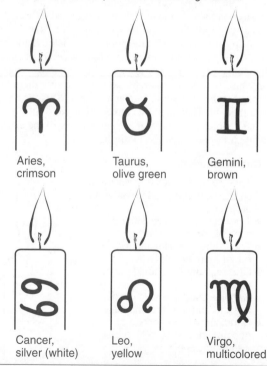

Aries,
crimson

Taurus,
olive green

Gemini,
brown

Cancer,
silver (white)

Leo,
yellow

Virgo,
multicolored

scratch into it the corresponding sign of the zodiac
also. Each of the twelve zodiac signs is shown here
together with the corresponding candle color and the
appropriate symbol.

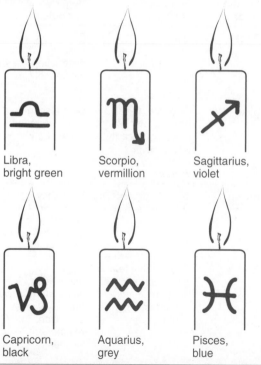

Libra,
bright green

Scorpio,
vermillion

Sagittarius,
violet

Capricorn,
black

Aquarius,
grey

Pisces,
blue

Working candles

Candles of varying colors are used when making different types of spell. Most candle colors have both positive and negative attributes and it is these

Candle color	Positive attributes	Negative attributes
Black	None	Confusion, despair, destruction, loss, melancholy, sadness
Blue	Devotion, fidelity, healing, inspiration, serenity, sincerity, spirituality, tranquillity, truth, wisdom	Coldness, gloom, lack of sympathy, melancholy, sorrow
Brown	Growth, practicality, solidarity, solidity	Hesitancy, melancholy, neutrality, sadness, sobriety, uncertainty
Green	Abundance, fertility, good luck, growth, harmony, immortality, joy, life, youth	Anger, depression, disharmony, envy, greed, jealousy, suspicion, resentment, sickness

attributes that are evoked during the burning of the
candle, depending on whether you are working good
or bad magic.

Candle color	Positive attributes	Negative attributes
Grey	Maturity, wisdom	Cancellation, dotage, mourning, neutrality, senility
Lavender	Affection, spirituality	None
Orange/gold	Adaptability, attraction, encouragement, justice, positive thinking,	None
Pink	Affection, beauty, friendship, honor, hope, gentleness, love, marriage, morality	None
Purple	Ambition, spiritual power, prestige, progress, psychic ability	Abuse of power, despotism, tyranny

continued

Working candles (continued)

Candle color	Positive attributes	Negative attributes
Red	Courage, creation, dynamism, enthusiasm, love, sexual energy, strength, vigor, warmth	Anarchy, bloodshed, cruelty, danger, hatred, revenge, uncontrolled lust, violence, war
Violet	Healing, innocence, love of truth, piety, spirituality	Melancholia, sadness, treachery
White	Cleanliness, goodness, hope, innocence, light, peace, purity, sincerity, truth	Corruption, cowardice, impotence, infirmity, impurity, weakness
Yellow	Charm, cheerfulness, communication, confidence, creative imagination, glory, joy, life, light, strength, warmth	Adultery, cowardice, decay, disease, dying, inconstancy, jealousy, sickness

Planetary candles
These are used in rituals that require the evocation of a spirit. Spirits have ruling planets and the planets have corresponding colors and symbols. To assist in the evocation of your chosen spirit, discern its governing planet then, using the table here, pick that candle which color corresponds to the ruling planet and scratch the planetary symbol into the candle to further assist your evocation.

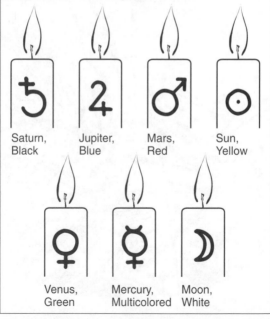

Saturn,
Black

Jupiter,
Blue

Mars,
Red

Sun,
Yellow

Venus,
Green

Mercury,
Multicolored

Moon,
White

CAULDRON

In Greek mythology, the witch goddess Medea restored
people to youth in a magic cauldron. According to
ancient Irish lore, magic cauldrons never ran out of

food at a feast. In the Middle Ages this was an iron pot into which poisons, ointments and philtres were brewed. As many ordinary people used this type of vessel for cooking, it was difficult to use this alone to identify a witch.

In modern witchcraft, the cauldron represents the creative aspects of the female goddess and symbolizes the female uterus. It is known as the Cauldron of Regeneration and may be used in a Yule ceremony. In witchcraft it is linked to Water and to the west. In other traditions it is linked to the "fifth element," ether (or spirit).

A cauldron with three legs is believed to represent the Triple Goddess and a cauldron with four legs, the four elements.

Uses of the cauldron

- It is filled with water and used for scrying (a method of divination).
- It is used to contain a candle.
- It is used to contain a small fire.
- In some cultures it is used to brew spells.

The nganga

Black witches of the Santería religion are known as mayomberos. They use a cauldron known as a *nganga*, an illegal object the making of which is punishable by imprisonment or a fine. Nevertheless, some ngangas are made following the complex ritual outlined on the next page.

Ritual for making a nganga

1 The mayombero and his assistant sprinkle rum in the shape of a cross on the grave of a criminal or someone who was insane, then remove the head, toes, fingers, ribs and tibias of the buried corpse.

2 In his home, the mayombero is covered in a sheet and his assistant lights four tapers around him. A knife is placed at his side heaped with seven amounts of gunpowder.

3 The mayombero goes into a trance, hoping the spirit of the defiled corpse will take over his body. If this happens, the gunpowder ignites.

4 If the possessing spirit agrees, its name is written on a piece of paper and this placed in the bottom of a cauldron with some coins, some grains of soil from its grave site, and blood dripping from the mayombero, cut from his arm using a white-handled knife.

5 Wax, a cigar butt, ashes, lime and a piece of bamboo are placed into the cauldron. The bamboo contains sand, seawater and quicksilver and is sealed at both ends.

6 To the cauldron are added ants, bats, bark, a centipede, chilli, cinnamon, frogs, garlic, lizards, onions, red pepper, rue, Spanish flies, termites, worms, the body of a small black dog, a tarantula, a wasp, and a scorpion. If the *nganga* is to be used for good spells as well as bad, a little holy water is added.

7 The cauldron is buried in the cemetery for three successive Fridays. After 42 days the cauldron is taken home and rum, pepper, dry wine, Caribbean cologne and fresh blood are added. The cauldron is now ready for use.

CENSER

The censer is a small container, such as a bowl or dish, used to burn incense, herbs, chemicals, wood, etc. In modern witchcraft it represents the element Air. Incense is widely used in magic rituals and comes in the form of cones, sticks and blocks, or scented oils, used to enhance magic spells.

Uses of incense and oils

- to cleanse and purify the air before rituals
- to exorcise unwanted energies away from the magic site
- to offer sweet air to the god and goddess
- to raise vibrational rates
- to summon energies
- to relax the senses
- to help contain and concentrate power

SCENTS USED TO ENHANCE DIFFERENT SPELLS

Spells for	Scent/oil used
Blessings	Benzoin, cumin, rue
Business	Benzoin, cinnamon, mint, peony
Clairvoyance	Lemongrass, saffron
Happiness	Lavender, lily of the valley, marjoram
Healing	Carnation, mimosa, rosemary, sandalwood
Love	Gardenia, jasmine, lavender, rose
Luck	Allspice, apple blossom, lemon balm (melissa), orange, nutmeg, violet
Lust	Basil, cinnamon, ginger, neroli, ylang ylang
Money	Clove, ginger, honeysuckle, nutmeg, pine
Peace	Lavender, gardenia, passion flower, skullcap
Prosperity	Almond, bergamot, honeysuckle, mint, peony
Protection	Basil, cypress, frankincense, lavender, myrrh
Purifying	Lavender, myrrh
Sleep	Chamomile, lavender, peppermint, thyme
Success	Bergamot, clove, ginger, lemon balm
Vitality	Bay, carnation, pennyroyal, Saint-John's-wort

CHALICE

Used in modern witchcraft, this is a cup or goblet associated with the element Water and the west. It is used to hold wine during rituals or for holding liquid potions and philtres when they are brought to the altar.

Characteristics of the chalice

- It was originally made from animal horn or even rock crystal, later from gold or silver inlaid with precious stones.
- It is today commonly made from stainless steel.

The chalice is associated with:

beauty
compassion
the earth
emotion
fertility
instinct
intuition
love
receptivity
the subconscious
the womb

CLOTHES

Witches have traditionally been represented wearing a
black cloak and tall pointed black hat; magicians, robes
adorned with silver stars. Many modern witches and
magicians do wear special clothes (such as a robe tied
with a cord) when performing ceremonies and magic
rituals, although they are not necessarily black or
ornate. Others believe that it is important to be naked
("sky clad").
The pointed hat so familiar as part of witches' apparel
was, in fact, an invention of the Christian church and
was known as a steeple-crowned hat. It was put on

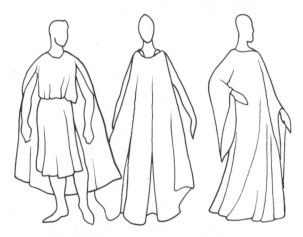

heretics or witches before they were burned in the hope that the church would somehow draw salvation into their souls.

Some magicians feel it is essential to wear a crown, cap or band around their head as a sign of their authority, important when dealing with evoked spirits. They may wear robes in colors corresponding to the planets governing the spirits they intend to evoke. (It was originally recommended that such garments be made only from silk woven by a virgin!)

Garments used in magic of any kind are never used for any other purpose by practicing witches and magicians and are often treated with the same respect as the various tools used.

Some of the grimoires contain elaborate rituals concerning the type of clothing that should be worn, methods of consecration, and the inscription of special signs and recitation of special words.

Spirits of the planet:	Corresponding robe color:
Saturn	Dark-violet
Jupiter	Blue
Mars	Purple
Sun	Yellow, gold or orange
Venus	Green
Mercury	Opalescent
Moon	Silver or white

CORDS

Cords are used by modern witches in many types of ceremony. If you are using cords in rituals requiring a particular planetary influence, you may wish to use a cord corresponding in color with that planet's color, as shown in the chart here.

Characteristics

- They are made from silk, other natural materials or even nylon.
- Different colored cords are used for different spells.

Uses

- A 9' red cord is used for initiation ceremonies.
- When casting spells, knots are tied in the cord in specific patterns and orders, and untied at specific times to release the spell's energy.
- Cords may be knotted by an individual or a group while chanting a spell.

Planet	Corresponding color cord
Saturn	Black
Jupiter	Deep sky blue
Mars	Red
Venus	Green
Mercury	Vermillion, yellow or silver
Sun	Gold
Moon	Silvery white
Earth	Olive, citrine, russet and black

DRUMS & RATTLES

Drums are an essential part of voodoo magic and ceremony. For example, during rada rites, three oxhide-covered drums are used, called *Manman*, *Second* and *Bou-Lah*, played by drummers called *houn'torguiers*. During Petro rites, two goatskin-covered drums are used, one relating to thunderbolts and their patron (*Quebiesou Dan Leh*), the other relating to the world that received thunderbolts (*Guinee*). Both drums are believed to be highly dangerous.

When the sacred drums need to be refreshed, they are sent to Ife, the Mecca of vodoun, in a ceremony symbolizing death, burial and resurrection.

A rattle known as an *asson* is also an important vodoun tool. This is made from a calabash, a type of squash, with a long handle. It represents the joining of the circle (at the round end) and the wand (at the handle). Inside the calabash are placed serpent bones and eight different colored sacred stones. These make the rattle "speak," indicating that the spirits have come down. Shaking or striking the rattle releases the power of the deities (known as *loas*).

MAGIC KNIFE

Called the athame, this was traditionally a ceremonial
sword about 30in long, shaped like a sabre. In
witchcraft it is linked to the element Fire. In other
traditions, it is linked to the element Air. In some
traditions, it is interchangeable with the sword.

Characteristics of the athame

- It is double-bladed with a black hilt.
- It is made from steel or iron. (Some witches
  believe metal should never be used in ritual tools
  as it interferes with the earth's energy and so
  recommend a blade made of flint.)
- The blade may be magnetized.
- Magic symbols are often inscribed on the blade.
- It should always be kept on the witch's person or
  kept wrapped in golden-yellow silk when not in
  use.

Uses of the athame

- In initiation ceremonies
- In the drawing of magic circles
- In the mixing of ingredients used in spell-making
- To direct and control the energy used in casting
  spells, in much the same way as the magic wand.
- Some say the athame should be used for ritual
  purposes only and never for cutting; others argue
  that it should be used as often as possible
- For some it symbolizes a phalluiuos, and may be
  plunged into a chalice of wine, for example, to
  signify the union of male and female

MAGIC LAMP

It is most important for magicians to work in an environment conducive to the spirits they are trying to evoke. Different spirits prefer different colored environments and these are achieved by the use of colored light bulbs or lamps fitted with colored glass or covered with colored cloths. A spirit lamp is the preferred type of lighting.

Spirits	Preferred color environment
Fire spirits	Red
Air spirits (fairies)	Dark blue
Water spirits (water nymphs)	Green
Earth spirits	Yellow
Higher spirits	White

Planetary spirits	Preferred color environment
Saturn	Violet or ultramarine
Jupiter	Blue
Mars	Red
Sun	Yellow
Venus	Green
Mercury	Opalescent
Moon	White

PEN, INK & PAPER

As for many other magic tools, early texts suggested careful or complex rituals for the preparation of the paper, pen and ink to be used in magic rituals. One source recommends using the first feather from the right wing of a swallow as a quill, keeping it wrapped in a white silk cloth when not in use. Ink was to be made by combining roasted peach kernals, soot, crushed gall-nut, gum arabic and river water. The best parchment was thought to be that produced from the skin of an animal that had not yet reproduced, such as an unborn kid.

Today, pens, inks and paper are bought specially for the use in magic ceremonies and are not used for any other purpose. As with other tools, they are often consecrated.

Spells and rituals for:	Preferred ink color
Abundance	Green
Banishing	Black
Communication	Blue
Courage	Red
Energy	Red
Fertility	Green
Healing	Blue
Mental powers	Blue
Prosperity	Green
Protection	Blue
Sex	Red

PENTACLE

This is a five-pointed star, a symbolic device used in modern witchcraft to represent the earth, material wealth, practicality, and stability. It may be written on paper or formed of more solid material. One source suggests that it should be made on a Wednesday, in the first quarter of the moon, at three o'clock in the morning, in a light and airy room in which the magician intends to live alone; three colored inks should be used— green, cinnamon and gold— all newly consecrated along with the quill.

For more information, see the section on magic signs and symbols.

Characteristics of the pentacle

- It may be shaped like a square or a disk.
- It is made from metal (usually copper or silver), wax, baked clay, earthenware or wood. It is inscribed with symbols and placed on the altar.

Uses of the pentacle

- It is used to ground energy.
- It may be used to serve food at the end of a coven's working session.

WAND

Also called a rod or blasting rod, in witchcraft this is linked to the element Fire and to the south. In other traditions, it is linked to the element Air.

Traditional uses of wands

- for transvection
- for divination
- to detect buried treasure
- to test virginity
- to identify thieves and murderers

Modern uses of wands

- to conjure and direct energy
- to bind the energy of a spell together
- to invoke spirits
- for casting a magic circle, in some circumstances

Characteristics

- Some say they should be made from fallen wood, others that they must be cut when the moon is waxing full, having asked the tree's permission and made an offering of thanks at its base. Some suggest they should be cut in the hour of Mercury from virgin wood—a branch with no offshoots and never having borne fruit—using a consecrated knife.
- Different woods are used for different purposes:

Type of wood	Uses
Apple	for binding love
Ash	for prosperity
Cypress	necromancy and for contacting Satan.
Elder	for evoking and exorcising spirits
Hazel	for drawing a magic circle
Oak	for strength and endurance
Rowan	for energy and protection
Willow	for enhancing wishes

- They should be 18" long or the length of the user's forearm, from fingertip to elbow.
- Some witches and magicians use wands made from crystal, silver, carved ivory, ebony or gold.
- They are usually tipped, perhaps with one end gold the other silver or both ends in steel which is then magnetized.
- They are wrapped in red silk when not in use.

Section 5
MAGIC SIGNS
AND SYMBOLS

Included in this section are astrological and
astronomical symbols, including kabbalistic symbols
for the planets and stars. The kabbalists used symbols
for seven planets and their corresponding spirits and
demons. It is not known when these symbols were first
invented, although they are likely to be of Sumerian or
Indian origin. Also provided are examples of
astrological symbols used by Cornelius Agrippa, a
famous occultist scholar and magician.

The kabbalists also modified certain alphabets to arrive
at their own system of letters, the meanings of which
were only known to the initiated. Symbols from the
Hebrew alphabet were widely used in magic and
symbols from both the ogham script and runes form
part of pagan and witch lore. The ogham staves, also
known as the tree alphabet or Celtic tree alphabet,
consist of 25 symbols used in magic and divination.
The 24 symbols of the runic alphabet were developed
in Northern Europe and used in divination. As well as
representing a letter, each symbol also represented a
concept.

5

The section on magic shapes covers the magic circle, triangles, the pentagram and pentacle, the hexagram and the square, all used by people practicing magic today.

In the section on spirits are symbols for those spirits most commonly evoked by people who practice magic: the seven angels of the week, the 72 spirits of Solomon (regarded as demons) and the Olympic spirits.

ASTROLOGICAL SYMBOLS

Common astronomical symbols

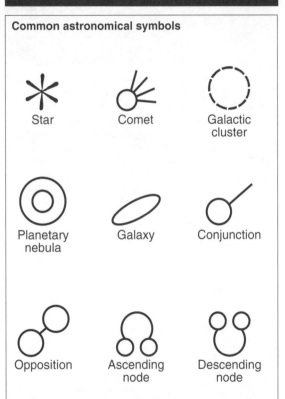

Star

Comet

Galactic cluster

Planetary nebula

Galaxy

Conjunction

Opposition

Ascending node

Descending node

Traditional planet symbols

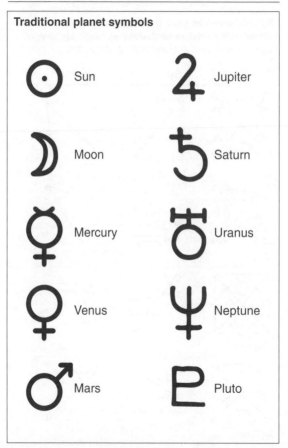

Symbol	Planet	Symbol	Planet
☉	Sun	♃	Jupiter
☽	Moon	♄	Saturn
☿	Mercury	♅	Uranus
♀	Venus	♆	Neptune
♂	Mars	♇	Pluto

Kabbalistic symbols for planets
Shown here are the kabbalistic symbols for seven
planets and their corresponding spirits and demons.

Planet	Spirit	Demon

Sun

Moon

Mercury

Venus

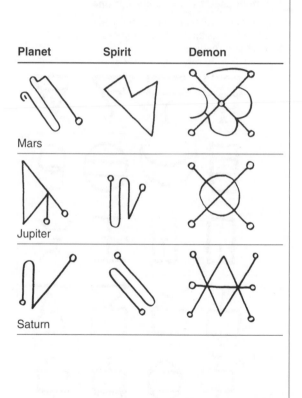

Planet	Spirit	Demon
Mars		
Jupiter		
Saturn		

Symbols used by Cornelius Agrippa

Shown here are examples of astrological symbols used by Cornelius Agrippa, a famous occultist scholar and magician.

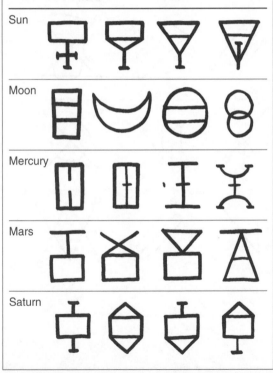

Sun

Moon

Mercury

Mars

Saturn

Zodiac signs

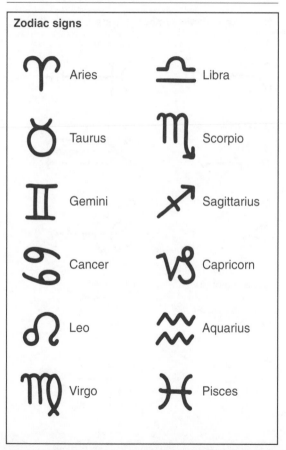

♈ Aries	♎ Libra
♉ Taurus	♏ Scorpio
♊ Gemini	♐ Sagittarius
♋ Cancer	♑ Capricorn
♌ Leo	♒ Aquarius
♍ Virgo	♓ Pisces

Some kabbalistic symbols for stars

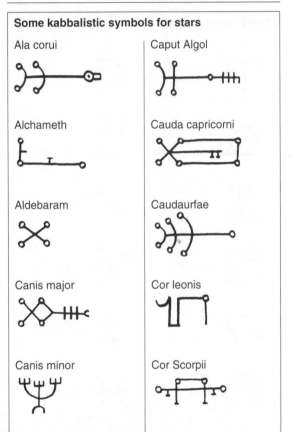

Ala corui

Caput Algol

Alchameth

Cauda capricorni

Aldebaram

Caudaurfae

Canis major

Cor leonis

Canis minor

Cor Scorpii

ALPHABETS

Example of a kabbalistic alphabet
This particular alphabet is believed to have been invented by Honorius, a Theban.

A	B	C	D	E	F
G	H	I	K	L	M
N	O	P	Q	R	S
T	V	X	Y	Z	

Hebrew alphabet

Hebrew was commonly used by magicians and converted by kabbalists into many other alphabets.

A	B	V	G	D	H
W	Z	H	T	Y	K
K	I	M	N	S	'
P	F	TS	Q	R	SH
S	T	T			

Ogham alphabet

The system of writing developed by the Celtic peoples of Britain and Ireland, and later used in magic and divination.

A	B	C	D	E	F
G	H	I	J	M	N
O	P	Q	R	S	T
U	V				

Runic alphabet

One of the earliest written alphabets used by the Germanic Peoples of Europe.

A	U	TH	O	R	K	
G		W	H	N	I	J
CH	P	EO	S	T	B	E
M	L	NG	OE	D	A	AE
Y	EA					

MAGIC SHAPES

The magic circle

Perhaps the best-known of
the magic symbols, the circle
is a symbol of eternity,
perfection and protection. It
was often drawn around
people or plants to protect
them from evil influences.
Formed according to specific
rituals (see the section on
Magic Rituals), for centuries
the circle has been used by
witches and magicians to
summon spirits. It represents
an impenetrable barrier,
keeping demons at bay.

The hexagram

This is a six-pointed star, also
known as the Star of David.
Composed of two
interlocking triangles it
represents the balance
between masculine and
feminine: the upward-
pointing triangle representing
man; the downward-pointing
triangle representing woman.
Additionally, the upward

triangle represents "above" and fire, the downward triangle, "below" and water. Black magic ceremonies were soften enacted within a hexagram.

A hexagram within a circle is known as the Star of Solomon, or the Seal of Solomon and is believed to help protect witches and magicians from demons.

The pentacle

This is a five-pointed star within a circle. It represented health to ancient physicians, but today represents the element Earth and is used as a means of protection by practicing witches and magicians. Such pentacles are made according to specific instructions involving the use of numbers, kabbalistic or Hebrew letters and the names of angels and demons. They may also be made on special days and at specific hours of the day, using specific materials and recitations.

Pentagram

This is a five-pointed star representing the four elements, Earth, Water, Air and Fire, and a fifth element, ether, or spirit. With a triangle pointing upwards it represents life and creativity; with a triangle pointing downward it looks a little like the face of a goat and symbolizes the Devil. (For uses, see Magic Rituals).

The square

"Magic" squares are used by witches and magicians in the making of talismans. For more information about this, see the section on Magic and Numbers.

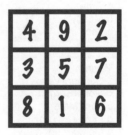

Triangle

Triangles may be used by magicians for "holding" demons. The upward-pointing triangle represents man; the downward-pointing triangle represents woman. Additionally, the upward triangle represents "above" and fire, the downward triangle, "below" and water.

ALCHEMISTS' SYMBOLS

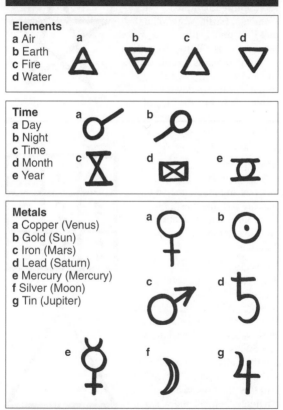

Elements
a Air
b Earth
c Fire
d Water

Time
a Day
b Night
c Time
d Month
e Year

Metals
a Copper (Venus)
b Gold (Sun)
c Iron (Mars)
d Lead (Saturn)
e Mercury (Mercury)
f Silver (Moon)
g Tin (Jupiter)

Alchemical instruments
a Crucible
b Furnace
c Glass container
d Receiver
e Retort
f Steam bath
g Water bath

Alchemic operations
a Amalgamate
b Distill
c Evaporate
d Extract
e Filter
f Precipitate
g Solution
h Sublimate

Substances used by alchemists

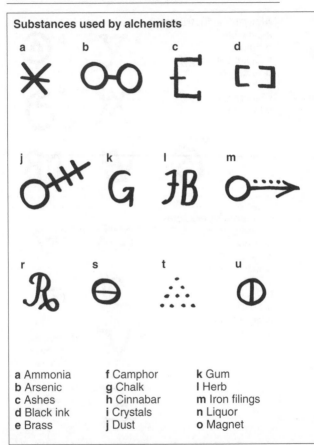

a Ammonia   **f** Camphor   **k** Gum
b Arsenic   **g** Chalk   **l** Herb
c Ashes   **h** Cinnabar   **m** Iron filings
d Black ink   **i** Crystals   **n** Liquor
e Brass   **j** Dust   **o** Magnet

e **f** **g** **h** **i**

n **o** **p** **q**

v **w** **x** **y** **z**

p Marcasite	**u** Soda	**z** Wax
q Oil	**v** Sugar	
r Roots	**w** Sulphur	
s Salt	**x** Urine	
t Sand	**y** Vinegar	

Alchemical Ciphers

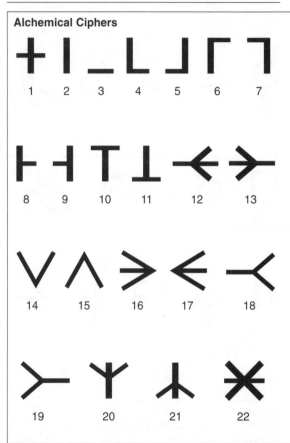

1	2	3	4	5	6
7	8	9	10	11	12
13	14	15	16	17	18
19	20	21	22	23	24

SIGILS OF SPIRITS

Sigils of the seven Olympic spirits

1 Aratron   **4** Och   **6** Phaleg
2 Bethor   **5** Ophiel   **7** Phul
3 Hagith

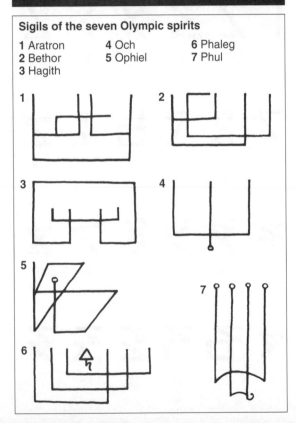

Sigils of the angels governing days of the week

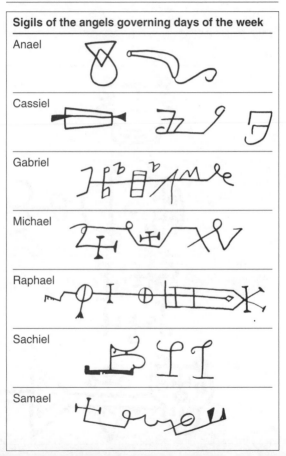

Anael

Cassiel

Gabriel

Michael

Raphael

Sachiel

Samael

Sigils for the the 72 spirits of Solomon
(Alternative names given in brackets)

Name	Sigil
Agares	

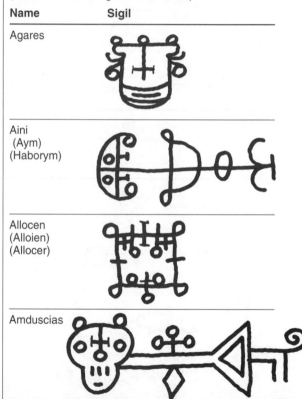

Aini (Aym) (Haborym)	

| Allocen
(Alloien)
(Allocer) | |

| Amduscias | |

Name	Sigil
Amon	
Amy	
Andras	
Andrealphus	

Sigils for the the 72 spirits of Solomon
(continued)

Name	Sigil

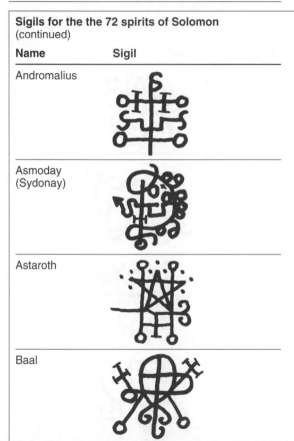

Andromalius	
Asmoday (Sydonay)	
Astaroth	
Baal	

Name	Sigil
Balam	
Barbatos	
Bathin (Bathym) (Marthim)	
Beleth (Byleth)	

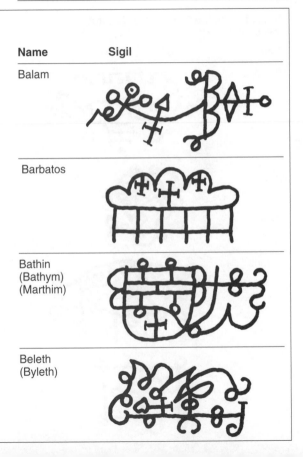

Sigils for the the 72 spirits of Solomon
(continued)

Name	Sigil

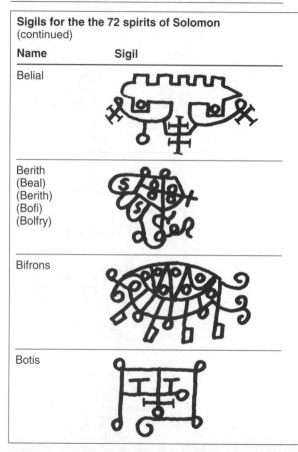

Belial

Berith
(Beal)
(Berith)
(Bofi)
(Bolfry)

Bifrons

Botis

Name	Sigil
Buer	
Bune	
Caim	
Cimeries	

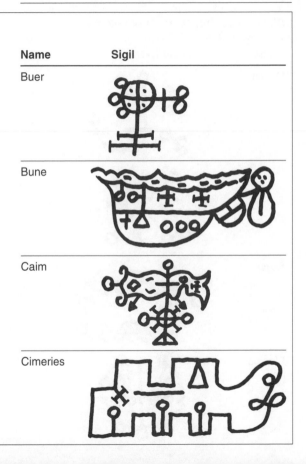

Sigils for the the 72 spirits of Solomon
(continued)

Name	Sigil

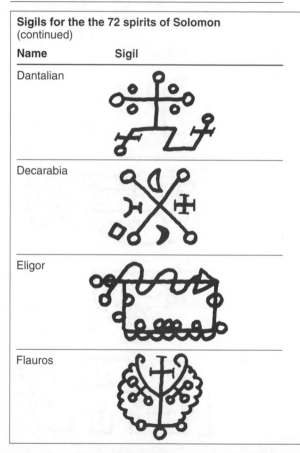

Dantalian

Decarabia

Eligor

Flauros

Name	Sigil
Focalor	
Foras (Forcas)	
Forneus	
Furcas	

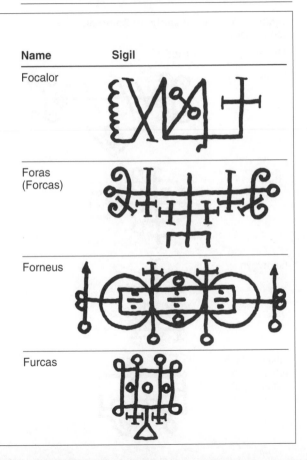

Sigils for the the 72 spirits of Solomon
(continued)

Name	Sigil
Furfur	
Gaap (Tap) (Goap)	
Gamygyn	
Glasyalabolas (Caacrinolaas) (Caassimola)	

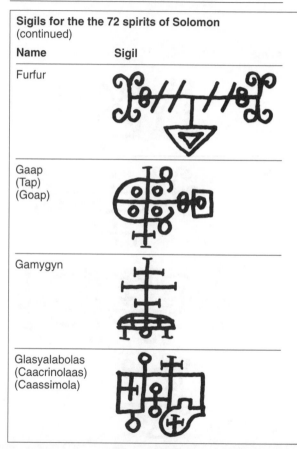

Name	Sigil
Gomory	
Gusion (Gusayn)	
Hagenti	
Halpas	

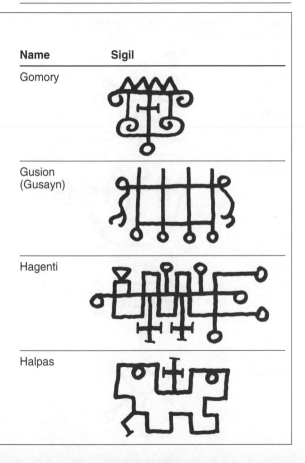

Sigils for the the 72 spirits of Solomon
(continued)

Name	Sigil
Ipos (Ipes) (Ayporos) (Aypeos)	
Lerajie	
Malpas	
Marbas (Barbas)	

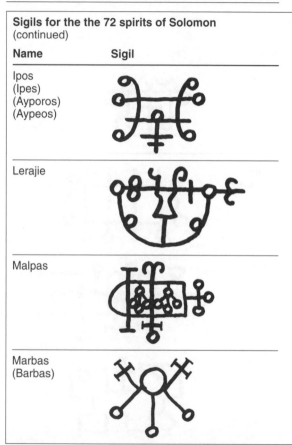

Name	Sigil
Marchosias	
Morax (Foraii) (Forfax)	
Murmur	
Naberius (Cerberus)	

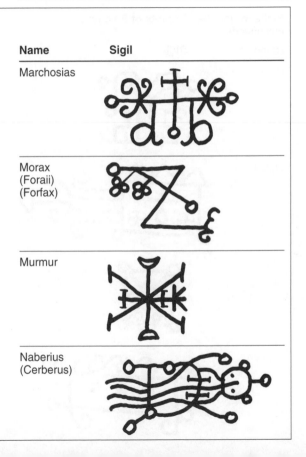

Sigils for the the 72 spirits of Solomon
(continued)

Name	Sigil

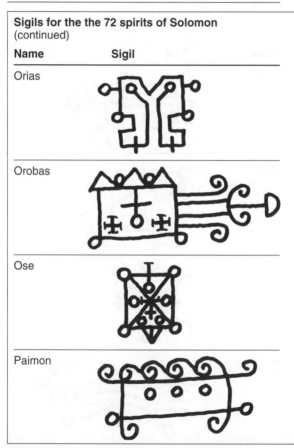

Orias

Orobas

Ose

Paimon

Name	Sigil
Phoenix	
Procel (Pucel)	
Purson (Curson)	
Raum	

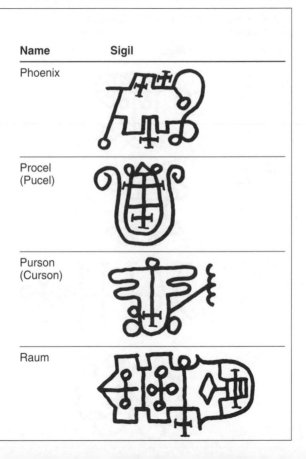

Sigils for the the 72 spirits of Solomon
(continued)

Name	Sigil
Ronobe (Roneve) (Ronove)	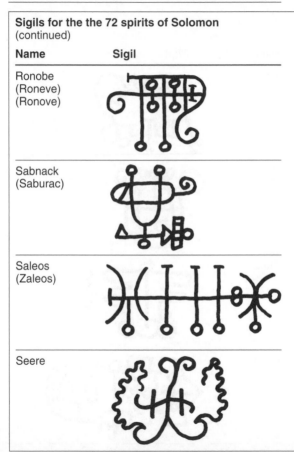
Sabnack (Saburac)	
Saleos (Zaleos)	
Seere	

Name	Sigil
Shax (Chax) (Scox)	
Solas (Stomas)	
Sytry	
Valac	

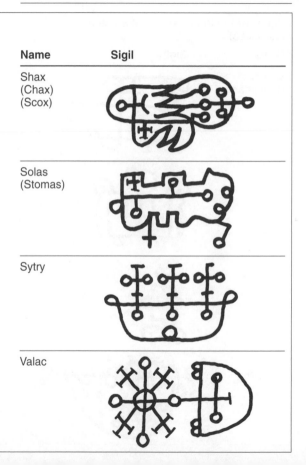

Sigils for the the 72 spirits of Solomon
(continued)

Name	Sigil
Valefor (Malaphar)	
Vapula	
Vassago	
Vepar (Separ)	

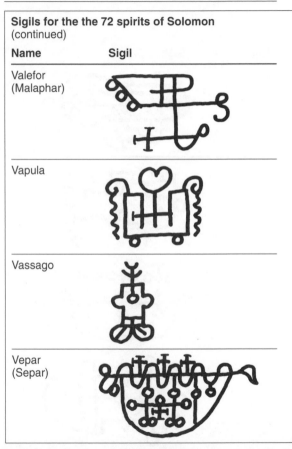

Name	Sigil
Vine	
Vual	
Zagan	
Zepar	

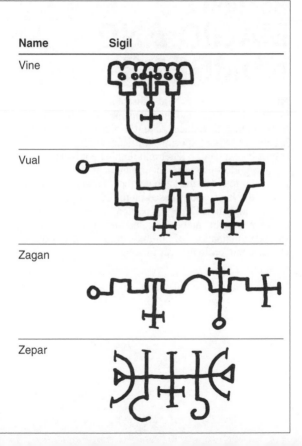

Section 6
MAGIC AND NUMBERS

Numbers have always held a fascination for those interested in magic and the occult. Words, names and numbers may be reduced to single digits, each of which is believed to have special significance. This section begins by explaining letter and number equivalents, a magico-philosophical science of numbers known as *gematria*, found in the kabbala, the secret and mystical lore of the Jews, and is based on the 22 letters of the Hebrew alphabet. There is a part on the relationship between numbers and colors, and on magic squares, special combinations of numbers used by medieval and classical numerologists for making talismans. Many magicians attempt to invoke the assistance of spirits and deities, which themselves relate to different numbers. An A–Z of deities and the numbers to which they correspond can be found in the part on numbers and deities. In the part on number significance are listed those items traditionally associated with different numbers. Superstitions about numbers are also included, as well as information about the practice of numerology, a form of divination still widely used today.

LETTER & NUMBER EQUIVALENTS

The kabbalists used a system in which numbers were
represented as letters. This system is called gemetria or
grammatyâ. Hebrew letters and their number
equivalents (see chart, *right*) can be used in the
construction of magic squares, themselves used for
making talismans.

In addition to the information provided in the chart
(*right*):

F relates to the number **6**
U relates to the numbers **3** and **21**
V relates to the numbers **3** and **21**
X relates to number **10**
Y relates to the numbers **1** and **10**
O is related to zero and the number **11**

The names of Hebrew letters themselves are words with
meaning. Numbers derived from the Hebrew can
therefore be used in magic where specific meanings are
required. A table of letter and number meaning
correspondences is also provided.

Hebrew letter and number equivalents

Hebrew letter	Name	European equivalent	Numerical value
א	Âleph	A	1
ב	Bêth	B	2
ג	Gîmel	G	3
ד	Dâleth	D	4
ה	Hê	He	5
ו	Wâw	W	6
ז	Zayin	Z	7
ח	Chêth	C	8

continued

Hebrew letter and number equivalents (continued)

Hebrew letter	Name	European equivalent	Numerical value
ט	Têth	T	9
י	Yôdh	Y	10
כ	Kâph	K	20
ל	Lâmedh	L	30
מ	Miem	M	40
נ	Nûn	N	50
ס	Sâmekh	S	60
ע	'Ayin	-	70

Hebrew letter	Name	European equivalent	Numerical value
פ	Pe	P	80
צ	Sâdhe	S	90
ק	Koph	K & Q	100
ר	Rêsh	R	200
שׂ	Sîn	S	300
שׁ	Shîn	Sh	300
ת	Tâw	T & Th	400
ן	Nûn	N	700

Hebrew letter and number meanings

Hebrew name	Numerical value	Meaning	Signifies
Âleph	1	Ox	• Independence • Creativity • Innovation
Bêth	2	House	• Family • Inheritance
Gîmel	3 & 4	Camel	• Survival • Change • Propagation
Dâleth	4	Door	• Authority • Access • Denial
Hê	5	Window	• Insight • Intuition • Meditation
Wâw	6	Peg, nail	• Fertility • Liberty
Zayin	7	Weapon	• Authority • Defense
Chêth	8	Enclosure	• Intellect • Female

Hebrew name	Numerical value	Meaning	Signifies
Têth	9	Snake	• Healing • Sexual energy
Yôdh	10	Hand	• Destiny
Kâph	20	Palm	• Healing
Lâmedh	30	Ox-goad	• Progress • Self-sacrifice
Miem	40	Water	• Completion • Destiny • Transition
Nûn	50	Fish	• Escape • Change • Opportunity
Sâmekh	60	Support	• Communion • Mutuality • Charity

continued

Hebrew letter and number meanings

Hebrew name	Numerical value	Meaning	Signifies
'Ayin	70	Eye	• Vision • Clairvoyance • Prediction
Pe	80	Mouth	• Immortality
Sâdhe	90	Fishing hook	meaning not known
Koph	100	Back of head	• Inspiration • Intuition
Rêsh	200	Head	• Identity • Individuality • Recognition
Shîn	300	Tooth	• Transformation
Tâw	400	Sign of cross	• Eternal life
Nûn	700	Fish	• Escape • Change • Opportunity

NUMBERS AND COLORS

In magic, all colors have number equivalents, shown in the table below. When using numbers it may therefore be of use to also employ the corresponding color association.

Color	Number	Color	Number
Aquamarine	11	Orange	8
Black	13	Pearl	9
Blue (dark)	2	Purple	7
Blue (light)	10	Red	5
Brown	4	Silver	9
Gold	6	White	1
Green	3	Yellow	12

MAGIC SQUARES

Magic squares were used by medieval and classical numerologists and by magicians for the making of talismans.

There are seven magic squares. Each one represents a planet or deity and each has particular attributes. They

The Square of Saturn

Added horizontally, vertically or diagonally, the numbers in this square total 15. The square totals 45, the number for 'Agîêl, the Spirit of Saturn, and Zâzêl the Demon of the Saturn. For use as a talisman, it is written with black squares and white numbers. Its alchemic metal is lead.

are used to help summon spirits or to afford protection against them. Each is traditionally made in certain colors and according to elaborate rituals. They are shown on the next seven pages, the first three (the Square of Saturn, the Square of Jupiter and the Square of Mars) with their Hebrew equivalents.

The Square of Jupiter
Added horizontally, vertically or diagonally, the numbers in this square total 34. The square totals 136, the number of Yôphîêl, the Spirit of Jupiter and Hasmâêl, the Demon of Jupiter. Its talismanic colors are blue for the squares, orange for the numbers. Its alchemic metal is tin.

4	14	15	1
9	7	6	12
5	11	10	8
16	2	3	13

ד	יד	יה	א
יב	ז	ו	ט
ח	י	יא	ה
יג	ג	ב	יו

The Square of Mars

Added horizontally, vertically or diagonally, the
numbers in this square total 65. The square totals 325,
the number for Graphîêl, the Spirit of Mars and
Barsâbêl, the Demon of Mars. For talismans, individual
squares are red and numbers green. Its alchemic metal
is iron.

11	24	7	20	3
4	12	25	8	16
17	5	13	21	9
10	18	1	14	22
23	6	19	2	15

גֿ	כֿ	ז	כד	יא
יֿו	חֿ	כה	יבֿ	ד
טֿ	הֿ	יג	כא	יֿו
כֿב	יד	א	יֿח	י
יֿה	כֿ	ב	יֿט	ו

Square of the Sun

Each line of this square adds up to 111, the number of the Spirit of the Sun, Nakîêl. The square totals 666, the number of Sôrath, the Demon of the Sun. Used as a talisman, the squares are yellow and the numbers purple or magenta. Its alchemic metal is gold.

6	32	3	34	35	1
7	11	27	28	8	30
24	14	16	15	23	19
13	20	22	21	17	18
25	29	10	9	26	12
36	5	33	4	2	31

Square of Venus

There are 49 squares here, the number of the Spirit of
Venus, Hagîêl. The sum of each line is 175, the number
of the Demon Kedemêl. The square totals 1225.
Traditional talismanic colors are dark green for the
background and yellow for the numbers. Its alchemic
metal is copper.

22	47	16	41	10	35	4
5	23	48	17	42	11	29
30	6	24	49	18	36	12
13	21	7	25	42	19	37
38	14	32	1	26	44	30
21	39	8	33	2	27	45
46	15	40	9	34	3	28

Square of Mercury

Lines of this square add up to 260. The square total is
2080, the number for Taphthârtharath, the Demon of
Mercury. As a talisman, it is orange with pale blue
numbers. Its alchemic metal is quicksilver.

8	58	59	5	4	62	63	1
49	15	14	52	53	11	10	56
41	23	22	44	45	19	18	48
32	34	35	29	28	38	39	25
40	26	27	37	36	30	31	33
17	47	46	20	21	43	42	24
9	55	54	12	13	51	50	16
64	2	3	61	60	6	7	57

Square of the Moon
Lines of this square total 369, the number for the
Demon of the Moon, Hasmôday. The square totals
3321, the number of Malka Betharshesîm, the Spirit of
the Moon and Shîedbarshemoth Sharthathan, the
Moon's Demon. As a talisman, it is purple with yellow
numbers. Its alchemic metal is silver.

37	78	29	70	21	62	13	54	5
6	38	79	30	71	22	63	14	46
47	7	39	80	31	72	23	55	15
16	48	8	40	81	32	64	24	56
57	17	49	9	41	73	33	65	25
26	58	18	50	1	42	14	34	66
67	27	59	10	51	2	43	75	35
36	68	19	60	11	52	3	44	76
77	28	69	20	61	12	53	4	45

A magic circle

Although talismans commonly contain a magic square, there is no reason why magic numbers should not be used within a circle, as the circle itself is a powerful magic symbol. This is a magic circle said to have been given to Benjamin Franklin. It's magic properties are produced by adding any circle or radial group and including the center number (12) always produces a total of 360.

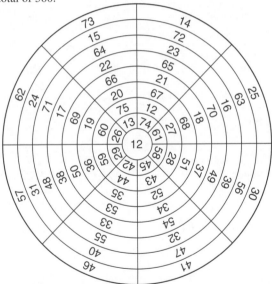

Summary of magic square information

Magic square	Number of squares	Total of each line	Total of all lines
Saturn	9	15	45
Jupiter	16	34	136
Mars	25	65	325
Sun	36	111	666
Venus	49	175	1225
Mercury	64	260	2080
Moon	81	369	3321

Corresponding metal	Colours squares	numbers
lead	black	white
tin	blue	orange
iron	red	green
gold	yellow	purple/magenta
copper	green	yellow
quicksilver	orange	pale blue
silver	purple	yellow

NUMBERS AND DEITIES

As the section on magic squares reveals, different
numbers were associated with different planets and
therefore with the spirits ruling them. In order to invoke
a particular spirit, a magician might concentrate on

Deity	Origin	Associated number
Allah	Islam	1
Amphitrite	Greek	6
Aphrodite (**a**)	Greek	1
Apollo (**b**)	Greek/Roman	1
Athena	Greek	6
Atlas	Greek	10
Bacchus (**c**)	Roman	6
Baldur (**d**)	Norse	12
Boreas	Greek	12
Ceres	Greek	2

a

b

c

using the corresponding magic number in some part of the magic ritual. Provided here are two tables: one lists deities in alphabetical order, their origins and the numbers with which they are associated; the other shows which deities are associated with the numbers 1–13.

Deity	Origin	Associated number
Coelus	Roman	10
Con Ticci	Inca	1
Cronos (e)	Greek	3
Cybele	Greek/Roman	8
Cythereia	Greek	5
Diana (f)	Roman	1
Dionysus	Greek	5
Frey	Norse	1
Freya	Nors	6
Frigga	Norse	2 & 7

d

e

f

Deity	Origin	Associated number
Gaea	Greek	8n
God the Father	Christianity	1
Hecate	Greek	3 & 9
Hades	Greek	13
Heimdal	Norse	8
Hella	Norse	9
Hephaestus	Greek	1
Hera	Greek	8
Hermes (**a**)	Greek	6
Holy Trinity	Christianity	3
Iduna	Norse	7
Ishtar	Babylonian	5
Janus (**b**)	Roman	12
Jehova	Judaism	1
Juno	Roman	9
Jupiter	Roman	4
Loki	Norse	2

a

b

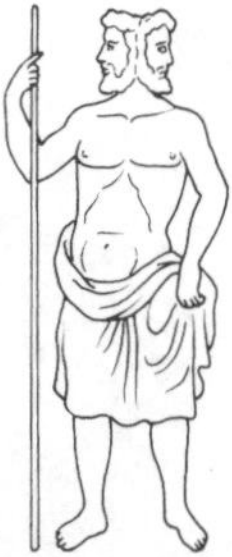

c

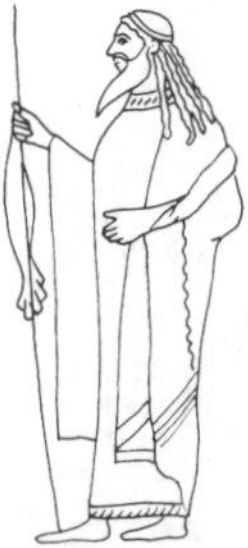

Deity	Origin	Associated number
Lucifer	Christianity	2
Luna	Roman	9
Magna Mater	Roman	8
Mars	Roman	5
Mercury	Roman	8
Minerva	Roman	7
Mithras	Babylonian	7
Neptune (c)	Roman	11
Neter	Egyptian	1
Niord	Norse	11
Odin (d)	Norse	4 & 9
Pangu	Chinese	1
Pluto (e)	Roman	3 & 13
Poseidon	Greek	11
Proserpine	Greek	9
Ptah (f)	Egyptian	1
Rhea	Greek	2

Deity	Origin	Associated number
Satan	Christianity	2
Saturn	Roman	3
Skuld	Norse	10
Sol	Roman	6
Terpsichore	Greek	9
Thor (**a**)	Norse	5
Tiw	Norse	3
Tyr	Norse	3
Uller	Norse	13
Uranus	Greek	10
Venus (**b**)	Roman	2
Vesta	Roman	1
Zeus (**c**)	Greek	4

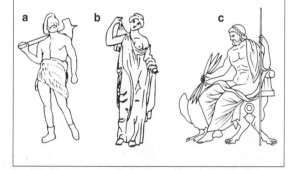

NUMBERS AND CORRESPONDING DEITIES

Number	Deities	Origin
1	Allah	Islam
	Aphrodite	Greek
	Apollo	Greek/Roman
	Con Ticci	Inca
	Diana	Roman
	Frey	Norse
	God the Father	Christianity
	Hephaestus	Greek
	Jehova	Judaism
	Neter	Egyptian
	Pangu	Chinese
	Ptah	Egyptian
	Vesta	Roman
2	Ceres	Greek
	Frigga	Norse
	Loki	Norse
	Lucifer	Christianity
	Rhea	Greek
	Satan	Christianity
	Venus	Roman
3	Cronos	Greek
	Hecate	Greek
	Holy Trinity	Christianity
	Pluto	Roman
	Saturn	Roman
	Tiw	Norse
	Tyr	Norse

NUMBERS AND CORRESPONDING DEITIES
(continued)

Number	Deities	Origin
4	Jupiter	Roman
	Odin	Norse
	Zeus	Greek
5	Cythereia	Greek
	Dionysus	Greek
	Ishtar	Babylonian
	Mars	Roman
	Thor	Norse
6	Amphitrite	Greek
	Athena (**c**)	Greek
	Bacchus	Roman
	Freya	Norse
	Hermes	Greek
	Sol	Roman
7	Frigga	Norse
	Iduna	Norse
	Minerva	Roman
	Mithras	Babylonian
8	Cybele	Greek/Roman
	Gaea	Greek
	Heimdal	Norse
	Hera	Greek
	Magna Mater	Roman
	Mercury	Roman

Number	Deities	Origin
9	Hecate	Greek
	Hella	Norse
	Juno	Roman
	Luna	Roman
	Odin	Norse
	Proserpine	Greek
	Terpsichore	Greek
10	Atlas	Greek
	Coelus	Roman
	Skuld	Norse
	Uranus	Greek
11	Neptune	Roman
	Niord	Norse
	Poseidon	Greek
12	Baldur	Norse
	Boreas	Greek
	Janus	Roman
13	Hades	Greek
	Pluto	Roman
	Uller	Norse

PLANETARY DEMONS AND THEIR NUMBERS

Name	spirit/ demon	Planet
'Agîêl	spirit	Saturn
Barsâbêl	demon	Mars
Graphîêl	spirit	Mars
Hagîêl	spirit	Venus
Hasmâêl	demon	Jupiter
Hasmôdây	demon	Moon
Kedemèl	demon	Venus
Malka Betharshesîm	spirit	Moon
Nakîêl	spirit	Sun
Shêdbarshemoth Sharthathan	demon	Moon
Sôrath	demon	Sun
Taphthartharath	demon	Mercury
Yôphîêl	spirit	Jupiter
Zâzêl	demon	Saturn

Number	Relates to
45	Total of numbers in the Square of Saturn
325	Total of numbers in the Square of Mars
325	Total of numbers in the Square of Mars
49	Number of squares in the Square of Venus
136	Total of numbers in the Square of Jupiter
369	Sum of a line in the Square of the Moon
175	Sum of a line in the Square of Venus
3321	Total of numbers in the Square of the Moon
111	Sum of a line in the Square of the Sun
3321	Total of numbers in the Square of the Moon
666	Total of numbers in the Square of the Sun
2080	Total of numbers in the Square of Mercury
136	Total of numbers in the Square of Jupiter
45	Total of numbers in the Square of Saturn

NUMBER SIGNIFICANCE

According to the practice of numerology, different numbers have different significance and often play an

NUMBER SIGNIFICANCE

Number	Signifies	Associated with
1	Unity	● God and the Sun ● New projects ● New beginnings ● Inspiration and ideas ● Confidence
2	Duality	● Balance and harmony ● Reaching out ● Caring and sharing ● Mothering
3	The Trinity	● The miracle of birth (man plus woman equals child) ● Communication ● Creativity & expression
4	Solidity	● Wholeness ● Hard work ● The seasons ● The four points of the compass

important part in character assessment. In magic such significances are especially important in divination (for more information see the section on Magic and Divination).

Number	Signifies	Associated with	
5	Man	● Marriage ● Freedom ● Curiosity ● The senses ● Expansion	● Fire ● Love ● Versatility
6	The path between Virtue and Vice	● Creation ● Balance & harmony ● Synthesis ● Family love ● Domesticity	
7	Mysticism	● The supernatural	
8	Justice; equilibrium	● The material aspects of existence ● Power ● Sorrow ● Worldly success	

NUMBER SIGNIFICANCE (continued)

Number	Signifies	Associated with
9	Experience	● Mastery over the lessons of life
10	Destiny	● Personal wholeness
11	Transformation	● Change
12	Transmutation	● Change
13	Resurrection	● Bad luck

NUMBERS & SUPERSTITION

Certain numbers are believed to be lucky and others unlucky; some are believed to be especially magical. According to Chinese numerologists, odd numbers are considered luckier than even numbers. Other examples are provided here.

LUCKY AND UNLUCKY NUMBERS

Number	Lucky or unlucky?
1	Considered an unlucky number by the Babylonians, it is today lucky, except as a house number.
2	Considered an unlucky number by the Babylonians, it is today lucky, except as a house number.
3	A lucky number considered to have magical powers. Superstitions include the sayings "Third time lucky" and "Accidents happen in threes." We often give three cheers or hope to have granted three wishes. Well-known triangles include "body, mind, and spirit," "earth, air, and water," "faith, hope, and charity," and "animals, vegetables, and minerals." It was lucky for the Babylonians and considered especially magical by the Romans, Celts, and in Vedic literature.

LUCKY AND UNLUCKY NUMBERS (continued)

Number	Lucky or unlucky?
4	Considered lucky by the Babylonians, it is today believed to be unlucky in the Far East, where it represents death.
5	A magic number often used in spells and charms. It was a lucky number for the Babylonians.
6	Although considered to be unlucky by the Babylonians, by some it is believed to be a "perfect number" because there were 6 days of creation. It is the sum of 1, 2 and 3.
7	This mystical number associated with the supernatural was a lucky number for the ancient Egyptians and Babylonians. Today it is thought to be particularly lucky by gamblers. The Roman's believed that if you broke a mirror you had seven years' bad luck, a superstition that remains to this day. It is especially magical in Vedic literature.
8	Little importance is placed on this number in superstition.

Number	Lucky or unlucky?
9	A lucky number used in many magic spells, especially those concerned with healing. It is a magic number (because 3 x 3 = 9), and if you multiply it by any number and then add together the digits of the product, you will always get nine or one of its multiples. For example, 3 x 9 = 27; 2 + 7 = 9. It was especially magical to the Romans and Celts.
10	Considered to be unlucky by the Babylonians, this is today generally believed to be beneficent.
11	Considered to be unlucky today, as it was for the Babylonians, this is a master number similar to 22 and 33.
12	Although thought to be unlucky by the Babylonians, this is today a lucky number, perhaps because it adds up to three. A magic number for the Romans.
13	Signifying resurrection, this number is generally considered to be unlucky, although for Americans it is officially lucky and appears in various guises on the back of the dollar bill (such as in the thirteen steps of a pyramid).

continued

LUCKY AND UNLUCKY NUMBERS (continued)

Number	Lucky or unlucky?
	Superstitions include the idea that it is especially unlucky when combined with a Friday and that it is unlucky to have thirteen to dinner.
15	A lucky number for the Babylonians.
21	A magic number in Vedic literature.
55	A magic number used in Indian spells.
77	A magic number in Vedic literature.
99	A magic number in Vedic literature.
666	The most evil of all numbers, associated with the devil.

NUMEROLOGY

This is a form of divination in which numbers exert an influence on every facet of our lives and personality. Also known as numeromancy or arithomancy. Modern numerologists tend to concentrate on character analysis and potential.

Primary numbers

Primary numbers 1 to 9 are thought to be of particular significance to all numerologists and form the basis of all numerological systems. All numbers can be reduced to primary numbers, and it is often necessary to do this when using numerology to assess character.

Reducing any number to its primary

Example: number 32 is reduced to the prime number

$$5 \ (3+2=5)$$

Example: the number 146 is reduced to the primary

$$2 \ (1+4+6=11; \ 1+1=2).$$

Dates are reduced to primary numbers in this way, as can be words, the letters of which are assigned numbers before being added together.

Birth numbers

The birth number is your most important number because it is unchangeable and shows the numerical influence at birth. You can calculate it by adding up the numbers in the date of your birth.

Calculating your birth number

Example: For someone born on February 14, 1954, add 2 (because February is the second month).

$$1+4+1+9+5+4+2 = 26$$

$$2+6 = 8$$

8 is the birth number for this person.

Once you have found your birth number, look up your natural characteristics and basic personality traits from the tables provided.

Name numbers

Name numbers show acquired or developed traits and can be changed.

Calculating your name number

Convert the name you usually use to numbers, using the number-letter equivalents chart below. Add up the numbers in the same way you would for calculating a birth number.

1	2	3	4	5	6	7	8	9
A	B	C	D	E	F	G	H	I
J	K	L	M	N	O	P	Q	R
S	T	U	V	W	X	Y	Z	

Example: Jo Green

j=1, o=6, g=7, r=9, e=5, e=5, n=5

1+6+7+9+5+5+5 = 38; 3+8 =11; 1+1 =2

Numerological analysis

1 Begin your analysis with the birth number. It is known as the "number of personality" and represents your subject's inborn characteristics.

2 Analyze the name number. This is known as the "number of development" and shows traits developed during life. If your subject uses another name at work, or is known by initials, calculate this also. This is known as the "number of attainment" and shows your subject's achievements.

3 Calculate the vowel number. Add up the number equivalents of vowels in your subject's name and reduce them to the primary number. This number is known as the "number of underlying influence."

4 Calculate the frequency number. Take into account any number that occurs frequently when you are calculating birth, name and vowel numbers. This is known as the "number of added influence" and has a modifying effect on the analysis.

Comparing birth and name numbers

It is considered ideal for a person's birth and name numbers to coincide, as this will reinforce the characteristics of the birth number. A serious mismatch between the two numbers indicates inner conflicts that remain unresolved.

Using numbers for prediction

You can use numbers for prediction in a variety of ways. For example, if you have an important meeting to go to, add the date on which the meeting is to be held, with your birth and name numbers and interpret your answer.

Symbol: the Sun
Day: Sunday
Characteristics: With strength, individuality, and creativity, these people are born leaders, ambitious, active, often aggressive. One is the number of innovators, leaders, winners, but also of tyrants.
Negative qualities: Number 1 people can be self-centered, ruthless, and stubborn if crossed.
Relationships: Number 1s will probably put more energy and attention into their chosen career than into their personal relationships.

Symbol: the Moon
Day: Monday
Characteristics: Gentle, passive and creative, these people are geared more to thought than to action. They are inventive but less forceful in carrying out their plans than number 1 people. They are likely to have charm and intuition.
Negative qualities: Lack of self-confidence. Can be changeable—even deceitful—as well as over-sensitive and depressive.
Relationships: They get on well with their opposites, the number 1 people.

3

Symbol: Jupiter
Day: Thursday
Characteristics: Energetic, disciplined, talented, these people are also conscientious, proud, and independent. Number 3 is the symbol of the Trinity and a superficial show may hide considerable spirituality.
Negative qualities: Number 3s love to be in control and may be too fond of telling other people what to do.
Relationships: They get on well with other 3s, and those born under 6 and 9.

4

Symbol: Uranus
Day: Sunday
Characteristics: Steady, practical, and with great endurance, these people are seldom interested in material things.
Negative qualities: Number 4—the square—contains its own opposite, and number 4 people often see things from the opposite point of view, making them rebellious and unconventional.
Relationships: Number 4s get on well with people whose numbers are 1, 2, 7 or 8, but making friends is hard and number 4s may feel isolated.

5

☿

Symbol: Mercury
Day: Wednesday
Characteristics: Lively, sensual, pleasure-seeking, impulsive and quick-thinking, these people are good at making money, especially by risk or speculation, and they bounce back easily from failure.
Negative qualities: Quick-tempered and highly strung, number 5s may have trouble with their nerves.
Relationships: Number 5s get on well with any number, but especially fellow number 5s.

6

♀

Symbol: Venus
Day: Friday
Characteristics: Lovers of family life and domesticity, these people are reliable, trustworthy, and romantic rather than sensual. They have a great love of beauty and are usually attractive. Dislike discord.
Negative qualities: May be obstinate.
Relationships: Number 6s get on well with any number.

7

Symbol: Neptune
Day: Monday
Characteristics: Original thinkers who are philosophical and spiritual, and not usually interested in material things. May be highly intuitive, even psychic. Often have a restless love of travel and the sea.
Negative qualities: Have a tendency to become too introverted.
Relationships: May exert an influence on others.

8

Symbol: Saturn
Day: Saturday
Characteristics: Incorporates the rebellious contradictions of number 4 symbolized by willpower and individuality. May mean sorrow, yet is also associated with worldly success. These people have deep and intense feelings.
Negative qualities: May appear cold.
Relationships: Are often misunderstood by others

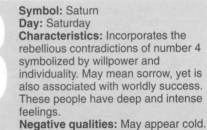

9

Symbol: Mars
Day: Tuesday
Characteristics: Fighters, active, and determined, these people usually succeed after a struggle.
Negative qualities: Prone to accident and injury; may be quarrelsome.
Relationships: Highly courageous, demonstrating brotherly love.

♂

Secondary numbers

In addition to the nine primary numbers, secondary numbers are taken into account by some numerologists, but usually only as additional information. Suppose, for example, that a person's birth number and name number are both 12. Both the birth number and name number will be 3 (1+2), but the occurrence of the number 12 for both results suggests that this number has special significance. Some numerologists have created a list of meanings for vast numbers of secondary numbers; others recognize only the secondary numbers up to 22 (note, there are 22 letters in the Hebrew alphabet). The secondary numbers most commonly thought to have significance are 11, 12, 13, 22 and 40.

Section 7
CORRESPONDENCES

Correspondences refers to the way things relate to each other. There are many different tables of correspondence, used by magicians over the centuries as part of their magic and rituals. Modern witches use correspondences, some traditional, others in keeping with a particular purpose.

This section lists some of the most common correspondences—those for the four elements, those relating to the seven planets, those relating to zodiac signs, and those relating to hours of the day and night. It should be noted that the zodiacal correspondences used by magicians are not necessarily the same as those

7

we have come to know as "lucky" correspondences.
For example, many people born under the sign of
Taurus believe their lucky gemstone to be topaz,
whereas according to some early magicians, the stones
associated with this sign are, in fact, emerald and
carnelian. There is also a chart showing the Arabic
associations relevant to the zodiac (as these differ from
the traditional Western version), and a chart listing the
associations relating to the 22 kabbalistic letters. More
information about kabbalistic letters and their
associations with numbers can be found in the section
on Magic and Numbers.

THE FOUR ELEMENTS

Element	Alchemic symbol	Color	Tarot suit
Earth		Green	Pentacles
Air		Yellow	Sword
Fire		Red	Wand
Water		Blue	Cups

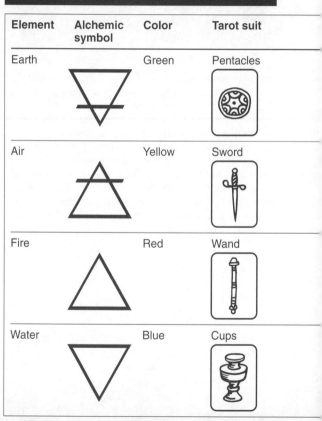

Compass point	Zodiac sign	Altar symbols
North	Taurus Virgo Capricorn	Flowers Herbs Earth Crystals Stones Money
East	Aquarius Libra Gemini	Feather Empty bowl Smoke of incense
South	Leo Sagittarius Aries	Burning candles Incense Fire
West	Scorpio Pisces Cancer	Bowl/chalice of water Seashells

continued

THE FOUR ELEMENTS (continued)

Element	Represents	Humor	Personality (after Jung)
Earth ▽	Solidity	Phlegmatic	Sensation
Air △	Intellect	Sanguine	Thinking
Fire △	Action	Choleric	Intuition
Water ▽	Fertility	Melancholic	Feeling

Virtues	Vices
Endurance	Dullness
Responsibility	Laziness
Thoroughness	Melancholy
Patience	Lack of conscience
	Boredom
	Stagnation
Diligence	Frivolity
Dexterity	Boasting
Optimism	Squandering
Joy	
Courage	Anger
Daring	Jealousy
Enthusiasm	Vindictiveness
Valor	Hatred
Compassion	Instability
Tenderness	Indifference
Receptivity	Spinelessness
Forgiveness	Uncommittedness
Creativity	Treachery

THE FOUR ELEMENTS (continued)

Element	Greco-Roman wind	Governing entity	Mythical being
Earth ▽	Boreas	Auriel	Gnome
Air △	Euros	Raphael	Sylph
Fire △	Notos	Michael	Salamander
Water ▽	Zephyros	Gabriel	Undine

Plant	Shape	Season
Red poppy Thrift	Cube 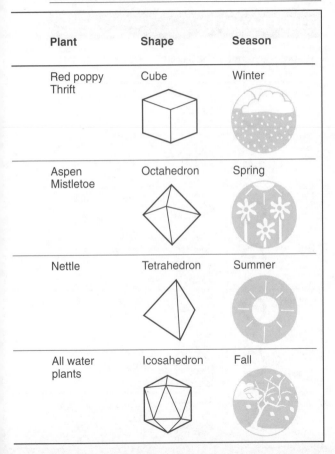	Winter
Aspen Mistletoe	Octahedron	Spring
Nettle	Tetrahedron	Summer
All water plants	Icosahedron	Fall

THE PLANETS

Planet	Symbol	Kabbalistic sign	Color	Metal
Saturn	♄		Black	Lead
Jupiter	♃		Blue	Tin
Mars	♂		Red	Iron
Sun	☉		Yellow	Gold
Venus	♀		Green	Copper
Mercury	☿		Multi-colored	Mercury
Moon	☽		White/silver	Silver

Day	Zodiac signs	Angel
Saturday	Capricorn Aquarius	Cassiel
Thursday	Sagittarius Pisces	Sachiel
Tuesday	Aries Scorpio	Samael
Sunday	Leo	Michael
Friday	Taurus Libra	Anael
Wednesday	Gemini Virgo	Raphael
Monday	Cancer	Gabriel

THE PLANETS (continued)

Planet	Olympic spirit	Kabbalistic spirit	Kabbalistic demon
Saturn	Aratron	'Agîêl	Zâziêl
Jupiter	Bethor	Yôphîêl	Hasmâêl
Mars	Phaleg	Graphîêl	Barsâbêl
Sun	Och	Nakîêl	Sôrath
Venus	Hagith	Hagîêl	Kedemèl
Mercury	Ophiel	Tiriel	Taphthârtharath
Moon	Phul	Malka Betharshesîm	Shîedbarshemoth Sharthathan

Stones	Tree	Perfumes
Onyx Obsidian Jet	Yew	Musk Alum
Sapphire Amethyst	Birch	Balm Nutmeg
Ruby	Holly	Benzoin Sulphur
Topaz	Oak	Myrrh Saffron
Emerald Turquoise	Myrtle	Ambergris Rose
Agate Opal	Olive	Storax Narcissus
Crystal Diamond Pearl	Walnut	Camphor Sandalwood

THE PLANETS (continued)

These three tables show the planetary magic squares for quick reference with other correspondences. More information about magic squares can be found in the section on Magic and Numbers.

Planet	Magic square	Square colors
Saturn	4 9 2 3 5 7 8 1 6	Black squares, white number
Jupiter	4 14 15 1 9 7 6 12 5 11 10 8 16 2 3 13	Blue squares, orange numbers
Mars	11 24 7 20 3 4 12 25 8 16 17 5 13 21 9 10 18 1 14 22 23 6 19 2 15	Red squares, green numbers

Planet	Magic square	Square colors
Sun	<table><tr><td>6</td><td>32</td><td>3</td><td>34</td><td>35</td><td>1</td></tr><tr><td>7</td><td>11</td><td>27</td><td>28</td><td>8</td><td>30</td></tr><tr><td>24</td><td>14</td><td>16</td><td>15</td><td>23</td><td>19</td></tr><tr><td>13</td><td>20</td><td>22</td><td>21</td><td>17</td><td>18</td></tr><tr><td>25</td><td>29</td><td>10</td><td>9</td><td>26</td><td>12</td></tr><tr><td>36</td><td>5</td><td>33</td><td>4</td><td>2</td><td>31</td></tr></table>	Yellow squares, purple numbers
Venus	<table><tr><td>22</td><td>47</td><td>16</td><td>41</td><td>10</td><td>35</td><td>4</td></tr><tr><td>5</td><td>23</td><td>48</td><td>17</td><td>42</td><td>11</td><td>29</td></tr><tr><td>30</td><td>6</td><td>24</td><td>49</td><td>18</td><td>36</td><td>12</td></tr><tr><td>13</td><td>21</td><td>7</td><td>25</td><td>42</td><td>19</td><td>37</td></tr><tr><td>38</td><td>14</td><td>32</td><td>1</td><td>26</td><td>44</td><td>30</td></tr><tr><td>21</td><td>39</td><td>8</td><td>33</td><td>2</td><td>27</td><td>45</td></tr><tr><td>46</td><td>15</td><td>40</td><td>9</td><td>34</td><td>3</td><td>28</td></tr></table>	Green squares, yellow numbers

THE PLANETS (continued)

Planet	Magic square								Square colors
Mercury	8	58	59	5	4	62	63	1	Orange squares, blue numbers
	49	15	14	52	53	11	10	56	
	41	23	22	44	45	19	18	48	
	32	34	35	29	28	38	39	25	
	40	26	27	37	36	30	31	33	
	17	47	46	20	21	43	42	24	
	9	55	54	12	13	51	50	16	
	64	2	3	61	60	6	7	57	

Planet	Magic square									Square colors
Moon	37	78	29	70	21	62	13	54	5	Purple squares, yellow numbers
	6	38	79	30	71	22	63	14	46	
	47	7	39	80	31	72	23	55	15	
	16	48	8	40	81	32	64	24	56	
	57	17	49	9	41	73	33	65	25	
	26	58	18	50	1	42	14	34	66	
	67	27	59	10	51	2	43	75	35	
	36	68	19	60	11	52	3	44	76	
	77	28	69	20	61	12	53	4	45	

THE ZODIAC

Sign	Symbol	Dates
Aries	♈	Mar 21–Apr 20
Taurus	♉	Apr 21–May 21
Gemini	♊	May 22–June 21
Cancer	♋	Jun 22–July 22
Leo	♌	July 23–Aug 23
Virgo	♍	Aug 24–Sept 23
Libra	♎	Sept 24–Oct 23
Scorpio	♏	Oct 24–Nov 22
Sagittarius	♐	Nov 23–Dec 21
Capricorn	♑	Dec 22–Jan 20
Aquarius	♒	Jan 21–Feb 19
Pisces	♓	Feb 20–Mar 20

Sign	Element	Color	Planet
Aries	Fire	Red	Mars
Taurus	Earth	Olive	Venus
Gemini	Air	Brown	Mercury
Cancer	Water	Silver	Moon
Leo	Fire	Yellow	Sun
Virgo	Earth	Multicolor	Mercury
Libra	Air	Green	Venus
Scorpio	Water	Vermillion	Mars
Sagittarius	Fire	Violet	Jupiter
Capricorn	Earth	Black	Saturn
Aquarius	Air	Grey	Saturn
Pisces	Water	Blue	Jupiter

Metal	Angel	Tarot card
Iron	Malahidiel	The Magician
Copper	Asmodel	The High Priest
Mercury	Ambriel	The Lovers
Silver	Muriel	The Chariot
Gold	Verchiel	Fortitude
Mercury	Hamaliel	The Hermit
Copper	Zuriel	Justice
Iron	Barchiel	Death
Tin	Advachiel	Temperance
Lead	Hanael	The Devil
Lead	Cambriel	The Star
Tin	Amnitziel	The Moon

Sign	Stones	Animal
Aries	Chalcedony, Sardius	Ram
Taurus	Emerald, Carnelian	Bull
Gemini	Sardonyx, Topaz	Magpie
Cancer	Sardius, Chalcedony	Crab
Leo	Chrysolite, Jasper	Lion
Virgo	Beryl, Emerald	Virgin
Libra	Topaz, Beryl	Elephant
Scorpio	Chrysoprase, Amethyst	Scorpion
Sagittarius	Jacinth	Centaur
Capricorn	Amethyst, Chrysoprase	Goat
Aquarius	Jasper, Rock crystal	Man
Pisces	Sapphire	Fish

Body system	Body parts
Cerebral	Head
-	Neck, throat
Nervous, pulmonary	Hands, arms, chest, lungs
Digestive	Breast, stomach
Cardiac	Heart, spine, arms, wrists
Alimentary	Abdomen, hands, intestines
Renal	Liver, kidneys
Generative	Pelvis, sexual organs
Hepatic	Hips, thighs, liver
Skeletal	Knees, bones, skin
Circulatory	Ankles, back, legs
Lymphatic, hepatic	Feet

CORRESPONDENCES ACCORDING TO EARLY ARAB MAGICIANS

Sign	Arabic name	English equivalent	Sex	Color
Aries	حمل	Hamal	Male	Brown
Taurus	ثور	Thaur	Female	Black
Gemini	جوزا	Jauza	Neuter	White
Cancer	سرطان	Saratan	Female	Red
Leo	اسد	Assad	Male	Yellow
Virgo	سنبلة	Sambula	Neuter	Green

Arabic number	English equivalent	Perfume	Attributes
١	1	Cinnamon	● Commerce ● Money matters ● Trade
٤	4	Amber	● Illness ● Strength ● Vitality
٢	2	Cloves	● Arcane knowledge ● Hidden things ● Invisibility
٣	3	Violets	● Games off chance ● Gambling ● Luck
٥	5	Lemon	● Bravery ● Strength
٩	9	Jasmine	● Knowledge ● Learning ● Study

CORRESPONDENCES ACCORDING TO EARLY ARAB MAGICIANS

Sign	Arabic name	English equivalent	Sex	Color
Libra	ميزان	Mizan	Female	Blue
Scorpio	عقرب	Aqrab	Male	Purple
Sagittarius	قوس	Qaus	Male	Orange
Capricorn	جدي	Jady	Neuter	Violet
Aquarius	دلو	Dalw	Neuter	Gold
Pisces	حوت	Hout	Male	Silver

Arabic number	English equivalent	Perfume	Attributes
١٠	10	Pepper	• Plans • Schemes • Success
٦	6	Musk	• Family • Marriage • Relatives
٧	7	Rose	• Against evil • Enchantment • Enemies
٨	8	Sandal	• Lawsuits • Lost property • Property
٤	4	Camphor	• Alchemy • Jewels • Metals
٥	5	Currants	• Movement • Travel • Visiting

ARAB JINNS

Name of Jinn	English equivalent	Attribute	Perfume
مَنی پِش	Aauoush	Enmity	Rosewater
دے نُوش	Badyoush	Love	Cinnamon
مَل اوش	Danoush	Passion	Syrup
اَوْا ایوش	Housh	Benevolence	Sandal
بِلے ارش	Kapoush	Neutrality	Honey
ھواش	Nuloush	Love	Saffron
کَے یوش	Puyoush	Good	Camphor
اکَ یوش	Qaypush	Amity	Aloes
بِیر یوش	Shaboush	Friendship	Musk
شَا یوش	Tawayush	Hatred	Sandalwood

KABBALISTIC LETTERS

Letter	Tarot card	
Aleph	0	The Fool
Beth	I	The Magician
Gimel	II	The High Priestess
Daleth	III	The Empress
He	IV	The Emperor
Vau	V	The Hierophant
Zayin	VI	The Lovers
Cheth	VII	The Chariot
Teth	VIII	Strength
Yod	IX	The Hermit
Caph	X	The Wheel of Fortune
Lamed	XI	Justice
Mem	XII	The Hanged Man
Nun	XIII	Death
Samekh	XIV	Temperance
Ayin	XV	The Devil
Pe	XVI	The Tower
Tzaddi	XVII	The Star
Qoph	XVIII	The Moon
Resh	XIX	The Sun
Shin	XX	Judgment
Tau	XXI	The World

HOURS AND DAYS

CORRESPONDING PLANETS

Hour	Sunday	Monday	Tuesday
1am	Sun	Moon	Mars
2	Venus	Saturn	Sun
3	Mercury	Jupiter	Venus
4	Moon	Mars	Mercury
5	Saturn	Sun	Moon
6	Jupiter	Venus	Saturn
7	Mars	Mercury	Jupiter
8	Sun	Moon	Mars
9	Venus	Saturn	Sun
10	Mercury	Jupiter	Venus
11	Moon	Mars	Mercury
12	Saturn	Sun	Moon
1pm	Jupiter	Venus	Saturn
2	Mars	Mercury	Jupiter
3	Sun	Moon	Mars
4	Venus	Saturn	Sun
5	Mercury	Jupiter	Venus
6	Moon	Mars	Mercury
7	Saturn	Sun	Moon
8	Jupiter	Venus	Saturn
9	Mars	Mercury	Jupiter
10	Sun	Moon	Mars
11	Venus	Saturn	Sun
12	Mercury	Jupiter	Venus

Wednesday	Thursday	Friday	Saturday
Mercury	Jupiter	Venus	Saturn
Moon	Mars	Mercury	Jupiter
Saturn	Sun	Moon	Mars
Jupiter	Venus	Saturn	Sun
Mars	Mercury	Jupiter	Venus
Sun	Moon	Mars	Mercury
Venus	Saturn	Sun	Moon
Mercury	Jupiter	Venus	Saturn
Moon	Mars	Mercury	Jupiter
Saturn	Sun	Moon	Mars
Jupiter	Venus	Saturn	Sun
Mars	Mercury	Jupiter	Venus
Sun	Moon	Mars	Mercury
Venus	Saturn	Sun	Moon
Mercury	Jupiter	Venus	Saturn
Moon	Mars	Mercury	Jupiter
Saturn	Sun	Moon	Mars
Jupiter	Venus	Saturn	Sun
Mars	Mercury	Jupiter	Venus
Sun	Moon	Mars	Mercury
Venus	Saturn	Sun	Moon
Mercury	Jupiter	Venus	Saturn
Moon	Mars	Mercury	Jupiter
Saturn	Sun	Moon	Mars

HOURS AND DAYS

CORRESPONDING ANGELS

Hour	Sunday	Monday	Tuesday
1am	Michael	Gabriel	Samael
2	Hanael	Cassiel	Michael
3	Raphael	Sachiel	Hanael
4	Gabriel	Samael	Raphael
5	Cassiel	Michael	Gabriel
6	Sachiel	Hanael	Cassiel
7	Samael	Raphael	Sachiel
8	Michael	Gabriel	Samael
9	Hanael	Cassiel	Michael
10	Raphael	Sachiel	Hanael
11	Gabriel	Samael	Raphael
12	Cassiel	Michael	Gabriel
1pm	Sachiel	Hanael	Cassiel
2	Samael	Raphael	Sachiel
3	Michael	Gabriel	Samael
4	Hanael	Cassiel	Michael
5	Raphael	Sachiel	Hanael
6	Gabriel	Samael	Raphael
7	Cassiel	Michael	Gabriel
8	Sachiel	Hanael	Cassiel
9	Samael	Raphael	Sachiel
10	Michael	Gabriel	Samael
11	Hanael	Cassiel	Michael
12	Raphael	Sachiel	Hanael

Wednesday	Thursday	Friday	Saturday
Raphael	Sachiel	Hanael	Cassiel
Gabriel	Samael	Raphael	Sachiel
Cassiel	Michael	Gabriel	Samael
Sachiel	Hanael	Cassiel	Michael
Samael	Raphael	Sachiel	Hanael
Michael	Gabriel	Samael	Raphael
Hanael	Cassiel	Michael	Gabriel
Raphael	Sachiel	Hanael	Cassiel
Gabriel	Samael	Raphael	-Sachiel
Cassiel	Michael	Gabriel	Samael
Sachiel	Hanael	Cassiel	Michael
Samael	Raphael	Sachiel	Hanael
Michael	Gabriel	Samael	Raphael
Hanael	Cassiel	Michael	Gabriel
Raphael	Sachiel	Hanael	Cassiel
Gabriel	Samael	Raphael	Sachiel
Cassiel	Michael	Gabriel	Samael
Sachiel	Hanael	Cassiel	Michael
Samael	Raphael	Sachiel	Hanael
Michael	Gabriel	Samael	Raphael
Hanael	Cassiel	Michael	Gabriel
Raphael	Sachiel	Hanael	Cassiel
Gabriel	Samael	Raphael	Sachiel
Cassiel	Michael	Gabriel	Samael

HOURS AND DAYS

CORRESPONDING GEMSTONES

Hour	Monday	Tuesday	Wednesday
1am	Moonstone	Hematite	Jasper
2	Turquoise	Diamond	Moonstone
3	Carbuncle	Coral	Turquoise
4	Hematite	Jasper	Carbuncle
5	Diamond	Moonstone	Hematite
6	Coral	Turquoise	Diamond
7	Jasper	Carbuncle	Coral
8	Moonstone	Hematite	Jasper
9	Turquoise	Diamond	Moonstone
10	Carbuncle	Coral	Turquoise
11	Hematite	Jasper	Carbuncle
12	Diamond	Moonstone	Hematite
1pm	Coral	Turquoise	Diamond
2	Jasper	Carbuncle	Coral
3	Moonstone	Hematite	Jasper
4	Turquoise	Diamond	Moonstone
5	Carbuncle	Coral	Turquoise
6	Hematite	Jasper	Carbuncle
7	Diamond	Moonstone	Hematite
8	Coral	Turquoise	Diamond
9	Jasper	Carbuncle	Coral
10	Moonstone	Hematite	Jasper
11	Turquoise	Diamond	Moonstone
12	Carbuncle	Coral	Turquoise

Thursday	Friday	Saturday	Sunday
Carbuncle	Coral	Turquoise	Diamond
Hematite	Jasper	Carbuncle	Coral
Diamond	Moonstone	Hematite	Jasper
Coral	Turquoise	Diamond	Moonstone
Jasper	Carbuncle	Coral	Turquoise
Moonstone	Hematite	Jasper	Carbuncle
Turquoise	Diamond	Moonstone	Hematite
Carbuncle	Coral	Turquoise	Diamond
Hematite	Jasper	Carbuncle	Coral
Diamond	Moonstone	Hematite	Jasper
Coral	Turquoise	Diamond	Moonstone
Jasper	Carbuncle	Coral	Turquoise
Moonstone	Hematite	Jasper	Carbuncle
Turquoise	Diamond	Moonstone	Hematite
Carbuncle	Coral	Turquoise	Diamond
Hematite	Jasper	Carbuncle	Coral
Diamond	Moonstone	Hematite	Jasper
Coral	Turquoise	Diamond	Moonstone
Jasper	Carbuncle	Coral	Turquoise
Moonstone	Hematite	Jasper	Carbuncle
Turquoise	Diamond	Moonstone	Hematite
Carbuncle	Coral	Turquoise	Diamond
Hematite	Jasper	Carbuncle	Coral
Diamond	Moonstone	Hematite	Jasper

USING CORRESPONDENCES

The tables in this part may be used in a variety of
ways—to increase the power of spells by incorporating
into the ritual as many elements as possible associated
with the spell, and to increase the power of invocations.
For example, if you are working a spell on a Monday, it
might be helpful to burn white candles in silver
candlesticks, inscribed with the sign of the Moon; if

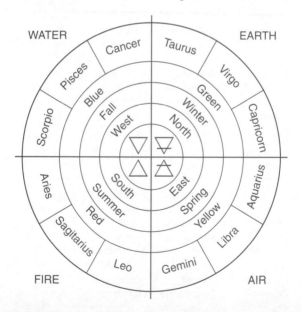

you need to work a spell to invoke the qualities of
water, you might do this facing west, wearing blue,
with items relating to the fall (such as fallen leaves and
berries) as these are all things relating to the element
Water.

Below are two charts using some of the information
from the sections on elements and the planets. Go
through the tables of correspondence and highlight the
information you find most useful. Use it to create your
own charts, similar to those shown below.

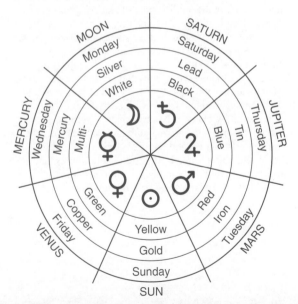

Section 8
MAGIC AND ASTROLOGY

Until the seventeenth century, astrology was considered synonymous with astronomy. The two disciplines are, however, quite different. Astrology involves understanding the significance of stars (using them to predict future events or personality types), astronomy is the study of the positions and movement of stars. Both have been practiced for centuries. The Assyrians, Babylonians, Egyptians and Mayans all employed astrologers to observe, record and predict the positions of stars and events that were believed to be important for their survival and prosperity. Early scientists—considered by many to be magicians—were fascinated with the planets and stars and their possible effects on our lives. Planetary and zodiac symbols were often incorporated into magic rituals and ceremonies, and today many modern witches take into account the significance of planets, especially the Moon.

Important conventions used in astrology
- Symbols are commonly used to represent the planets and signs of the zodiac.
- The Sun and Moon are referred to as planets.
- The Earth is seen as the center of the universe.
- How the planets influence us is determined by the signs of the zodiac, each based on a constellation of stars.

THE PLANETS

Until the eighteenth century, astrological treaties described and illustrated the influence of only seven planets: the Sun, the Moon, Mercury, Venus, Mars, Jupiter and Saturn, all visible to the naked eye. The so-called "modern" planets can only be seen with a telescope. They are Uranus, Neptune and Pluto. Early magicians were fascinated by the effect these planets might have on our lives.

Today, witches—many of whom practice pagan rituals—are particularly concerned with phases of the Moon. They often make banishing spells by a waning moon and spells to increase and grow during a waxing moon. A full moon is believed to be a particularly powerful time for all kinds of magic.

In order to use the planets as part of their magic and ritual, magicians drew up tables of correspondence showing those things with which they believed each planet was associated (such as colors, gemstones, etc.),

but did not always agree on what these things were.
The illustration (below) shows which parts of the body
Robert Fludd believed to be influenced by different
planets. These are listed in the first column of the table
(right). Also listed in the table are those body parts two
other writers believed to be associated with the planets.
You can see that there is considerable difference.
The seven planetary tables which follow (overleaf)
highlight some of the things believed to be *generally*
associated with each of the seven planets.

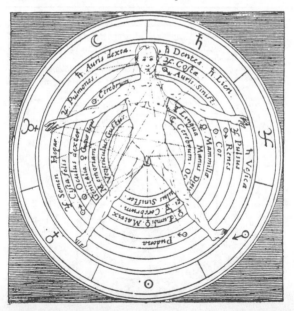

Planet	Fludd	Writer 1	Writer 2
Saturn	Right ear Teeth Spleen Bladder	Brain	Left foot
Jupiter	Liver Lungs Ribs Pulse Semen	Forehead	Stomach
Mars	Left ear Kidneys Sex organs Gall bladder	Lungs	Testicles
Sun	Brain Heart Right eye	Heart	Head
Venus	Loins Womb Testicles Throat Liver Breasts	Stomach	Left arm
Mercury	Tongue Right hand Brain	Liver	Right foot
Moon	Brain Left eye Digestion Gout	Intestines	Right arm

THE SEVEN TRADITIONAL PLANETS

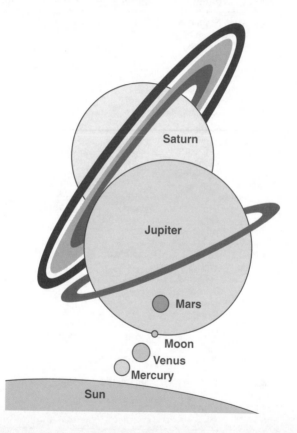

SATURN

Symbol

Color	Black
Metal	Lead
Day	Saturday
Angel	Cassiel
Olympic spirit	Aratron
Kabbalistic spirit	'Agîêl
Kabbalistic demon	Zâziêl
Zodiac signs	Capricorn Aquarius
Stones	Onyx Obsidian Jet
Tree	Yew
Perfumes	Musk, alum
Symbolism	Lawgiver

Associated with

- truth
- aging
- ambition
- responsibility
- the capacity for a career
- the lessons life can teach us

Hours & days

Sun	5am, 12pm, 7pm
Mon	2am, 9am, 4pm, 11pm
Tues	6am, 1pm, 8pm
Wed	3am, 10am, 5pm, 12pm
Thurs	7am, 2pm, 9pm
Fri	4am, 11am, 6pm
Sat	1am, 8am, 3pm, 10pm

JUPITER

Symbol

2

Color	Blue
Metal	Tin
Day	Thursday
Angel	Sachiel
Olympic spirit	Bethor
Kabbalistic spirit	Yôphîêl
Kabbalistic demon	Hasmâêl
Zodiac signs	Sagittarius Pisces
Stones	Sapphire Amethyst
Tree	Birch
Perfumes	Balm Nutmeg
Symbolism	Prophet

Associated with

- expansion
- philosophy
- benevolence
- prosperity
- optimism
- growth
- long-distance travel

Hours & days

Sun	6am, 1pm, 8pm
Mon	3am, 10am, 5pm, 12pm
Tues	7am, 2pm, 9pm
Wed	3am, 9am, 6pm
Thurs	1am, 8am, 3pm, 10pm
Fri	5am, 12am, 7pm
Sat	1am, 9am, 4pm, 11pm

MARS

Symbol

Color	Red
Metal	Iron
Day	Tuesday
Angel	Samael
Olympic spirit	Phaleg
Kabbalistic spirit	Graphîêl
Kabbalistic demon	Barsâbêl
Zodiac signs	Aries Scorpio
Stones	Ruby
Tree	Holly
Perfumes	Benzoin Sulphur
Symbolism	Warrior

Associated with

- action and drive
- power
- physical movement
- construction
- sexual energy
- courage
- self-assertion
- strength
- initiative

Hours & days

Sun	7am, 2pm, 9pm
Mon	4am, 11am, 6pm
Tues	8am, 3pm, 10pm
Wed	5am, 12am, 7pm
Thurs	2am, 9am, 4pm, 11pm
Fri	6am, 1pm, 8pm
Sat	3am, 10am, 5pm, 12pm

SUN

Symbol

Color	Yellow
Metal	Gold
Day	Sunday
Angel	Michael
Olympic spirit	Och
Kabbalistic spirit	Nakîêl
Kabbalistic demon	Sôrath
Zodiac signs	Leo
Stones	Topaz
Tree	Oak
Perfumes	Myrrh
Symbolism	Source of life

Associated with

- personality
- dignity
- health
- leadership
- ego
- the capacity for experience

Hours & days

Sun	10am, 8am, 3pm, 10pm
Mon	5am, 12am, 7am
Tues	2am, 9am, 4pm, 10pm
Wed	6am, 1pm, 8pm
Thurs	3am, 10am, 5pm, 12pm
Fri	7am, 2pm, 9pm
Sat	4am, 11am, 6pm

VENUS

Symbol

Color	Green
Metal	Copper
Day	Friday
Angel	Anael
Olympic spirit	Hagith
Kabbalistic spirit	Hagîel
Kabbalistic demon	Kedemèl
Zodiac signs	Taurus Libra
Stones	Emerald Turquoise
Tree	Myrtle
Perfumes	Ambergris Rose
Symbolism	Goddess of love

Associated with

- feelings and values
- love
- the arts
- affections
- pleasures
- possessions
- morality
- marriage
- socialbility

Hours & days

Sun	2am, 9am, 4am, 11am
Mon	6am, 1pm, 8pm
Tues	3am, 10am, 5pm, 12pm
Wed	7am, 2pm, 9pm
Thurs	4am, 11am, 6pm
Fri	1am, 8am, 3pm, 10pm
Sat	5am, 12am, 7pm

MERCURY

Symbol

Color	Multicolored
Metal	Mercury
Day	Wednesday
Angel	Raphael
Olympic spirit	Ophiel
Kabbalistic spirit	Tiriel
Kabbalistic demon	Tapthâthatath
Zodiac signs	Gemini Virgo
Stones	Agate Opal
Tree	Olive
Perfumes	Storaz Narcissus
Symbolism	Messenger

Associated with

- thoughts
- reason
- the capacity for emotion
- local travel
- dexterity
- words and intellect
- communication

Hours & days

Sun	3am, 10am, 5pm, 12pm
Mon	7am, 2pm, 9pm
Tues	3am, 11am, 6pm
Wed	1am, 8am, 3pm, 10pm
Thurs	5am, 12am, 7pm
Fri	2am, 9am, 4pm, 11pm
Sat	6am, 1pm, 8pm

MOON

Symbol

Color	Moon
Metal	White/silver
Day	Monday
Angel	Gabriel
Olympic spirit	Phul
Kabbalistic spirit	Malka Betharshesîm
Kabbalistic demon	Shîedbarshemoth Sharthathan
Zodiac signs	Cancer
Stones	Crystal Diamond Pearl
Tree	Walnut
Perfumes	Camphor Sandalwood
Symbolism	Mirror of life

Associated with

- moods
- fluctuations
- cycles
- habits
- reflex actions
- desires
- fertility
- the need to touch

Hours & days

Sun	4am, 11am, 6pm
Mon	1am, 8am, 3pm, 10pm
Tues	5am, 12am, 7pm
Wed	2am, 9am, 4pm, 11pm
Thurs	6am, 1pm, 8pm
Fri	3am, 10am, 5pm, 12pm
Sat	7am, 2pm, 9pm

THE MOON IN WITCHCRAFT

The Moon has been worshipped for centuries, and lies
at the heart of the witches' calendar. Hecate, the Greek
moon goddess, is the patroness of witchcraft, and many
modern witches worship the Moon by paying homage
to the goddess Isis.

It takes 27.3 days for the Moon to complete one orbit of
Earth. Because it takes exactly the same time for the
Moon to turn once on its own axis, the Moon always
points the same face to Earth. The far side of the Moon
can only be seen from space.

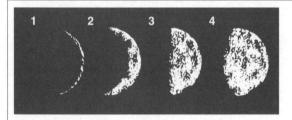

Phases of the Moon

The Moon produces no light of its own: it shines
because it reflects sunlight. Half the Moon is always
in sunlight. The amount of the lit half that can be seen
from Earth changes from day to day. These regular
changes are known as phases of the Moon. Shown
here is the Moon as it appears on selected nights
within the month. The interval between one new
Moon and the next is 29 days 12 hours 44 minutes 3
seconds.

A waxing Moon is one that is becoming increasingly visible. For witches this is a time for casting spells to make wishes come true. A waning Moon is becoming less visible and is the Moon by which banishing spells are often cast. A gibbous ("humped") Moon is between half and full. During the full Moon phase, a witch may make statements about how he or she wishes her life to be. There are thirteen full-moon rituals called esbats. During these the ceremony of "drawing down the moon" is performed.

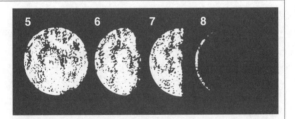

Names of the phases
1 New Moon
2 Waxing crescent Moon
3 Half Moon, first quarter
4 Waxing gibbous moon
5 Full Moon
6 Waning gibbous Moon
7 Half Moon, last quarter
8 Waning crescent Moon

THE ZODIAC

The twelve groups of stars which early astrologers identified as forming a broad band were called the zodiac and were distinguished with traditional symbols.

Guide to the 12 zodiac tables

The twelve tables which follow show the things with which each Zodiac sign is believed to be associated according to early astrologers and magicians. Modern "lucky" associations (lucky colors, stones and flowers) are included for comparison. Associations made by Arab magicians were often different from those that came to be used in the West, and these have been listed separately at the bottom of each table. It should be noted, however, that many of the associations vary

The twelve constellations

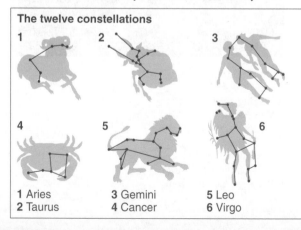

1 Aries   3 Gemini   5 Leo
2 Taurus   4 Cancer   6 Virgo

between sources.

How to use the tables

These tables are particularly useful if you are working spells for someone for whom you know the zodiac sign. Use the tables to gather as much information about the sign as possible. For example, if your subject is an Arian, you might chose to decorate you altar with a red cloth (the associated color), and to place on it some red candles (Fire being the associated element), the sign for Aries and Mars (the associated planet), some of the associated stones, a geranium (an associated plant), and to burn some cinnamon incense (the associated Arab perfume).

More information on this subject can be found in *The Little Giant Encyclopedia of the Zodiac.*

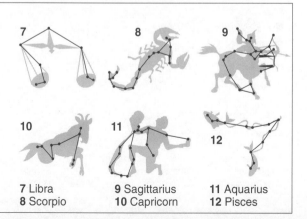

7 Libra
8 Scorpio
9 Sagittarius
10 Capricorn
11 Aquarius
12 Pisces

ARIES

Symbol

Dates	Mar 21–Apr 20
Element	Fire
Planet	Mars
Color (magic)	Red
Colors (lucky)	Red, black, white
Metal	Iron
Angel	Malahidiel
Tarot card	The Magician
Stones (magic)	Chalcedony, sardius
Stones (lucky)	Ruby, diamond
Animal	Ram
Body system	Cerebral
Body parts	Head
Plants	Geranium, sage, primrose
Plants (lucky)	Tiger lily

Arabic associations

Color	Brown
Sex	Male
Number	1
Perfume	Cinnamon
Attributes	Commerce, money matters, trade

TAURUS Symbol

Dates	Apr 21–May 21
Element	Earth
Planet	Venus
Color (magic)	Olive
Colors (lucky)	Pastel shades and blues
Metal	Copper
Angel	Asmodel
Tarot card	The High Priest
Stones (magic)	Emerald, carnelian
Stones (lucky)	Topaz
Animal	Bull
Body system	-
Body parts	Neck, throat
Plants	Vervain, clover, lilac
Plants (lucky)	Mallow

Arabic associations

Color	Black
Sex	Female
Number	4
Perfume	Amber
Attributes	Illness, strength, vitality

GEMINI   Symbol

Dates	May 22–June 21
Element	Air
Planet	Mercury
Color (magic)	Brown
Color (lucky)	Orange
Metal	Mercury
Angel	Ambriel
Tarot card	The Lovers
Stones (magic)	Sardonyx, topaz
Stones (lucky)	Tourmaline, garnet
Animal	Magpie
Body system	Nervous, pulmonary
Body parts	Hands, arms, chest, lungs
Plants	Orchid, gladiolus, verbena
Plants (lucky)	Orchid and hybrids

Arabic associations

Color	White
Sex	Neuter
Number	2
Perfume	Cloves
Attributes	Arcane knowledge, hidden things, invisibility

CANCER   Symbol

Dates	Jun 22–July 22	
Element	Water	69
Planet	Moon	
Color (magic)	Silver	
Colors (lucky)	Yellow-orange, indigo	
Metal	Silver	
Angel	Muriel	
Tarot card	The Chariot	
Stones (magic)	Sardius, chalcedony	
Stones (lucky)	Pearl, amber, moonstone	
Animal	Crab	
Body system	Digestive	
Body parts	Breast, stomach	
Plants	Lotus, comfry, iris	
Plants (lucky)	Lotus, moonwort, almond	

Arabic associations

Color	Red
Sex	Female
Number	3
Perfume	Violets
Attributes	Games of chance, gambling, luck

LEO

Symbol

Dates	July 23–Aug 23
Element	Fire
Planet	Sun
Color (magic)	Yellow
Colors (lucky)	Yellow, orange
Metal	Gold
Angel	Verchiel
Tarot card	Fortitude
Stones (magic)	Chrysolite, jasper
Stones (lucky)	Chrysolite, cats eye
Animal	Lion
Body system	Cardiac
Body parts	Heart, spine, arms, wrists
Plants	Sunflower, cyclamen, heliotrope
Plants (lucky)	Sunflower, laurel

Arabic associations

Color	Yellow
Sex	Male
Number	5
Perfume	Lemon
Attributes	Bravery, strength

VIRGO   **Symbol**

Dates	Aug 24–Sept 23
Element	Earth
Planet	Mercury
Color (magic)	Multicolored
Colors (lucky)	Yellow-green, brown, cream
Metal	Mercury
Angel	Hamaliel
Tarot card	The Hermit
Stones (magic)	Beryl, emerald
Stones (lucky)	Peridot, opal, agate
Animal	Virgin
Body system	Alimentary
Body parts	Abdomen, hands, intestines
Plants	Snowdrop, jasmine
Plants (lucky)	Narcissus, vervain, herbs

Arabic associations

Color	Green
Sex	Neuter
Number	9
Perfume	Jasmine
Attributes	Knowledge, learning, study

LIBRA   Symbol

Dates	Sept 24–Oct 23
Element	Air
Planet	Venus
Color (magic)	Green
Colors (lucky)	Green, purple, pink
Metal	Copper
Angel	Zuriel
Tarot card	Justice
Stones (magic)	Topaz, beryl
Stones (lucky)	Emerald
Animal	Elephant
Body system	Renal
Body parts	Liver, kidneys
Plants	Aloe, rose
Plants (lucky)	Aloe, rose, myrtle

Arabic associations

Color	Blue
Sex	Female
Number	10
Perfume	Pepper
Attributes	Plans, schemes, success

SCORPIO   **Symbol**

Dates	Oct 24–Nov 22
Element	Water
Planet	Mars
Color (magic)	Vermillion
Colors (lucky)	Deep red, blue-green
Metal	Iron
Angel	Barchiel
Tarot card	Death
Stones (magic)	Chrysoprase, amethyst
Stones (lucky)	Turquoise, snakestone, ruby
Animal	Scorpion
Body system	Generative
Body parts	Pelvis, sexual organs
Plants	Cactus, hound's-tongue, hawthorn
Plants (lucky)	Cactus, ivy, oak

Arabic associations

Color	Purple
Sex	Male
Number	6
Perfume	Musk
Attributes	Family, marriage, relatives

SAGITTARIUS   Symbol

Dates	Nov 23-Dec 21
Element	Fire
Planet	Jupiter
Color (magic)	Violet
Colors (lucky)	Blue, royal blue, purple, white
Metal	Tin
Angel	Advachiel
Tarot card	Temperance
Stones (magic)	Jacinth
Stones (lucky)	Jacinth, lapiz lazuli
Animal	Centaur
Body system	Hepatic
Body parts	Hips, thighs, liver
Plants	Rush, pimpernel, stock
Plants (lucky)	Rush, oak, fig, hyssop

Arabic associations

Color	Orange
Sex	Male
Number	7
Perfume	Rose
Attributes	Against all evil, enchantment and enemies

CAPRICORN   **Symbol**

Dates	Dec 22–Jan 20
Element	Earth
Planet	Saturn
Color (magic)	Black
Colors (lucky)	Green, black, grey, indigo, violet
Metal	Lead
Angel	Hanael
Tarot card	The Devil
Stones (magic)	Amethyst, chrysoprase
Stones (lucky)	Jet, black diamond, onyx, ruby
Animal	Goat
Body system	Skeletal
Body parts	Knees, bones, skin
Plants	Thistle, sorrel, coltsfoot
Plants (lucky)	Yew, ash, hemp, weeping willow

Arabic associations

Color	Violet
Sex	Neuter
Number	8
Perfume	Sandal
Attributes	Lawsuits, lost property, property

AQUARIUS   Symbol

Dates	Jan 21–Feb 19
Element	Air
Planet	Saturn
Color (magic)	Grey
Colors (lucky)	Violet, light yellow
Metal	Lead
Angel	Cambriel
Tarot card	The Star
Stones (magic)	Jasper, rock crystal
Stones (lucky)	Glass, onyx, topaz, sapphire
Animal	Man
Body system	Circulatory
Body parts	Ankles, back, legs
Plants	Fennel, buttercup, rosemary
Plants (lucky)	Olive, aspen

Arabic associations

Color	Gold
Sex	Neuter
Number	4
Perfume	Camphor
Attributes	Alchemy, jewels, metals

PISCES

Symbol

Dates	Feb 20–Mar 20
Element	Water
Planet	Jupiter
Color (magic)	Blue
Colors (lucky)	Violet, light green, blue
Metal	Tin
Angel	Amnitziel
Tarot card	The Moon
Stones (magic)	Sapphire
Stones (lucky)	Pearl, amethyst, beryl, aquamarine
Animal	Fish
Body system	Lymphatic, hepatic
Body parts	Feet
Plants	Opium, birthwort, thyme
Plants (lucky)	Opium poppy, lotus, water plants

Arabic associations

Color	Silver
Sex	Male
Number	5
Perfume	Currants
Attributes	Movement, travel, visiting

Qualities of the signs

One of three qualities is attributed to each sign.

Quality	Describes	Signs
Cardinal	Signs that use their abilities to achieve ambitions.	Aries Cancer Libra Capricorn
	♈ ♋ ♎ ♑	
Fixed	Signs that hold on to what they have and resist change.	Taurus Leo Scorpio Aquarius
	♉ ♌ ♏ ♒	
Mutable	Signs that are always searching and often changing.	Gemini Virgo Sagittarius Pisces
	♊ ♍ ♐ ♓	

The four elements

One of four elements is attributed to each sign.

Element	Description	Signs
Fire ♈ ♌ ♐	A process, not a substance, fire is glowing and volcanic, difficult to contain. Once burning, fire will use up air, boil water, or scorch earth.	Aries Leo Sagittarius
Earth ♉ ♍ ♑	Earth can be used for planting or building; solid or sandy, it can channel water, make a fireplace, and co-exist with air.	Taurus Virgo Capricorn
Air ♊ ♎ ♒	Always on the move and invisible, air is windy or balmy; it rises above earth, makes bubbles in water, and is transformed by fire, to which it is essential.	Gemini Libra Aquarius
Water ♋ ♏ ♓	Water seeks its own level, can be clear or muddy, can evaporate, freeze, and reflect rainbows; it can put out a fire, flood earth, and dampen air.	Cancer Scorpio Pisces

Combining qualities and elements

Combining qualities and elements gives an indication of a sign's positive and negative qualities.

Sign	Positive characteristics	Negative characteristics
Aries ♈	Dynamic Independent	Hasty Arrogant
Taurus ♉	Stable Loyal	Stubborn Possessive
Gemini ♊	Communicative Adaptable	Gossipy Scheming
Cancer ♋	Sensitive Sympathetic	Touchy Manipulative
Leo ♌	Generous Self-assured	Pretentious Pompous
Virgo ♍	Humane Discriminating	Insular Petty

Sign	Positive characteristics	Negative characteristics
Libra	Diplomatic Refined	Fickle Apathetic
Scorprio	Passionate Probing	Jealous Suspicious
Sagittarius	Honest Enthusiastic	Blunt Big-headed
Capricorn	Economical Responsible	Mean Inhibited
Aquarius	Just Altruistic	Two-faced Vague
Pisces	Intuitive Sacrificing	Unreliable Lazy

Section 9
MAGIC AND DIVINATION

Divination is the ascertaining of future events by magical means and has been practiced for centuries. Some authorities believed divination to be a legitimate means of finding answers to questions, others thought it an integral part of witchcraft and punished anyone found practicing it.

In this section, you will find a complete glossary of divination methods, and a fortune finder which lists those things that have been used for divination, such as stones, tea leaves, water and wax.

A full description of many of the different types of divination can be found in *The Little Giant Encyclopedia of Fortune Telling*.

9

GLOSSARY OF DIVINATION METHODS

Aeromancy
Divination by atmospheric conditions. There are several different forms, including austromancy, ceraunoscopy, chaomancy, and meteormancy.

Ailuromancy
Divination from cats.

Alectryomancy
A form of augury, in this case divination from the eating patterns of sacred chickens.

Aleuromancy
Divination using slips of paper baked in dough balls. The modern equivalent are Chinese fortune cookies.

Alphitomancy
Divination using cakes made of wheat or barley flour.

Antinopomancy
Divination using the entrails of women and children.

Arachnomancy
A form of augury, in this case divination from the appearance and behavior of spiders.

Arithomancy
A form of divination in which numbers are believed to exert an influence on our lives and personality. This is also called numerology or numeromancy.

Astragalomancy
A form of sortilege which in this case is divination using the bones of sheep.

Astrology
Divination using stars and planets and involving signs of the zodiac (e.g. Aries, Taurus, Gemini, etc).

Augury
Divination based mainly on the appearance and behavior of animals and includes alectryomancy, arachnomancy, cephalomancy, entomomancy, ichthyomancy, myomancy, ophiomancy, scapulomancy, and zoomancy, and also oenomancy and tephromancy. Haruspicy is sometimes considered part of augury.

Austromancy
A form of aeromancy, in this case divination using the wind.

Axinomancy
Divination by saws.

Belomancy
A form of sortilege which in this case is divination by arrows.

Bibliomancy
A form of sortilege which in this case is divination from books and which includes rhapsodomancy. It is also called stichomancy.

Botanomancy
A form of pyromancy which in this case is divination by burning leaves and branches.

Capnomancy
A form of pyromancy which in this case is divination by smoke.

Carromancy
Divination by melting wax.

Cartomancy
Divination using modern playing cards.

Catoptromancy
A form of scrying which in this case involves divination by gazing into a mirror.

Catoxtromancy
Divination by looking glasses.

Cattabomancy
Divination using vessels made of metal.

Causinomancy
A form of pyromancy which in this case is divination by objects cast into the fire.

Cephalomancy
A form of augury, in this case divination from the skull or head of a donkey or goat.

Ceraunoscopy
A form of aeromancy, in this case divination using thunder and lightning.

Ceromancy
Divination from melted wax.

Chaomancy
A form of aeromancy, in this case divination using aerial visions.

Chartomancy
Divination using writing papers.

Chirognomy
Divination using the palm of the hand but which also includes an analysis of hand shape, fingers and fingernails. It is also called chirology, chiromancy, and palmistry.

Chirology
Divination using the palm of the hand but which also includes an analysis of hand shape, fingers and fingernails. It is also called chirgnomy, chiromancy, or palmistry.

Chiromancy
Divination using the palm of the hand but which also includes an analysis of hand shape, fingers and fingernails. It is also called chirgnomy, chirology, or palmistry.

Clairaudience
A form of clairvoyance which in this case is hearing the future ahead of time.

Clairvoyance
Divination by seeing the future ahead of time. There are many different forms of clairvoyance, including clairaudience, metagnomy, precognition, and psychometry.

Cleidomancy
A form of radiesthesia which in this case is divination using a suspended key. It may be used in dowsing.

Cleromancy
An alternative name for sortilege.

Coscinomancy
A form of radiesthesia which in this case is divination using a suspended sieve.

Crithomancy
Divination using the markings on freshly baked bread.

Cromniomancy
Divination using onions.

Crystallomancy
A form of scrying which in this case involves divination with a crystal ball.

Dactylomancy
A form of radiesthesia which in this case is divination

using a suspended ring. Dactylomancy may be used in dowsing.

Demonomancy
Divination by the suggestion of demons.

Daphnomancy
A form of pyromancy which in this case is divination by the burning of laurel leaves.

Dowsing
A method of divination used to locate things under the earth, including water, mineral deposits, bodies, archeological sites, cables, pipes, tunnels, lost property or hidden treasure. Dowsing may involve radiesthesia.

Entomomancy
A form of augury which in this case is divination from the appearance and behavior of insects.

Gastromancy
Divination using the sounds or signs upon the belly.

Geomancy
Divination by the earth. This can mean use of actual earth, or earth-like substances such as sand.

Graphology
A method of assessing a person's character from his or her handwriting.

Gyromancy
Divination by rounds or circles.

Halomancy
A form of pyromancy which in this case is divination by casting salt into a fire.

Haruspicy
Divination from the entrails of animals, one form of which is hepatoscopy. It is sometimes considered part of augury.

Hepatoscopy
A form of haruspicy which in this case is divination using the liver.

Hippomancy
Divination from horses.

Hydromancy
A form of scrying which in this case is divination by water. Pegomancy is a form of hydromancy.

I Ching
An ancient Chinese text (also known as the *Book of Changes*) from which one's fortune can be predicted.

Ichthyomancy
A form of augury which in this case is divination from the shape and entrails of fish.

Idolomancy
Divination using idols, images or fingers.

Lampadomancy
Divination using a single oil lamp or a torch flame.

Lecanomancy
Divination using a basin of water.

Lithomancy
Divination using precious stones.

Livanomancy
Divination by burning frankincense.

Logarithmancy
Divination by logarithms.

Lychnomancy
Divination from the flames of three wax candles.

Macharomancy
Divination by knives or swords.

Metagnomy
A form of clairvoyance which in this case is seeing future events when in a hypnotic trance.

Meteormancy
A form of aeromancy, in this case divination using meteors and shooting stars.

Metoposcopy
A method of assessing character and fortune from lines on the forehead.

Moleoscopy
A method of assessing character from moles on the body.

Molybdomancy
Divination using molten tin or lead.

Myomancy
A form of augury which in this case is divination from the color and movement of mice.

Necromancy
Asking the dead to answer questions about the future using methods such as automatic writing or a ouija board, or a working through a medium.

Numerology
A form of divination in which numbers are believed to exert an influence on our lives and personality. This is also called numeromancy or arithomancy.

Numeromancy
A form of divination in which numbers are believed to exert an influence on our lives and personality. This is also called numerology or arithomancy.

Oenomancy
A form of augury which in this case is divination from the patterns made by wine.

Oinomancy
Divination by wine.

Omphilomancy
Divination by the navel.

Oneiromancy
Divination using dreams.

Onomatomancy
Divination by names.

Onychomancy
Divination by nails.

Ophiomancy
A form of augury which in this case is divination from the color and movement of snakes.

Oriental astrology
A form of Eastern divination based on a 12-year cycle and involving 12 animals which, unlike the zodiac signs of Western astrology, are not based on the configuration or movement of planets or stars.

Ornithomancy
Divination using the sound, appearance, and flight of birds.

Palmistry
Divination using the palm of the hand but which also includes an analysis of hand shape, fingers and fingernails. It is also called chirognomy, chirology, or chiromancy.

Pegomancy
A form of hydromancy which in this case is divination using a sacred pool or spring.

Pessomancy

A form of sortilege which in this case is divination by drawing or casting of specially marked pebbles. This is also called psephomancy.

Phyllorhodomancy

Divination using rose petals.

Phrenology

Assessing character from the presence of bumps on the head.

Physiognomy

Character analysis using facial features.

Podomancy

Divination by feet.

Psephomancy

A form of sortilege which in this case is divination by the drawing or casting of specially marked pebbles. This is also called pessomancy.

Precognition

A form of clairvoyance which in this case is an inner paranormal knowledge of the future.

Psychomancy

Divination by men's souls, affections, wills, religious or moral dispositions.

Psychometry

A form of clairvoyance which in this case involves

divination about a specific person, brought about by holding an object belonging to them.

Pyromancy
Divination by fire. There are many different forms, including, botanomancy, capnomancy, causinomancy, daphnomancy, halomancy, pyroscopy, and sideromancy.

Pyroscopy
A form of pyromancy, which in this case is divination by burning a sheet of paper on a white surface and examining the resulting stains.

Radiesthesia
Using a pendulum for divination. There are different forms, including cleidomancy, coscinomancy, and dactylomancy. Radiesthesia is often used when dowsing.

Rhapsodomancy
A form of bibliomancy which in this case is divination from a book of poetry.

Roadomancy
Divination by stars.

Runes
The symbols of an ancient alphabet that are used for divination.

Scapulomancy
A form of augury which in this case is divination from

the patterns or cracks and fissures on the burned shoulder blade of an animal.

Sciomancy
Divination by shadows.

Scrying
Divination by gazing into a reflective surface. There are many different forms, including crystallomancy, catoptromancy, and hydromancy.

Sideromancy
A form of pyromancy which in this case is divination by casting an odd number of straws onto iron brought to red heat in a fire and reading the patterns formed by straws, their movements, and the nature or the flames and smoke.

Sortilege
Divination by the casting or drawing of lots. There are many different types including astragalomancy, belomancy, bibliomancy, pessomancy (also known as psephomancy), rhapsodomancy and stichomancy. It is also called cleromancy.

Spatalamancy
Divination using skin, bone or excrement.

Stareomancy
Divination using the elements.

Sternomancy
Divination from the breast to the belly.

Stichomancy
A form of sortilege which in this case is divination using books. This is also called bibliomancy. Rhapsodomancy is a form of stichomancy.

Sycomancy
Divination using figs.

Tasseography
Divination using tea leaves.

Tephromancy Divination using the patterns formed in the ashes of burnt offerings made to the gods.

Theomancy
Pretending to divine by the revelation of the words of God.

Theriomancy
Divination by beasts.

Tuphramancy
Divination by ashes.

Tyromancy
Divination from cheese.

Zoomancy
A form of augury which in this case is divination from the appearance and behavior of any animal.

FORTUNE FINDER

This list can be used in two ways. First, it can be of use if you know what a particular method of fortune-telling involves, but can't remember its name. For example, let's say you know that the method involves bones, but you can't remember what sort of bones or the name of the method of divination you have in mind. Looking up "bones" in the list gives you the name of three possible methods: astragalomancy, cephalomancy and scapulomancy. You can then look these up in the glossary for a quick definition.

Second, if you have an interest in a particular type of fortune-telling, the list can be used to help identify related methods. For example, you could look up "Animals," "The body" or "Fire," and would find a list of related methods which you could then investigate further.

What does the method involve?	See:
Aerial visions	Chaomancy
Ancient alphabet	Runes
Animals	Ailuromancy
	Alectryomancy
	Arachnomancy
	Astragalomancy
	Cephalomancy
	Entomomancy
	Haruspicy
	Hippomancy
	Ichthyomancy
	Myomancy
	Ophiomancy
	Oriental astrology
	Ornithomancy
	Scapulomancy
	Zoomancy
Arrows	Belomancy
Ash	Pyroscopy
	Tephromancy
	Tuphramancy
Atmospheric conditions	Aeromancy
	Austromancy

What does the method involve?	See:
	Ceraunoscopy
	Chaormancy
	Meteomancy
Birds	Ornithomancy
The body	Antinopomancy
	Chirognomy
	Chirology
	Chiromancy
	Gastromancy
	Metoposcopy
	Moleoscopy
	Omphilomancy
	Palmistry
	Phrenology
	Physiognomy
	Podomancy
	Sternomancy
Bones	Astragalomancy
	Cephalomancy
	Scapulomancy
Books	Bibliomancy
	I Ching
	Rhapsodomancy
	Stichomancy

What does the method involve?	See:
Burning	Botanomancy Capnomancy Causinomancy Daphnomancy Pyromancy
Bread	Aleuromancy Crithomancy
Cakes	Alphitomancy
Candles	Lychnomancy
Cards	Cartomancy Tarot
Cats	Ailuromancy
Cheese Chickens	Tyromancy Alectryomancy
Circles	Gyromancy
Crystal ball	Crystallomancy
The dead	Necromancy
Demons	Demonomancy

What does the method involve?	See:
Donkey	Cephalomancy
Dreams	Oneiromancy
Earth	Geomancy
Entrails	Antinopomancy Haruspicy Hepatoscopy Ichthyomancy
Face	Metoposcopy Physiognomy
Feet	Podomancy
Figs	Sychomancy
Fire	Botanomancy Capnomancy Causinomancy Daphnomancy Halomancy Pyromancy Pyroscopy Sideromancy
Fish	Ichthyomancy

What does the method involve?	See:
Flames	Lampadomancy Lychnomancy Pyromancy Sideromancy
Flower	Phyllorhodomancy
Food	Aleuromancy Alphitomancy Crithomancy Cromniomancy Sycomancy Tyromancy
Forehead	Metoposcopy
Goat	Cephalomancy
Hands	Chirognomy Chirology Chiromancy Palmistry
Handwriting	Graphology
Head	Phrenology
Hearing	Clairaudience

What does the method involve?	See:
Horses	Hippomancy
Idols	Idolomancy
Insects	Entomomancy
Intestines	Haruspicy Ichthyomancy
Key	Cleidomancy
Knives	Macharomancy
Lamp	Lampadomancy
Leaves	Botanomancy Daphnomancy
Lightning	Ceraunoscopy
Liver	Hepatoscopy
Logarithms	Logarithmancy
Lots	Sortilege
Metal	Cattabomancy Molybdomancy

What does the method involve?	See:
Meteors	Meteormancy
Mice	Myomancy
Mirror	Catoptromancy Catoxtromancy
Moles	Moleoscopy
Nails	Onychomancy
Names	Onomatomancy
Navel	Omphilomancy
Numbers	Arithomancy Numerology Numeromancy
Oil lamp	Lampadomancy
Onions	Cromniomancy
Paper	Chartomancy
Paranormal knowledge	Precognition
Pebbles	Pessomancy Psephomancy

What does the method involve?	See:
Pendulum	Cleidomancy Coscinomancy Radiesthesia
Petals	Phyllorhodomancy
Planets	Astrology
Playing cards	Cartomancy
Poetry	Rhapsodomancy
Pool	Pegomancy
Precious stones	Lithomancy
Reading	Bibliomancy Rhapsodomancy Stichomancy
Ring	Dactylomancy
Reflective surface	Catoptromancy Hydromancy Pegomancy Scrying
Rose	Phyllorhodomancy

What does the method involve?	See:
Salt	Halomancy
Sand	Geomancy
Saws	Axinomancy
Shadows	Sciomancy
Sheep	Astragalomancy
Shooting stars	Meteormancy
Sieve	Coscinomancy
Skull	Cephalomancy
The sky	Aeromancy Ceraunoscopy Chaomancy Meteormancy
Smoke	Capnomancy Sideromancy
Snakes	Ophiomancy
Soil	Geomancy
Souls	Psychomancy

What does the method involve?	See:
Space	Astrology
Spiders	Arachnomancy
Spring water	Pegomancy
Stars	Astrology Meteormancy Roadomancy
Stones	Lithomancy Pessomancy Psephomancy
Straws	Sideromancy
Thunder	Ceraunoscopy
Tea leaves	Tasseography
Torch	Lampadomancy
Trance	Metagnomy
Twigs	Dowsing
Water	Hydromancy Lecanomancy Pegomancy

What does the method involve?	See:
Wax	Ceromancy Carromancy
The weather	Aeromancy Austromancy Ceraunoscopy
Wine	Oenomancy Oinomancy
Wind	Austromancy Aeromancy
Words	Bibliomancy Rhapsodomancy Stichomancy
Writing	Graphology

Section 10
ALCHEMY

The forerunner to modern chemistry, alchemy has always played an important part in the magic arts.

The word *alchemy* is Arabic, although its origins are obscure. It may be derived from *Khem*, the name Arabs gave to Egypt where they obtained knowledge of this science, or it may derive from the Greek *chymia*, which means the art of alloying metals.

Gold has long been regarded as a valuable metal, prized for its beauty, an indication of wealth and power. Over time it came to stand for wisdom, light and perfection, and therefore had both a real and symbolic meaning. The job of the alchemist was therefore twofold: to turn base metals into gold *and* to attain a kind of spiritual perfection.

Although alchemists made some important chemical discoveries, unlike chemists, they often made wild suppositions on the basis of just one or two experiments.

This section begins with a brief introductin to the history of alchemy and goes on to explain the lessons needed to become a true alchemist, the kinds of things found in an alchemist's laboratory, the symbolism employed by practitioners, and alchemic concepts and processes. The section ends with brief descriptions of some well-known alchemists.

HISTORY

The origins of this strange science are unclear.
According to one Arabic legend, God revealed to
Moses and Aaron the secrets of alchemy. Another
theory is that it was founded by the Egyptian god
Hermes (Thoth) (and is therefore sometimes referred to
as the Hermetic Art). According to the third century
alchemistical writer Zosimus Panopolis, alchemy was
an art taught by fallen angels to the women they
married.

Whatever its true origins, it was first practiced among
the Egyptians around the time that Christ was born. It
reached the Greeks, Romans and Arabs, then from
Spain spread throughout western Europe. Many
alchemists drew the attention of kings who were eager
to profit from the achievements of these early chemists.
Charles II of England had a laboratory under his
bedroom, for example, and James IV of Scotland
encouraged his alchemist to fly. Such alchemists—
secretive by nature—were often imprisoned and
tortured for failing to turn metal into gold.

Many learned men took an interest in the art (such as
Sir Isaac Newton and Francis Boyle), as did many
fraudsters. A list of some of the people involved in
alchemy is provided at the end of this chapter.

Right An alchemist being tortured in front of a
monarch, perhaps for refusing to reveal the secrets of
his trade.

BECOMING AN ALCHEMIST

Alchemy was not just a physical science. In order to be successful, one had to be honest and upright and skilled in many fields. For true alchemists, the creation of gold was of secondary importance to their real goal, attaining spiritual perfection. Alchemists who concentrated solely on turning base metals into gold were frowned upon by true practitioners, and came to be known as puffers. This term was later applied to most alchemists, perhaps because they used a bellows to fan their furnaces.

Arab alchemists believed that gold may be produced in two ways, either as a result of some actual, physical change brought about by chemical processes or as a result of the alchemist's having such dedication and concentration that he came to *believe* he had turned metal into gold, and that such a belief in the power of God resulted in the alchemist's ability to transfer this belief into others who would look at the base metal and also see gold.

Cornelius Agrippa von Nettesheimm may have been someone with the ability to convince others of his gold-making powers. He always traveled in style, but it was claimed that "golden" coins with which he sometimes paid his bill later turned out to be pieces of horn or shell.

In his book, *Magus* (1801), Francis Barrett set out ten lessons (overleaf) for the would-be alchemist.

Right The alchemist Heinrich Khunrath praying at the altar in his laboratory.

Barrett's lessons for becoming an alchemist

1
- Keep secrets
- Respect the poor
- Do not court favors

2
- Avoid levity, deceit, vain people and profanity of speech

3
- Give to the poor

4
- Have mercy
- Avoid being vengeful
- Practice forgiveness

5
- Do not condemn others
- Avoid gossip

6
- Study hard

7
- Do not get drunk

8
- Do not be a glutton

9
- Do not covet wealth

10
- Read these ten lessons to prepare yourself as an alchemist

THE ALCHEMIST'S LABORATORY

By the end of the sixteenth century, the alchemist's laboratory was highly sophisticated, containing many materials and much equipment. It was probably situated underground so that any light showing after dark would not attract attention, and may have been covered in symbols and inscriptions in Arabic, Greek, Hebrew or Latin.

Contents of the laboratory

- Medicinal herbs hanging from the ceiling
- Several furnaces
- Bellows to fan the furnace flames
- Fuel for the furnace, such as animal dung, charcoal, peat or rushes
- A glass mask to protect the alchemist's face
- An altar for prayer and meditation
- Animal skeletons
- Books and parchments
- A still
- Supplies of metals

- Supplies of other ingredients such as acid, arsenic, bile, lime, potash, pyrites, salt, sulphur, urine, and vinegar
- Chemical apparatus such as glass jars, tripods, beakers, flasks, spatulas, funnels, crystalizing dishes, pestles and mortars and filters

Alchemic laboratory equipment
Neapolitan alchemist Giambattiste della Porta believed
that alchemic vessels should relate to things in nature
and be used with reference to certain animals. For
example, delicate spirits should be drawn through
vessels with long slender necks like those of the ostrich,
because ostriches were themselves "gentle" and of
"thin spirits."

Some alchemic vessels
a Vessel relating to an
   ostrich, for delicate
   spirits
b Alembic, like a bear,
   part of distilling
   equipment
c A pelican, for
   continuous distillation,
   after the bird of the
   same name

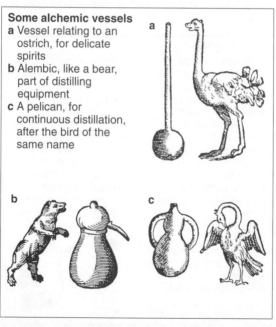

SYMBOLISM IN ALCHEMY

Alchemists enjoyed shrouding their writings in mystery and symbolism, drawing inspiration from astrology, religion and magic. They were generally very secretive people, perhaps because they did not want to be accused of sorcery, perhaps because they did not want their work to fall into the hands of the "wrong" kind of alchemists. Some symbols were used to describe laboratory processes, others for different stages of the soul. A king stood for gold and a queen for silver, but there was generally no consistency to alchemic writing, with different writers using different symbols.

Symbolism used to describe a chemical process
A green lion (royal water, comprisingf nitric and hydrochloric acid) devouring (dissolving) the sun (gold). The lion is green because the gold used often contained copper and colored the acid blue-green.

For additional information see the section on Signs and Symbols.

SOME ALCHEMIC SYMBOLS AND MEANINGS

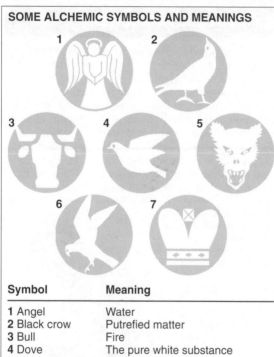

Symbol	Meaning
1 Angel	Water
2 Black crow	Putrefied matter
3 Bull	Fire
4 Dove	The pure white substance achieved by sublimation
5 Gray wolf	Antimony
6 Eagle	Earth
7 King (red)	Gold (or philosopher's sulphur)
8 Lion	Air or sulphur
Lion (red)	The fermenting of material

Symbol	Meaning
Lion (white)	May stand for the realization of the Elixir of Life
9 Lion (winged)	Mercury
10 Moon	Silver (philosopher's mercury)
11 Newborn baby with a crown	The Philosopher's Stone
12 Sun	Gold (or philosopher's sulphur)
13 Toad	Earth
14 Queen (white)	Silver (philosopher's mercury)

ALCHEMIC CONCEPTS

Theory of transmutation

Greek alchemists believed that all substances were
composed of one type of matter—the *prima materia*—
onto which other properties were imposed. They
believed that by removing the other properties, the
prima materia would be obtained. By then adding other
properties to the *prima materia*, new substances would
be formed.

Prima materia was identified with the mercury of the
philosophers, quite different from ordinary mercury.
The mercury of the philosophers was mercury from
which Earth, Air, Fire and Water had been removed. In
practice, this meant the alchemist having to remove an
earth principle or duality, a liquid quality, and an air or
volatile property.

Once the *prima materia* had been obtained, it then had
to be treated with a special kind of sulphur as it was
believed that metals were composed of mercury and
sulphur, an idea that survived to the seventeenth
century.

> *'He that has once the Flower of the Sun,*
> *The perfect ruby which we call Elixir...*
> *Can confer honour, love, respect, long life,*
> *Give safety, valour, yea, and victory,*
> *To whom he will. In eight-and-twenty days*
> *I'll make an old man of fourscore a child.'*
>
> Ben Jonson, *The Alchemist*, 1612

Elixir of Life or Philosopher's Stone

The Elixir of Life was a substance alchemists attempted to make to restore youth, prolong life and turn metals into gold. The idea that you could create such a substance may have originated in China as here it was part of early alchemic practice. The magician Li Chao Ti told the emperor Wu Ti (born AD 141) that the powder of cinnabar could be made into "yellow gold" which could then be used to make utensils that would give long life, and the legend of Wei Po-Yang (in the second century AD) tells how he became immortal after taking a "pill of immortality." The words *Hsien tan* (sulphide of mercury) when translated means "the Philosopher's Stone." It was this that was supposed to bestow everlasting life.

Although the alchemists never succeeded in making the Philosopher's Stone, their findings paved the way for modern chemistry.

There were two varieties of the Philosopher's Stone, one red, used in the production of gold, the other white, to make silver. In addition to being able to transform metals, the stone was believed to have magical properties:

- it helped you see the heavens
- it embued you with perfect health
- it brought great wealth
- it helped you understand everything concerning animals, vegetables and minerals

Correspondences

Alchemists made use of a system of correspondences in which all things are linked to all other things. For example, the planets are linked to metals and are also linked to numbers and colors and attributes. Such correspondences were widely used in magic and occult practices. (For more information, see the section on Magic Rituals).

ALCHEMIC PROCESSES

All alchemists accepted Aristotle's theory that all material things were made up of four elements, Earth, Air, Fire and Water, and that they could be transformed into other substances by applying either wetness, dryness, cold or heat. A whole variety of chemical processes were employed, many of which involved heating and cooling. Sometimes a substance might simply be left to rot, but most often it was combined, separated or solidified in some way.

Common alchemic processes	
Calcination	Reducing minerals and metals to fine powder.
Distillation	Converting a liquid to a vapor by first boiling, then condensing it back into a liquid by cooling.
Sublimation	Heating a substance until it vaporizes, and then returning it to a solid state by rapid cooling.

Alchemical color changes
All alchemists believed that the process of changing things into gold underwent certain very specific color changes.

1 Black (*nigredo*). This indicated that a substance has been reduced to first matter.
2 The material is reborn and lightens and may pass through many different colors as follows.
3 White (*albedo*)
4 Yellow
5 Red (*rubedo*). This was the final stage in the alchemic process, indicating that the Philosopher's Stone had been achieved that could turn base metals into gold.

ALCHEMISTS

Many people attempted to turn base metals into gold. Listed here are some of the more well-known or notorious.

Cornelius Heinrich Agrippa (1486–1535). After practicing as an alchemist himself, Agrippa later became disillusioned with such work and criticized other alchemists.

Saint Thomas Aquinas (1224–1274). A pupil of Albertus Magnus, a Christian philosopher and alchemist who believed that celestial virtue was needed to make gold alchemically.

Roger Bacon (1220–1292). Distinguished between theoretical and practical alchemy and argued that in their attempts to make gold, men brought to light many useful inventions and experiments. He insisted on the need for recording the results of experiments properly so that they could be repeated and verified.

Armand Barbault (1920–1970's). French alchemist who began his career as an enginee,r and who later wrote *Gold of a Thousand Mornings*.

Robert Boyle (1627–1691). Although Boyle believed in the possibility of transmutation, he tried to establish chemistry independently of alchemy. He attacked Aristotle's notion that all matter was made up of the four elements, and disputed the alchemic ideas regarding salt, sulphur and mercury.

Eugene Canseliet (1920–1950). French alchemist and writer on alchemy.

Cleopatra (69–30 BC). Some credit Cleopatra with being an alchemist as she had a gold-making process.

Archibald Cockren (1900–1945). An osteopath living in London who claimed to have made the Philosopher's Stone, but who was killed during the Blitz, taking his secret with him.

Dunikovski (c. 1900's–1930's). Polish engineer who claimed in the 1930s to have discovered a new form of radiation ("Z-rays") that could turn sand or quartz into gold. He raised 2 million francs in investment before being brought to trial for fraud.

Nicholas Flamel (1330–1418). A scribe believed to have discovered the Philosopher's Stone in the late fourteenth century, using it to turn base metals into gold, and making many charitable donations as a result.

Johann Rudolf Glauber (1604–1668). A physician and chemist and believer in alchemy. On discovering what we now know to be sodium sulphate, Glauber believed he had discovered the Philosopher's Stone.

Jabir ibn Hayyan (721–776). An Arab alchemist who made many important chemical observations and wrote treatises on geometry, logic, magic squares and poetry.

John Baptist van Helmot (1580–1644). A respected scientist who was also an alchemist and who claimed to have successfully carried out transmutation.

Edward Kelley (1555–1595). An alchemist who professed to have discovered the Philosopher's Stone and who teamed up with the respected scientist John Dee.

Heinrich Khunrath (1560–1605). A deeply mystical alchemist whose laboratory was half church, adorned with many spiritual inscriptions.

Gottfried Wilhelm Leibniz (1646–1716). A philosopher who spent some years as secretary to an alchemical society in Nürnberg and who was always preoccupied with the nature of the Philosopher's Stone.

Saint Albertus Magnus (1200–1280). A thirteenth-century alchemist, scholar and churchman who was first to describe the composition of white lead, minium, cinnabar, and other substances.

Michel Maier (1568–1622). A physician who abandoned medicine in pursuit of the Philosopher's Stone and collected alchemical writings. He claimed to be a member of the Rosicrucian Order, but this may have been contemporary disinformation or hoaxes designed to discredit those interested in alchemy and the occult.

Sir Isaac Newton (1642–1727). Although best known for propounding the law of gravity, Newton spent much time speculating on the magical nature of things, including alchemy.

Philippus Aureolus Paracelsus (1493–1541). Real name Philippus Aureolus Theophrastus Bombast von Hohenheim. Using his understanding of alchemy, this fifteenthth-century scientist developed a range of medicines.

Al-Razi (866–925). A Persian alchemist and physician who wrote books on alchemy, astronomy, mathematics, medicine, natural science, philosophy and theology.

George Ripley (1415–1490). An alchemist who wrote *Vision*, a poem describing the alchemic process, disguised as a description of the death of a toad.

Emperor Rudolf II (1552–1612). Although not an alchemist himself, this European monarch became obsessed with the science of alchemy and set up a laboratory in Prague, eventually neglecting his state duties. The alchemists who worked for the king lived nearby, in the Golden Lane, also known as the Street of the Alchemists.

Alexander Seton (c. 1540–1604). An alchemist who demonstrated the art of transmutation wherever he went. He was summoned by the Emperor Rudolf II who demanded Seton reveal his secret, as did Christian II of Saxony. He died after being imprisoned and tortured for refusing to disclose his method.

Franz Tausend (1890's–1940's). German alchemist who in the 1920s claimed to have successfully changed iron oxide and quartz into gold and used subsequent investments to finance the Nazi party.

Leonhard Thurneysser (1531–1596). An alchemist
and fraudster who used to pretend to have been able to
turn an iron nail into gold. He did this by making a nail
that was half iron and half real gold, and painting the
gold part black. When this part was dipped into a
solvent, the nail appeared to have been changed into
gold.

Solomon Trismosin (c. 1450–1510). An alchemist
whose real name is not known but who was believed by
some to have been successful in preparing a tincture
that was the Philosopher's Stone.

Section 11
SPELLS

Spells have been inherent to witchcraft for centuries and take many different forms. Used by cunning persons, magicians and wizards as part of ritual healing, charms were often corruptions of Christian prayers. They could be very simple, such as writing out the charm three times on a piece of paper, reciting it out loud and then burning the paper. Or the charm might be written on a piece of paper and worn about the person. Other spells involved potions and lotions and sometimes complex rituals.

Sorcerers could make money from spells by threatening to cast a spell on a farmer's crop or livestock, for example, and thereby extract money from him. Or, the sorcerer could use spells to provide local community cures that were beyond the scope of a physician. Sometimes a witch offered to free a bewitched person from the spells of another witch.

This section provides examples of love spells, spells used for protection, spells used as cures and for the prevention of illness, spells used for empowerment, evil spells and death spells.

More information on the use of spells—and their supposed effects—can be discovered from other books on this subject. It is not recommended that anyone try these spells for themselves.

WHEN TO CAST SPELLS

DAYS ON WHICH TO CAST SPELLS

Day	Spells relating to	
Sunday	● ambition ● career ● healing	● sport ● success
Monday	● childbirth ● clairvoyance ● feminine qualities	● home ● psychic powers
Tuesday	● courage ● men ● sexual energy	● war
Wednesday	● acting ● communication ● education	● mental agility ● travel
Thursday	● business ● expansion ● insurance	● law ● political power
Friday	● arts ● beauty ● entertainment ● environment	● love ● music
Saturday	● agriculture ● inheritance ● karma	● property

LUCKY AND UNLUCKY DAYS FOR SPELLS

Lucky and unlucky days for spell-casting according to the *Grand Grimoire*

Month	Lucky days	Unlucky days
January	3, 10, 27, 31	13, 23
February	7, 8, 18	2, 10, 17, 22
March	3, 9, 12, 14, 16	13, 19, 23, 28
April	5, 17	18, 20, 29, 30
May	1, 2, 4, 6, 9, 14	10, 17, 20
June	3, 5, 7, 9, 13, 23	4, 20
July	2, 6, 10, 23, 30	5, 13, 27
August	5, 7, 10, 14	2, 13, 27, 31
September	6, 10, 13, 18, 30	13, 16, 18
October	13, 16, 25, 31	3, 9, 27
November	1, 13, 23, 30	6, 25
December	10, 20, 29	15, 26

HOURS ON WHICH TO CAST SPELLS

Hour of	Appropriate for spells concerning
Saturn	hatred, enmity, discord
Mars	necromancy
Mercury	speculation, games of chance
Venus	love, poisons, philtres
Jupiter	unknown experiments
Moon	water, sleep.

Casting spells by Moon movements

Some believe that spells should be cast according to when the Moon is in certain zodiac signs:

Moon in	Examples	Appropriate for spells concerning
Fire sign	Aries Leo Sagittarius	love, invisibility
Water sign	Scorpio Pisces	hatred, destruction
Air sign	Gemini Libra Aquarius	peculiar spells, unknown spells

METHODS OF SPELL–CASTING

Ensuring the effectiveness of a spell

It was once believed that spells worked best if some part of the intended recipient were incorporated into them, such as body fluids (**a**), nail trimmings (**b**), teeth (**c**), a lock of hair (**d**), garments (**e**), a footprint (**f**), the straw on which a victim slept (**g**). This was especially true of love and death spells. Appeals would also be made to the Devil (**h**) (perhaps within the safety of a magic circle) to help ensure the efficacy of a spell.

a b c

d e

f g h

MODERN METHOD OF SPELL–CASTING

Witches today use a variety of methods for
spell–casting, one example of which is set out here.

1 Create the right environment: a quiet place where
   you won't be disturbed.
2 Choose an appropriate time for spell casting.
   Many people prefer to cast spells at night time.
   (Consult the two charts on the previous
   pages.)The phase of the Moon is important, too,
   as some spells are believed to work better by a
   waning Moon than by a waxing one. (See the
   section on Magic and Astrology.)
3 Assemble your equipment, such as candles,
   incense, a pentacle (see the section on Magic
   Tools).
4 Decide on what to wear. Many modern witches
   cast their spells naked, as they believe this
   heightens their powers.
5 Get into the right frame of mind, perhaps by
   meditating.
6 Ritually cleanse your working area.
7 Cast your magic circle (see the section on Magic
   Rituals).
8 State the intention of your work.
9 Raise the power by chanting or dancing.
10 Direct the power and cast your spell.
11 Once you have finished, ground yourself,
   perhaps by eating or drinking something.

Items previously used in spell–making

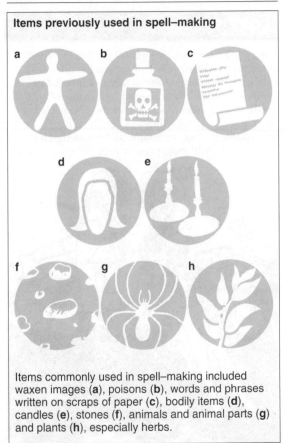

Items commonly used in spell–making included waxen images (**a**), poisons (**b**), words and phrases written on scraps of paper (**c**), bodily items (**d**), candles (**e**), stones (**f**), animals and animal parts (**g**) and plants (**h**), especially herbs.

LOVE SPELLS

One of the most popular forms of spell in medieval times was the love spell. This section provides examples, both ancient and modern, of love potions, spells to procure love, a method for enhancing love spells, spells to secure fidelity, spells to bring back a lover, a spell to cause illness or death to an unconsenting lover, an antidote to love spells, and a spell to make you more popular with the opposite sex.

LOVE POTIONS

Known as philtres, these were originally made from wine with herbs and drugs added and were believed to induce love when slipped into someone's drink or given to them to eat. There are numerous examples of how love potions were made, four of which are outlined here.

FOUR LOVE POTIONS

Love potion 1
Slip a few drops of bat's blood or a lark's eye into someone's drink.

Love potion 2
Powder together the heart of a dove, the liver of a sparrow, the womb of a swallow, the kidney of a hare. Next, add an equal part of your own blood, dried and powdered.

Love potion 3
Mix together powdered root of Enula campana, gathered on St John's Eve, an orange, some ambergris and a piece of paper with the word "sheva" written on it.

Love potion 4
In Iraq, the brain of the hoopoe bird was once powdered and used in a cake to incite love.

SPELLS TO PROCURE LOVE

If a love potion was unavailable or didn't work, there
were others ways to procure love, some more complex
than others. Below are several examples of how they
might have been used.

To procure love using an orange

For a boy to procure the love of a girl, he must prick
an orange all over using a needle and then sleep
with the fruit under his armpit. The following day it
should be presented to the girl, and if she eats it she
will return his love.

To procure love using a love ball

1 Make a love ball from straw, incense, virgin wax,
  rosemary, and hairs from the head of the desired
  man.
2 Carry the charm in the right pocket to attract your
  lover.

To procure love by touching

Rub your hands with the juice of vervain and touch
the man or woman you wish to inspire with love.

To procure love using a pentacle

Pentacles had been used for all kinds of magic
purposes and were believed to be especially useful
for protecting against evil. They could, however, also
be used to procure love. This is an example of a
love pentacle from the *Clavicles of Solomon*. Around
the edge it says "*This is now bone of my bones, and
flesh of my flesh...And they shall be one flesh.*" .

To procure love using herbs

1 Gather some rosemary sticks on the morning of St John.
2 Light a fire in the kitchen.
3 Remove some sticks from the fire and place on them three twigs of rosemary.
4 Recite the following verse three times.

> *I burn rosemary;*
> *But I am not burning rosemary.*
> *Then what am I burning?*
> *The heart of (name your lover) I burn;*
> *That he may neither be able to stop nor rest*
> *Until he comes to be with me and to stay.*

To procure love using a candle

Pierce a lit candle wick using two pins saying:

> *'Tis not the candle alone I stick,*
> *But (the lover's name)'s heart I mean to prick.*
> *Whether he/she be asleep or awake,*
> *I'll have him/her come to me and speak.*

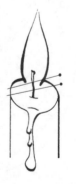

To procure love using an effigy

1 Make a model of your intended using wax, clay, earth or lead.
2 Stick it with pins to "draw the heart."

or

1 Make a waxen image using the desired partner's bodily secretions (blood, saliva, or semen).
2 Write the name of the person on the forehead of the wax image and your name on the breast, using blood from the third finger of the left hand.
3 Using four new needles, pierce the figure in the back, the head, the heart and the pelvis.
4 Sprinkle with salt and mustard seed.
5 Lay in a fire which has been kindled with a piece of paper on which is a sample of the desired person's handwriting.
6 When the fire is spent, write the desired person's name in the ashes.

To procure love using wax hearts

1 Make two hearts from wax.
2 Baptize the hearts in the names of the two persons involved.
3 Join the hearts together using three pins with no heads.
4 Wear the hearts against your own heart to attract your lover.

To procure love using a diamond ring

1 Get a new gold ring set with a diamond.
2 Wrap the ring in a piece of silk.
3 Wear it for nine days and nine nights against your skin, next to your heart.
4 On the ninth day, use a new graver and engrave the word "sceva."
5 Take three hairs from the person you wish to be loved and join them with three of your own saying,

"O Body, may thou love me, and by thy design, succeed as ardently as mine, by the efficacious virtues of sceva."

6 Tie the hairs in knots.
7 Wrap them round the ring.
8 Wrap the ring in silk and wear it against your heart for the next six days.
9 On the seventh day, remove the lovers' knots and give the ring to your intended lover, before sunrise and before eating anything.

To procure love using two needles

1 Take two needles, representing man and woman.
2 Name and bless them.
3 Insert the point of the "male" needle into the eye of the "female" needle.
4 Bind together the two needles using thread in an appropriate color.

HOW TO PROCURE LOVE ACCORDING TO TRADITIONS FROM THE AMERICAN SOUTH

You could have anyone you desired providing:

- you could eat a crab apple without frowning
- you held an apple in your armpit until it was warm before eating it
- you could tie a vine into a lover's knot
- you cut your nails for nine Sundays
- you had curly hair

Methods to procure love using hair

- Wearing a lock of your intended's hair in your hat.
- Burying a hair of your intended along with one of your own, and he or she would love you forever.
- Pulling a hair from a girl's head.
- Burying a photograph of your intended along with some of their hair, and your love would be returned.

Methods to procure love using a wasps' nest

If a woman wore a wasps' nest in her clothing, her lover wouldl love her more deeply.

To procure love using a mandrake

The root of the mandrake plant was believed to be
particularly potent in love spells as it resembles the
human body, and medieval herbals often show "male"
and "female" roots. Below is an example of how it
was used.

1 Dig up a mandrake before dawn when the Moon is
waxing, reciting the words,

"Blessed be this earth, this root, this night."

2 Whittle the root into the figure of your desired lover.

3 Hold the root in your left hand and form a
pentagram over it with your right hand saying,

"I name you (the
name of your
lover)."

Mandrake the male.

4 Bury the root in
the garden.

5 Pour a mixture of
water, milk and
your own blood
over the buried
root saying,

> *"Blood and milk upon the grave*
> *will make (your lover's name) evermore my slave."*

Leave the root buried until the next new Moon.

6 At the next new Moon, an hour before sunrise, dig
up the root saying,

> *"Moon above so palely shining*
> *Bestow this night thy sacred blessing*
> *on my prayer and ritual plea*
> *To fill (your lover's name)'s heart with love for me."*

7 Dry out the root, passing it through incense
associated with the planet Venus saying,

> *"This fruit is*
> *scorched by that*
> *same heat*
> *Which warms my*
> *heart with every*
> *beat."*

€Mandrake the female.

8 When the root is
thoroughly dry,
pierce its heart
with a silver pin.

9 Leave the
mandrake
exposed to the
Moon.

A modern love spell

This spell could be cast over several days, beginning on
a Friday (which is ruled by Venus, the planet of love
and wisdom). It is in three parts: the first was designed
to promote feelings of love, by identifying fears and
stale relationships; the second encouraged letting go

Identifying fear and stale relationships

1 On a Friday evening, light a pink candle.

2 Meditate on how you feel. Try to
clear away any unpleasant thoughts
or fears. List these, including anyone
you have an unpleasant relationship
with.

3 Clear out the northeast corner of
every room. According to Feng Shui,
this is the area governing marriage
and relationships.

4 On another Friday evening, when the
Moon is waning, light a pink candle
and meditate once more on how you
feel. Add to your list of fears or
problem relationships. Imagine these
fears and difficulties being
transformed by beams of love. Carry
your list of fears for three days and
nights.

Dispelling fears

5 On the next Monday set up your altar, light candles,
and once more meditate on your list of fears. Try to
release them. Forgive anyone who needs forgiving.

any unpleasant feelings. Once this was done, the idea was to concentrate on those qualities admired in a prospective partner and casting a spell to attract one. Below is an example of how this spell might have been used.

6 Light your list of fears and allow it to burn.
7 Either scatter the ashes of the list to the night wind or bury it.
8 Return to your altar and meditate on what you have done. Allow any candles to burn themselves out completely.

Identifying new relationship needs

9 Over the next three days make a list of all the attributes you admire in a prospective partner.
10 On a Friday night, during a new Moon phase, set up your altar: anoint two pink candles with appropriate essential oils. Score into them your initials.
11 Draw your heart. Pin to it the qualities of the partner you seek. Meditate on what you need. Imagine your new partner.
12 Once you have an image, burn your paper heart and list or bury it.

ENHANCING LOVE SPELLS

These were methods for enhancing a love spell once it had been cast.

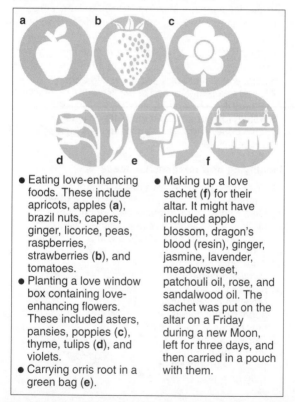

- Eating love-enhancing foods. These include apricots, apples (**a**), brazil nuts, capers, ginger, licorice, peas, raspberries, strawberries (**b**), and tomatoes.
- Planting a love window box containing love-enhancing flowers. These included asters, pansies, poppies (**c**), thyme, tulips (**d**), and violets.
- Carrying orris root in a green bag (**e**).

- Making up a love sachet (**f**) for their altar. It might have included apple blossom, dragon's blood (resin), ginger, jasmine, lavender, meadowsweet, patchouli oil, rose, and sandalwood oil. The sachet was put on the altar on a Friday during a new Moon, left for three days, and then carried in a pouch with them.

SPELLS TO SECURE FIDELITY

Once they had the man or woman of their dreams, fidelity was ensured by using the following methods.

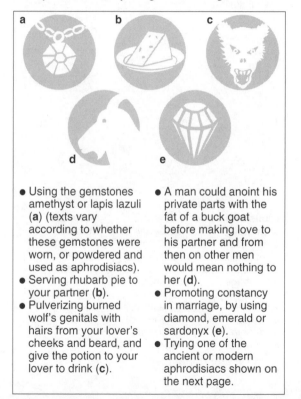

- Using the gemstones amethyst or lapis lazuli (**a**) (texts vary according to whether these gemstones were worn, or powdered and used as aphrodisiacs).
- Serving rhubarb pie to your partner (**b**).
- Pulverizing burned wolf's genitals with hairs from your lover's cheeks and beard, and give the potion to your lover to drink (**c**).

- A man could anoint his private parts with the fat of a buck goat before making love to his partner and from then on other men would mean nothing to her (**d**).
- Promoting constancy in marriage, by using diamond, emerald or sardonyx (**e**).
- Trying one of the ancient or modern aphrodisiacs shown on the next page.

Ancient and modern aphrodisiacs

Aphrodisiacs are substances believed to increase sexual desire.

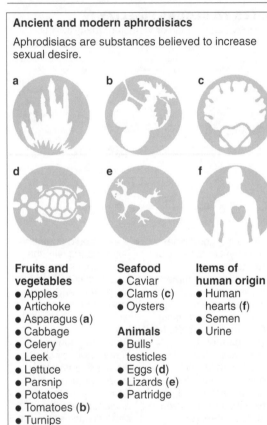

Fruits and vegetables
- Apples
- Artichoke
- Asparagus (**a**)
- Cabbage
- Celery
- Leek
- Lettuce
- Parsnip
- Potatoes
- Tomatoes (**b**)
- Turnips

Seafood
- Caviar
- Clams (**c**)
- Oysters

Animals
- Bulls' testicles
- Eggs (**d**)
- Lizards (**e**)
- Partridge

Items of human origin
- Human hearts (**f**)
- Semen
- Urine

Charm to bring back a sweetheart

Gather a piece of oak with an acorn on it and a
piece of the ash tree with some of the seeds (keys),
lay them under the pillow for three consecutive
nights, and say:

> *Acorn cup and ashen key,*
> *Bid my true love come to me –*
> *between moonlight and firelight,*
> *Bring him over the hills to-night;*
> *Over the meadows, over the moor,*
> *Over the rivers, over the sea,*
> *Over the threshold and in at the door,*
> *Acorn cup and ashen key,*
> *Bring my true love back to me.*

To reconcile an estranged husband

According to Hindu magic you could reconcile an estranged husband by drawing a diagram on bark using sandal paste, and placing it in a small earthen pot. The pot was filled with ghee and worshipped daily.

SPELL TO CAUSE ILLNESS OR DEATH TO AN UNCONSENTING LOVER

If after trying love potions, love spells and aphrodisiacs your lover was still unconsenting you might have stuck pins into a hare's heart and buried it near a newly-dug grave. This spell was believed to bring about an unconsenting lover's death.

ANTIDOTE TO LOVE SPELLS

As an antidote to love spells you might have:

- eaten pistachio nuts or lizards dipped in urine
- prevented the amorous advances of a male lover by putting a glow-worm into his bedtime glass of milk which would have turned him into a eunuch

SPELLS TO BE MORE POPULAR WITH THE OPPOSITE SEX

If you didn't have a particular person in mind for a love spell and simply wished to be more popular with the opposite sex you could:

- Carry a dried toad's tongue or a lark's eye wrapped in wolfskin in your right pocket
- Wear cloves
- Girls wear a sprig of valerian

- Use agate, amber (which makes a woman smell more desirable to her lover), beryl, lodestone, ruby, sapphire, turquoise

SPELLS FOR PROTECTION

This section gives examples of a variety of spells
traditionally thought to help protect against witches, the
Evil Eye, the Devil, demons, ghosts, vampires, incubi,

PROTECTION AGAINST WITCHES

Methods which protected your home:

- Planting olive, birch, elder or bay trees around your house
- Digging a stream around your house. (Witches couldn't cross running water).
- Hanging green branches or hawthorn over the doorway
- Nailing an iron amulet to the outside of your house (**a**).
- Placing a dime under the hearth.
- Keeping a bull's heart stuck with pins in the chimney piece.
- Hanging the diseased leg of a calf near the chimney.
- Never keeping eggshells (**b**), but always smash them (witches used the shells to go to sea and would seek them out).

a

b

c

nightmares and a whole host of dangerous situations
which included foul weather, fire, death by drowning,
insect attack, plagues, poison and shipwreck. Some
spells involved reciting protective words or phrases,
others simply relied on the use of everyday objects;
some required special talismans to be made.

- Keeping ash leaves or ash wood in the house.
- Keeping bright new iron in the house (**c**).

On corner walls, a glittering row,
Hang fire-irons—less for use than show;
With horseshoe brightened, as a spell,
Witchcraft's evil powers to quell

- Hanging this Hindu charm in your house

٣٣	٣١	٢	٨
٦	٣	٣٨	٣٧
٣٠	٣٥	٩	١
٣	٤	٣٤	٣٨

Methods which protected you from witches:

- Carrying a red talisman
- Carrying mugwort, rosemary wood or yarrow
- Carrying a penny (**a**)
- Wearing amber or crystal
- Wearing oak leaves (**b**) or a sprig of rowan
- Weaingr a piece of rattlesnake skin
- Wearing your hat the wrong way round (**c**)
- Standing beneath an oak tree (**d**)
- Never stepping on a crack in the sidewalk (otherwise a witch will appear and grab you)
- Never carrying a witch hazel leaf (witches used it for conjuring)
- Chewing tobacco
- Sleeping with a Bible under your head (**e**)
- Lying on the ground and drawing a circle around yourself using a fork made from willow (**f**)

a   b   c

d   e   f

Methods which broke a witch's spell on you:

- Ritually roasting a sheep's heart
- Wearing a chaplet made from the leaves of deadly nightshade
- Bathing in mimosa
- Wearing jet
- Gathering nine twigs. By removing a twig each day, the spell would finally be removed.
- Drawing the image of the witch who was tormenting you. By shooting it through the heart using a silver bullet, preferably over running water, the witch would die.
- Drawing the image of the witch who is tormenting you. By driving a nail into the heart of the picture and striking the nail once each day for nine days, the witch would die.
- Boiling ragweed, beating it all the time. Traditionally, the witch could break this counter charm by borrowing from you or having a member of her family borrow from you.
- Inscribing the following Hindu charm on gold plate.

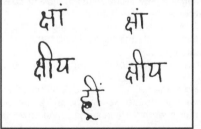

Methods which protected livestock:

- Nailing a severed fox's head, a dead barn owl or some mountain ash (rowan) to the barn door.
- Placing a birch tree adorned with red and white ribbons against the barn door.
- Scattering primroses on the ground or planting lilies.
- Taring cows behind the ears and at the root of the tail. This prevented witches from stealing their milk.
- Burning a calf alive. This placated the witch and protected the rest of the herd.
- Driving sheep under an arch or rowan tree.
- Having cattle step over an axe when taken out of the pasture for the first time in spring.
- Bleeding or branding cattle on May Day.
- Keeping a piece of silver in water. Every few days, the cows would be sprinkled with this water.

Traditional waysto break a spell cast on a cow:

- Cutting the cow's tongue using a silver coin sharpened on a grindstone.
- Shutting the barn door. Not giving your cow anything to eat, and then milking her without looking up.
- Burning the whisp of the bushy part of the cow's tail.
- Taking some hair from the back of the cow, throwing it into the fire, and boiling some more of the hair over this fire in some of the cow's own milk.

Methods which prevented horses from being hag-ridden:

- Placing a stone with a hole in it in the stable
- Braiding the horses' tails.

Traditional ways believed to torment witches:

- Ringing a bell (this caused flying witches to fall to the ground).
- Placing walnuts beneath a witch's chair (to rob her of movement).
- Sleeping with a sieve over your face. When a witch came to bewitch you she would exhaust herself by being forced to pass in and out of every mesh hole.
- Using this written spell. A witch would be unable to remain in the same room with it.

```
S A T O R
A R E P O
T E N E T
O P E R A
R O T A S
```

Methods which protected the dairy from witches:

Witches sometimes hindered the process of buttermaking. To ensure that butter would come, the following verse was recited:

Come, butter, dash,
Cow's gone to t'marsh.
Peter stands at the toll gate,
begging butter for his cake,
Come, butter, come.

- Throwing a pinch of salt into a fire before you begin buttermaking (**a**).
- Waiting until the tide came in (**b**).
- Placing a silver coin in the churn (**c**).
- Placing three white hairs from a black cat's tail into the churn.
- Plunging a red-hot poker (or a heated horseshoe) into the cream (**d**).
- Dipping the hand of a dead man into the cream.
- Using a churn made of rowan wood.

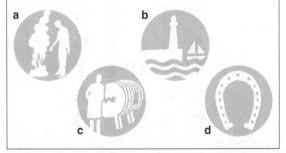

PROTECTING AGAINST THE EVIL EYE

For thousands of years people have believed that there
were certain individuals who could cause illness,
property damage, and even death simply by looking at
you.

Superstition about the Evil Eye reached its peak during
the seventeenth century when many were accused of
being witches, having the power to "overlook" their
enemies. When the great plague was prevalent in
Britain, it was commonly believed that people with the
Evil Eye could spread the disease simply by looking at
a victim.

> *Write "Lord have mercy on us" on those three:*
> *They are infected; in their heart it lies;*
> *They have the plague, and caught it of your eyes.*

> *Love's Labour's Lost.*
> Shakespeare

Names for the Evil Eye

The notion of the Evil Eye occurs all over the world
and is known by many different names:

baskania	Greek
fascinum	Roman
al-'ayn (the Eye)	Arabic
an-nazar (the Glance)	Arabic
mauvais oeil	French
chashm-i-bad	Persian
jettadore	Italian
aojadura	Spanish
ipso facto	Armenian

Identifying people with the Evil Eye

Some people were thought more likely to have the Evil Eye than others. They included:

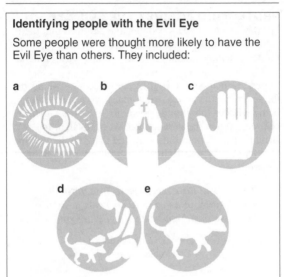

- People who were cross-eyed (**a**).
- People whose eyes were of a different color from everyone else's in the district.
- People with deep-set eyes.
- People who squinted (Asia, Italy, Africa)
- People with blue or green eyes (Armenian)
- Members of the clergy (**b**).
- Left-handed people (**c**).
- People who were able to tame animals (**d**).
- Some animals, especially the cat (**e**), hare, rabbit, dog and fox, but also wolves, snakes and peacocks.

Methods to protect children from the Evil Eye:

- Children who had been hexed could be held upside down each morning by their clothes.
- Washing children who had been hexed in water into which a silver coin borrowed from a neighbor had been placed.
- Children who were ragged and dirty would be protected because the Evil Eye generally only fell on those who were attractive.
- If someone praised a child, a Jew might say immediately *kayn aynhorah*, meaning "May no Evil Eye harm you."
- In China, if someone praised a child, the Chinese would dispute this so as to ward off evil from their beautiful or intelligent child.
- Engraving the charm below on a copper disc and giving it to the child to wear as a necklace.

۲۸	۱۸	۳۳	۲۳
۹۸	۸۲	۹	۱۱.
۲۵	۲۷	۹۹	۵۰
۸۵	۲۷	۹	۱

Customs used to protect against the Evil Eye:

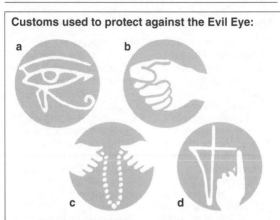

- Carring an eye symbol such as this one used by the ancient Egyptians (**a**).
- Drawing a circle around your eye using eye shadow so that evil can't enter.
- Making the sign of the fig by putting your thumb between your index finger and middle finger (**b**).
- Carring blue worry beads (**c**).
- Spitting in the eye of the "overlooked."

- Burning an animal that has died as the result of being looked at, so the person who laid the curse would have a similar fate.
- Making the sign of the cross (**d**).
- Sticking pins into an effigy of the person with the Evil Eye.
- If someone praised you, you would say, *"Kayn aynhorah"* (which, loosely translated from the Yiddish means: May no Evil Eye harm you).

- Making the sign of the "Devil's horns" by holding down the middle two fingers of the hand with the thumb and directing the horns at the overlooker.
- Wearing an arrowhead.
- Carring a found nail.
- Keeping a stag's horn.
- Keeping rosemary wood or birch tree branches in the house.
- Wearing birch twigs or pieces of larch.
- Hanging hawthorn over the porch.
- Bringing willow branches into the house on May Day morning.
- Wearing agate, sapphire, topaz or turquoise.
- Decorating using the fleur-de-lis pattern.
- Hanging glass "witch balls" in the window.
- Wearing the charm (*above*). The name of the victim was in the middle and "Hrim" written in each of the nine cells.

Protecting horses from the Evil Eye

Horse brasses were traditionally used to protect horses from witch spells and the Evil Eye. Although one or two brasses were worn on a daily basis, a full set consisted of 19 or 20 pieces, usually reserved for special occasions. It was important that the brasses were polished so that they shone brightly, as shiny objects dazzle evil spirits. Popular motifs include items often found in lucky charms: acorns, birds, crescent moons, flowers, hands, hearts and wheels, examples of which are shown here.

TO PROTECT AGAINST VAMPIRES

A vampire is a corpse that returns to life at night in order to suck people's blood. They were thought to be particularly dangerous and evil beings because their victims later became vampires themselves, doomed to a life of eternity, having to seek out their own victims from whom they in turn drew blood. Belief in vampires is particularly strong in eastern Europe, but occurs all over the world.

Identifying a vampire

A vampire traditinally had all or some of the following traits:

- Body did not decompose after death
- Bad breath
- Eyebrows met across the nose
- Hairy palms
- Sharp-pointed tongue (Poland)
- Only one nostril (Bulgaria)
- Red hair (in countries where this was unusual)
- Blue eyes (in countries where this was unusual)
- Middle finger of the hand is the same length as the index finger or third finger
- Materialized in the form of an old woman with two heels on the same foot (India)
- Cast no shadow
- Had no reflection
- Could transform into a bat
- Needed to return to a coffin each night; the coffin was lined with soil from the vampire's birthplace
- Fed by sinking its teeth into the blood vessels of human hosts, usually at the neck

People who would become vampires included:

- Anyone bitten by a vampire
- Babies born with teeth
- A person buried with their mouth open
- A suicide not buried at a crossroads

Ways to prevent a corpse becoming a vampire:

- Breaking the spine of the corpse (California)
- Rubbing the corpse with the lard from a hog slaughtered on St Ignatius' Day (Romania)
- Decapitating the body, destroying the head or placing it between the corpse's legs, perhaps with garlic stuffed in the mouth (Transylvania)
- Tearing out the corpse's heart and dissolving it in vinegar (Greece)
- Driving a stake through the corpse's heart (**a**)
- Driving a nail into the skull and covering the corpse in a wild rose bush to tangle it (Romania)
- Using a wizard to entice the vampire into a bottle, corking it, and throw it into a fire (Bulgaria)
- Ensuring that suicide victims were always buried at a crossroads (Britain) (**b**)

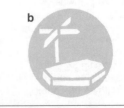

a

b

A vampire was detered from leaving the grave by

- Scattering iron around the grave (**a**)
- Scattering garlic around the grave (**b**)
- Stabbing nine spindles into the grave three days after the death (Romania)
- Burning tow on top of the grave
- Fencing in the tomb
- Heaping stones on top of the tomb
- Pouring boiling water on the grave (Greece)

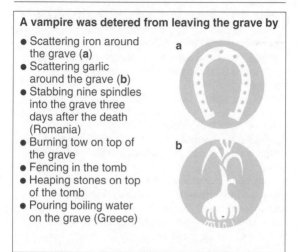

Traditional ways to kill a known vampire:

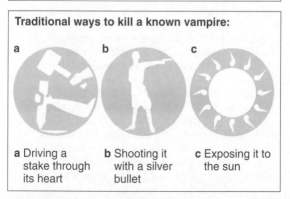

a Driving a stake through its heart

b Shooting it with a silver bullet

c Exposing it to the sun

SPELLS TO PROTECT AGAINST ZOMBIES

Zombies are similar to vampires in that they are corpses
that return to life but, unlike vampires, zombies were
brought back to life by voodoo sorcerers (known as
bokor) who used the robot-like creatures for evil
purposes.

To obtain a zombie, a *bokor* chose a live victim (a man,
woman or even a child) and, putting his mouth to the
crack of the victim's door, sucked out his victim's soul
(known as the *ti bon ange*, or "little good angel"). The
victim then died and was buried. The *bokor* visited the
new grave at midnight, carrying the stolen soul either in
his hand or secured in a bottle. The corpse was roused
when the *bokor* passed the stolen soul under its nose
and banged it on the head.

Alternatively, the *bokor* would capture the soul as it
hovered about the grave for seven days after death.
During the process of obtaining a zombie, the *bokor*
might feed a person or a corpse a special poison.

Once raised from the dead, zombies were often put to
work in the fields or made to perform other manual
jobs. They might be turned to stone and kept outside a
bokor's house, or turned into an animal and sold as
meat.

It is because zombies were doomed to a life of work
and torture on behalf of their masters that relatives
would try a whole host of spells to prevent a sorcerer
gaining control over a recently deceased loved one.
Once persons becames zombies, there was little that
could be done for them, except to give them salt, which
resultedS in their regaining their willpower.

How a zombie was identified

- Seemed dazed and acted mechanically.
- Spoke in a nasal tone
- Had no enjoyment, intelligence or willpower

Traditionally, a loved one was protected from becoming a zombie by:

- Strangling the corpse
- Beheading the corpse
- Cutting open the corpse
- Firing bullets into the brain of the corpse
- Poisoning the corpse
- Allowing the corpse to decompose before being buried
- Burying the corpse face down with a dagger for protection
- Sewing up the mouth (the corpse couldn't be summoned if it didn't reply)
- Distracting the corpse by putting things into its coffin (such as an eyeless needle which cannot be threaded)

SPELLS TO PROTECT AGAINST THE DEVIL

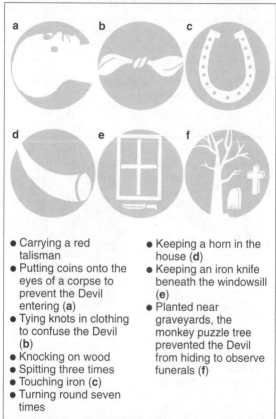

- Carrying a red talisman
- Putting coins onto the eyes of a corpse to prevent the Devil entering (**a**)
- Tying knots in clothing to confuse the Devil (**b**)
- Knocking on wood
- Spitting three times
- Touching iron (**c**)
- Turning round seven times
- Keeping a horn in the house (**d**)
- Keeping an iron knife beneath the windowsill (**e**)
- Planted near graveyards, the monkey puzzle tree prevented the Devil from hiding to observe funerals (**f**)

SPELLS TO PROTECT AGAINST DEMONS

- Hanging green branches over the doorway
- Scattering the flowers of a bean plant about the house
- Covering your mouth with your hand when yawning to prevent demons from entering your body
- Wearing a peach pit necklace
- Holding a branch of tamarisk and scatter the leaves

SPELLS TO PROTECT AGAINST GHOSTS

- Keeping dung in the house
- Eating wolf meat (to prevent you from seeing ghosts)
- Planting lilies in the garden
- Carrying a cross made of rowan wood, fastened with red thread, in the lining of your coat
- Planting bay trees
- Keep ing this talisman

SPELLS TO PROTECT AGAINST EVIL

Wearing:
- a tortoiseshell bracelet
- a wolf's tooth (**a**)
- a white apron
- a garland of deadly nightshade
- a bamboo charm
- rowan (mountain ash) berries as a necklace
- a snakestone, a naturally-occurring stone with glass-like qualities, believed to be the hardened saliva of adders
- oak leaves (**b**)
- carnelian, chrysolite, coral, diamond, lodestone, olivine, pearl, peridot, ruby or sapphire

Placing:
- Saint-John's-Wort over doorways on Midsummer's Eve
- mountain ash around the door of your home on Good Friday
- plum branches over the door and windows
- ash leaves or ash wood in the house
- twigs of papaya over the door
- branches of buckthorn near doors and windows
- pine needles all over the floor (**c**)

Keeping:
- a pet chameleon (**d**)
- wren feathers (**e**)
- a big red tomato on the windowsill
- a charm wand in the house, a glass rod filled with seeds.

Carry:
- a molucca bean
- a hollowed-out pumpkin on Halloween

Burn:
- mistletoe
- juniper
- an oil lamp

Plant
- blackthorn thickets
- elder trees

Trying to:
- stand beneath an oak tree
- knock on a willow tree
- ring church bells (**f**)
- spit on the ground
- tie a knot in your handkerchief
- use vervain
- sleep with a key under your pillow
- say the following verse, very quickly, three times, in one breath:

Three blew beans in a blew bladder,
Rattle, bladder, rattle.

PROTECTING YOUR HOME

Methods to protect a house from storms

Keeping:
- a live bunches of hazel gathered on Palm Sunday
- a walnut branch
- opine or a fern in the house
- an acorn on the windowsill

Trying to:
- ring a church bell during a storm
- use rosemary wood
- scatter ashes over the roof of your house

Growing:
- holly nearby
- bay trees
- a hawthorn tree in the garden
- an olive tree
- stonecrop or houseleek on the roof of your house
- a date palm tree to protect the local community

Methods to protect a house from fire

- hanging a dried snakeskin from the roof
- keeping pieces of larch
- driving hazel pins into a house
- keeping a three-colored cat
- allowing stonecrop or houseleek to grow on the roof

Methods to protect a new home from evil:

- burying the bones of a horse in the foundations
- burying a cock beneath the foundations

PROTECTING YOURSELF

To protect against being struck by lightning:

- wearing agate, amethyst, carnelian, garnet, malachite or red coral
- carrying nettle
- sheltering under an elder tree

Methods to protect against animals:

- suspending a herring from the ceiling on Good Friday (flies)
- keeping a wolfskin in the house (flies)
- growing a walnut tree (flies)
- wearing garnet (flying insects)
- wearing amethyst or coral (locusts)
- carrying a raw onion (snake attack)
- wearing jet or sardonyx (snake attack)
- smoke from burning tamarisk branch detered snakes (snake attack)
- divers should wear a pearl (sharks and octopusses)

PROTECTION AGAINST NIGHTMARES

- Sleeping with a wolf's head under your pillow
- Leaving your shoes in the shape of a "T" at night
- Leaving your shoes by the bedroom door, one coming in to the room and the other going out
- Wearing the root of the violet plant about your neck
- Wearing a glass ball
- Burning cedar-wood incense
- Hanging a snakeskin over the bed
- Wearing amber, amethyst, chrysolite, coral, crystal, jade, olivine, peridot or ruby

- Hanging a stone with a hole in it over the bed
- Pinning your socks in the shape of a cross at the end of your bed
- Keeping a knife or other metal object nearby
- Placing your shoes under the bed, with the toes pointing out
- Sleeping with your hands crossed and straw crosses fixed to each corner of the bed
- Placing a garland of holly around a horse (to protect it from nightmares)

- Saying:

Jesu Christ and Saint Benedict,
Bless this house from every wicked wight

or

St George, St George,
He walks by day, he walks by night.

ANGLO-SAXON DEFENSE AGAINST AN INCUBUS

1 Collect hops, wormwood, bishopwort, lupin, ashthroat, henbane, harewort, viper's bugloss, heathberry plants, cropleek, garlic, grains of hedgerife, githrife, fennel.
2 Put them in a jar beneath an altar.
3 Sing nine Masses over them.
4 Boil them in butter and sheep's grease.
5 Add salt.
6 Strain the mixture through a cloth.
7 Throw the worts into running water.
8 Anoint yourself with the salve, on the eyes and making the sign of the cross.

PROTECTION AGAINST DANGER

- Carrying the tip of a calf's tongue
- Spitting loudly three times if you were frightened
- Wearing a bloodstone
- Wearing a garnet or turquoise, both of which would change color in the presence of danger
- Wearing a pearl, as this lost its lustre in the presence of danger
- Touching a key, especially if it was made of iron
- Wearing a carbuncle, as this would grow dim in the presence of danger
- Wearing the eye of a cockerel, or a mascot in the shape of a cockerel's eye

Protection against death by drowning

- Carrying a molucca bean
- Wearing a bloodstone
- Wearing an Iona stone, a small stone found on the western shores of Scotland

Protection against poison

- Wearing amethyst (which changed color), emerald (when worn as a ring), jacinth (zircon), opal (which turned pale) or ruby (which turned pale)
- Using mugwort

Protection against accidents

- Wearing turquoise

Protection against thieves

- Wearing amethyst or olivine

Protection against injury in battle

- Rubbing leeks over your body

Protection against plague

- Wearing amethyst

PROTECTING SHIPS

Protect a ship from storms at sea by
- Fixing a goatskin or whole goat to the ship's mast
- Carrying rowan wood

Protect a boat from evil by
- Passing the entire boat through a rope circle

Protect against shipwreck by
- Wearing hazel sprigs or a moonstone at sea

PROTECTION AGAINST GREMLINS

Gremlins are mythical creatures invented by a British Royal Air Force bomber squadron stationed in India before the Second World War. These creatures tampered with all kinds of machinery, which resulted in mechanical breakdown. To prevent their meddling, an empty beer bottle was laid nearby and the gremlins crawled inside and stayed there.

FLYING SPELLS

These included recipes for preparing flying ointment, magic garters, and the use of a magic square. Below are examples of how they might have been used.

To prevent air sickness when flying
Before setting out, take three drops of blood in a glass of wine.

To make magic flying garters

1 Make two round garters from the skin of a stag.
2 Using the blood of a hare killed on the 25th of June, inscribe magic signs and symbols on the inside of the garters.
3 Fill the garters with green mugwort gathered before sunrise on the 25th of June.
4 Insert into each end of each of the garters the eye of a Barbel fish.
5 Rise before sunrise and wash in running water before placing the garters above the knee on each leg.
6 Cut a rod of oak on the 25th of June.

When you wish to travel, turn to the direction you desire and write your destination on the ground. You shall have the power of flight.

When you wish to stop, beat the ground with the wand saying "amech."

Flying ointment

1 Boil together the following ingredients:

> 2 ounces human fat
> 1 ounce oil of horn
> 1 ounce bay tree oil
> 1 ounce natural mummy
> 1/2 chopine spirit of wine
> 7 vervain (verbens) leaves

2 Reduce by half
3 Make into plasters. When applied to the feet, you will be able to fly

---

To fly as a crow

Use the following magic square

R O L O R
O B U F O
L U A U L
O F U B O
R O L O R

SPELLS FOR INVISIBILITY

Spells for invisibility could be found in the grimoires, including the *Grand Grimoire*, *The Key of Solomon* and the *Secret of Secrets*. They often involve reciting long verses in Latin.

A particularly gruesome spell for invisibility from the *Grand Grimoire*

1 Light a fire.
2 Put a black cat into a new pot and fill with water you have collected from a fountain at the stroke of midnight.
3 Hold down the lid of the pot using your left hand. Do not look behind you.
4 Boil the cat for 24 hours.
5 Take the boiled cat meat and throw it over your left shoulder saying *Accipi quod tibido et nihil cumplius.*
6 Place the bones, one at a time, between the teeth at the left side of the mouth and gaze into a mirror. If you have no reflection you know the spell has worked.

Spell for invisibility, from a Greek papyrus

1 Obtain the egg of a hawk.
2 Gild one half.
3 Coat the other half with cinnabar.
When you carry this egg, you will be invisible.

Spell for invisibility according to Spanish witch custom

1 Place a bean in the head of a black cat.
2 Bury the head.
3 When the bean plant grows the beans it produces, when worn under the arm, will make you invisible .

Quick ways of becoming invisible

- Keeping the right eye of a bat in your waistcoat pocket
- Using the Hand of Glory (see the Glossary of Magic)
- Carrying chicory or a fern seed
- Carrying the heart of a bat, black hen or frog under your right arm
- Witches mixed sow thistle with frog spittle to become invisible
- Wearing opal or agate
- Wearing the ring of gyges.

Making the ring of gyges

The ring had to be made of mercury set with a stone found in a lapwing's nest around which was inscribed the words:

"Jesus, passing through the midst of them, went this way."

SPELLS AS CURES

Some of the most common spells were those for
"curing" physical ills, many of which are listed here.
They remained popular for many years because many
of them were simple, relying on the use of readily
available objects and substances. Some required those
who were ill to carry an item about their person, such as
a common plant or a gemstone; others involved
ingesting something or rubbing in an ointment made
from everyday ingredients such as honey, blood or fat.
Some spells required the use of special mandalas;
others involved simply repeating a certain phrase over
and over again. Although people often sought out a
local witch or wise woman to help them prepare spells
with animal ingredients, many such spells were
prepared in the home, as they relied on the use of
common animals, such as livestock, spiders, cats or
mice.

WARNING

Remember that these "cures", though traditionally
believed to be of value, are often highly unpleasant
and may even be dangerous or deadly.

**Information provided here is for reference only.
Under no circumstances should you attempt to
use these spells for the purposes of treatment.**

Aches and pains	● Apply bear fat
Ague	● Pass beneath the belly of a donkey and over its back ● Swallow a live sheep tick every morning for nine mornings ● Hammer a nail into a stile ● Swallow cobweb pills ● Eat sage before breakfast on 7 or 9 successive mornings ● Wear a snakestone
Alcoholism	● Eat burned and powdered swallow
Arthritis	● Carry a buckeye (chestnut)
Asthma	● Eat carrots ● Use the gemstones amber, cat's-eye or topaz ● Carry a buckeye (chestnut)
Backache	● Sleep on a bearskin ● Wear a snail in a bag around you neck for nine days then throw it into a fire ● Carry a buckeye (chestnut)
Bad breath	● Gargle with honey and mouse ashes
Baldness	● Rub bear or fox fat onto the scalp

	• Sprinkle parsley on your head • Stuff cyclamen up your nostrils • Use oil of cloves or onions
Bed sores	• Use elm bark
Bed wetting	• Swallow live frogs • Use garlic cloves or ash keys (seeds of the ash tree)
Bites	• Rub with the dead body of a snake or with snake fat • Carry the heart and right foot of an owl under your left armpit • Use onions, elder, or the gemstones agate, jade or pearl • Spit • Apply toadstone, a small, dark gray or light brown stone resembling a toad (perhaps a fossilized fish tooth)
Blackheads	• Crawl through an arch made of brambles
Bleeding	• Carry powdered bat heart • Wrap the wound in linen cloths steeped in frog spawn

- Chew periwinkle leaves
- Apply thick cobwebs to the wound
- Use betony or yarrow plants or the gemstones agate, bloodstone, carnelian or jasper
- Repeat this phrase:

"Our Blessed Saviour was born in Bethlehem and baptized in the river Jordan.
the water were wild and rude,
the child Jesus was meek, mild and good.
He put his foot into the waters and the water stopped and so shall thy blood."

Boils	 • Be near or in an open grave • Apply lilies or the leaves of a periwinkle • Crawl through an arch made of brambles
Breast cancer	• Rub a live toad on the skin
Bronchitis	• Use oil of cloves
Burns	• Apply elder or elm bark
Cancer	• Touch the hand of a corpse • Bury yourself in soil • Use vervain

Cataracts	● Put a fox's tongue on your eyes
Chilblains	● Use horses' teeth or onions
Colds	● Use a dried rat's tail or goose grease mixed with turpentine ● Eat beets
Colic	● Apply wolf dung to limbs ● Draw the following diagram on a Sunday. Mix it into water which you drink while standing, facing the sun. 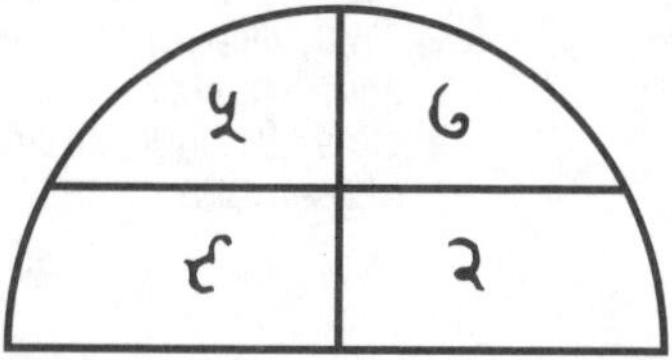

Consumption	● Eat gravy made with stewed black cat ● Have a cow breathe on you ● Swallow live frogs ● Eat snails mixed in the milk of a red cow ● Use moonstone

Convulsions	● Use hairs from a donkey's back
Coughs	● Eat fox's liver ● Use goose grease mixed with turpentine or syrup made from holly bark
Cramp	● Wear an eelskin garter ● Carry the paws of a mole ● Sleep with a moleskin on the affected part ● Wear a sheep's shoulder blade ● Keep a piece of coffin in your pocket ● Wear a peony root necklace ● Tie periwinkle leaves or a red ribbon around the affected part ● Wear a ring made from metal taken from a coffin ● Repeat this phrase:

"There came three Angells out of the East.
The one brought fire, the other brought frost;
Out, fire; in, frost,
In the name of the Father, and Son, and Holy
Ghost Amen"
As Our Lady was sinless,
When she bare Jesus."

Deafness	● Apply a whole eel to your ear

Depression	● Wear hawthorn
Diarrhea	● Use oil of cloves
Dizziness	● Use a comb made from rosemary wood ● Carry a buckeye (chestnut)
Dropsy	● Wear the ashes of a dead toad ● Use juniper or moonstone
Drunkenness	● Keep a live eel in your drink ● Eat five almonds ● Use the betony plant ● Drink liquid distilled from acorns
Dysentery	● Mix powdered bones with red wine ● Use emerald
Earache	● Put snail froth into your ear ● Use goose grease mixed with turpentine, onions or garlic ● Dab the ear with cotton wool dipped in black pepper

Epilepsy

- Wear a fragment of deer hoof in a ring
- Wear a ring made from the nails and screws from a coffin
- Wear a peony root necklace
- Wear a wolfskin
- Eat goat's brain that has been passed through a golden ring
- Eat cooked hedgehog
- Eat swallow broth or grated skull mixed with food
- Swallow mole's blood on a lump of sugar or a toad's heart
- Drink from the skull of a person who has committed suicide
- Drive a nail into the ground where the epileptic had his or her last fit
- Wrap boiled bear's fur around your feet
- Apply elder bark
- Use vervain, juniper, or the gemstones emerald, jade, jasper, jet, lapis lazuli or topaz
- Bury a cockerel beneath the bed

Erysipelas	• Use beeswax dissolved in water • Use amber
Eye diseases	• Blow the ashes from the burned head of a black cat into the eye • Use crocodile blood • A volunteer must lick the eyes of a frog and then lick the eyes of the infected person • Apply rain collected on Ascension Day • Eat eagle's bile • Use lily of the valley, the distilled water made from marigold blossoms or the gemstones agate, emerald, lapis lazuli or turquoise
Female ailments	• Drink water in which a flint arrowhead has been dipped.
Fever	• Use horses' hooves or onions • Keep a cut onion under the bed • Wear a bag containing splinters taken from a gibbet • Pull nettle up by the root • Carry a caterpillar

- Eat a spider with jam, syrup or an apple
- Use agate, garnet or moonstone
- Tie a feather of the Aulak bird with white thread to the left ear.
- Draw a circle with sixteen radii, making a circle at the end of each radii, on a peepal leaf. Give it to the patient to wear around the neck.

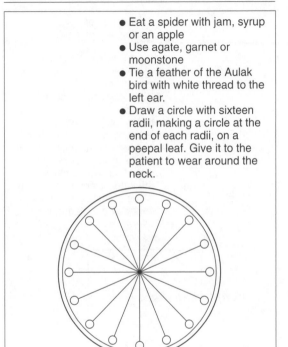

- Pin a lock of the patient's hair to an aspen tree saying

"Aspen tree, apsen tree, I prithee to shake and shiver instead of me."

- Apply turtle oil
- Apply dead pigeons to the feet
- Seal some of the patient's nail parings within an aspen tree
- Poke elder twigs into the ground
- Using the juice of the Dhatura plant on the 8th or 14th day of the month, draw the following diagram of eight triangles, each with the letter "Ram" in it. Put the name of the patient in the centre of the diagram.

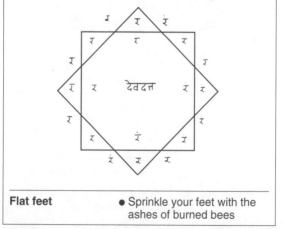

Flat feet

- Sprinkle your feet with the ashes of burned bees

Fractures	● Use oil from swallows
Freckles	● Use pumpkin mixed with oil rubbed on the skin
Gallstones	● Eat carrots
Goiter	● Eat the hair from a horse's tail ● Bite into the bark of a peach tree at midnight on Ascension Day ● Use amber
Gout	● Eat salted owl ● Wrap the sinews of a stork about the feet ● Use lily of the valley, hemlock of the gemstones amethyst, lodestone or topaz ● Tie a knot in a fir tree twig
Gray hair	● Eat owl egg broth
Hangovers	● Use onions
Headaches	● Drive a nail into the skull of a dead man ● Wrap the corner of a corpse's sheet around the head ● Wear the diagram (left) as a talisman ● Eat beets or wild lettuce

Diagram (in Headaches row):

43	82
311	60

	• Wear a red ribbon borrowed from a loved one as a headband • Drive nails into an old skull • Use amethyst or sapphire
Hernia	• Use oil of cloves • Embrace an oak tree
Hiccups	• Repeat the following verse: *"Hickup, hickup, go away,* *Come again another day.* *Hickup, hickup, when I bake,* *I'll give you a butter cake"*
Hysteria	• Eat swallow broth
Impotence	• Use lizards • Eat figs
Indigestion	• Use cloves
Incontinence	• Be in or near an open grave
Infertility	• Eat figs
Insomnia	• Place a goat's horn under your pillow • Eat wild lettuce • Use onions
Kidney complaints	• Eat swallow broth • Use jade or moonstone

Jaundice

- Apply a poultice made from a dog's head and wine
- Gaze into the eye of stone curlew
- Hold a yellowhammer close to your face
- Eat three yellowhammers
- Swallow a spoonful of head lice
- Eat nine lice on a piece of bread and butter or in some boiled milk
- Eat a live spider in a pat of butter
- Use pearl
- Draw the following diagram with the name of the patient in the center.

Liver problems

- Use juniper or aquamarine

Measles	● Drink tea made from plantain
Mumps	● Rub a child's head on a pig's back and the mumps will be transferred to the pig
Nerve pains	● Make a cross on your shoe using your finger ● Use bee stings or amethyst
Nightmares	● Use horses' teeth or the betony plant
Nosebleeds	● Wear a dried toad in a silk bag
Pain	● Use tortoise oil ● Rub with soil
Palsy	● Eat swallow broth
Piles	● Use vervain ● Recite the following spell 21 times and then tie a knot in a piece of red thread:

Om Umati Umati Chal Chal Swaha

Repeat this process a further two times so that there are three knots in total tied in the thread. Tie the thread to your toe and you will no longer be troubled with piles.

Pimples	● Pass a cloth over the pimples when a shooting star goes by
Plague	● Wear the ashes of a dead toad ● Use garnet or the fumes from burning jet
Pneumonia	● Place a sheep's lung at the foot of the patient ● Place a dead dove on the chest
Poisoning	● Use spoons made from rosemary wood ● Use cyclamen or emerald
Quinsy	● Drink water in which mice have been boiled
Respiratory problems	● Drink the ashes of a fox in wine ● Carry a buckeye (chestnut)
Rheumatism	● Apply melted dog fat ● Apply bee stings ● Carry the paws of a mole ● Carry an old, blackened potato in your pocket ● Carry an elder twig tied in knots in your pocket ● Wear the ashes of a dead toad ● Wear red garters

	• Rub affected parts with the yellow meat of a turtle • Lean against a bellows • Eat carrots • Chew parsley • Bury yourself in soil • Crawl through an arch made from brambles • Use the betony plant, juniper, hazel, hemlock or willow • Carry a buckeye (chestnut)
Rickets	• Use ash trees
Ringworm	• Apply grease from a church bell • Rub with soil
Scarlet fever	• Feed a donkey the hairs from a patient
Sciatica	• Carry a piece of lodestone
Scrofula	• Wear a dried dog's tongue around the neck • Be touched by a king • Use vervain
Shingles	• Use cat's blood mixed with milk
Skin sores	• Have the sores licked by a dog • Touch the hand of a corpse

Skin diseases	● Use lizards, cloves or the gemstones agate or lapis lazuli ● Wear a toad's hind leg

Smallpox	● Use garlic ● Place the following diagram under the patient's pillow

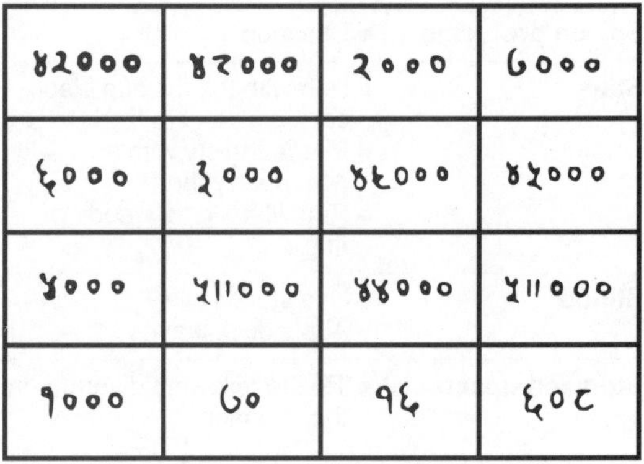

82000	87000	2000	6000
6000	3000	86000	87000
8000	811000	88000	811000
9000	60	98	605

Snakebites	● Use crocodile blood ● Wrap with fresh sheepskin ● Apply adder's-tongue fern ● Use elder or the gemstones agate, emerald, pearl or ruby

Sore throat	• Drink the juice of live crabs mixed with horse saliva • Sleep with a left stocking around the throat • Apply plaster made from the leaves of a violet • Eat walnuts • Tie a red ribbon around the throat
Spleen problems	• Use jade
Sties	• Rub with the tail of a black cat • Pierce the sty with a gooseberry thorn • Rub with a gold wedding ring
Stings	• Use stork's bile • Apply dock leaves
Stomach upsets	• Tie the following diagram on the stomach

६२३	१स	८६
६सी	५प्	३6
२म	६८	४स

- Use yarrow
- Write he spells "Yam" and "Hrim" in the centre of a simple square. Wear it to cure stomach disorder.

Stuttering	• Drink from an upturned bell
Swollen eyes	• Place crab eyes on the back of your neck
Swollen limbs	• Wrap the limb in the corner of a corpse's sheet
Syphilis	• Use lizards
Teething trouble in infants	• Use hairs from a donkey's back • Rub wolves' teeth against the gums
Thrush	• Place a live frog in the patient's mouth
Toothache	• Wear a bear's tooth • Wear a bag containing splinters taken from a gibbet • Carry the nail from a coffin • Carry the paws of a mole • Be in or near an open grave • Hold a dried cat's skin over the face

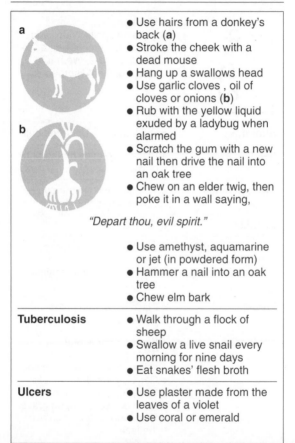

a

- Use hairs from a donkey's back (**a**)
- Stroke the cheek with a dead mouse
- Hang up a swallows head
- Use garlic cloves , oil of cloves or onions (**b**)
- Rub with the yellow liquid exuded by a ladybug when alarmed

b

- Scratch the gum with a new nail then drive the nail into an oak tree
- Chew on an elder twig, then poke it in a wall saying,

"Depart thou, evil spirit."

- Use amethyst, aquamarine or jet (in powdered form)
- Hammer a nail into an oak tree
- Chew elm bark

Tuberculosis	• Walk through a flock of sheep • Swallow a live snail every morning for nine days • Eat snakes' flesh broth
Ulcers	• Use plaster made from the leaves of a violet • Use coral or emerald

Warts

- Catch moonbeams in a metal basin and "wash" your hands in them saying

"I wash my hands in this thy dish
O man in the moon, do grant my wish,
And come and take this away"

- Stroke with the tail of a tortoiseshell cat in the month of May
- Apply cat's, eel's, mouse, pig or mole blood
- Rub a live frog on the wart (**a**) and then impale it on a tree to die
- Rub with bacon
- Rub the wart with a pod containing nine peas
- Rub a web on the wart then burn the web
- Rub with a gold wedding ring
- Rub the wart with the inner lining of a bean pod, throw the pod away or bury it in a secret place. As it rots, so too will the wart.
- Rub with bacon which you hide in an aspen tree
- Prick a snail using a thorn and anoint the wart with snail froth (**b**)

	• Stroke the wart with a black snail before impaling it on a tree • Wear a toad's hind leg • Pierce the wart with a gooseberry thorn • Stick a pin in the ground • Touch the hand of a corpse • Use lizards • Use ash or elder trees
Weakness	• Swallow live frogs
Whitlows	• Use lilies
Whooping cough	• Swallow nine hairs from the tail of a black cat • Drink milk that has been sipped by a ferret or a fox • Put a trout's head into a patient's mouth • Drink beer in which a trout has been drowned • Drink milk in which live trout have swum • Drink milk from a cup made from holly wood • Eat frog soup • Eat owl egg broth • Inhale horse breath • Be breathed on by a sheep • Hang a snail in a tree or in the chimney

- Wear a nest of mice in a bag around the neck
- Wear a caterpillar in a bag about your neck
- Wear a snakeskin
- Wear the shoelaces or garters of godparents
- Crawl through an arch made from brambles
- Sit on the back of a donkey that circles nine times
- Pass under the belly of a donkey and over its back
- Use amber or coral

Worms
- Eat a single horse hair with bread and butter

SPELLS PREVENTING ILLNESS

Just as there were many spells for curing illness, so too
there were spells for preventing it. Listed here are some
common ailments and spells once used for their
prevention.

WARNING

Remember that these methods of "prevention",
though traditionally believed to be of value, are often
highly unpleasant and may even be dangerous or
deadly.

**Information provided here is for reference only.
Under no circumstances should you attempt to
use these spells for preventing disease.**

Asthma	● Wear amber on your throat
Bleeding	● Wear bloodstone
Cancer	● Eat raw beets each day
Catarrh	● Wear a piece of amber on your throat
Cholera	● Carry an acorn ● Wear malachite
Colds	● Wear a necklace of blue beads ● Eat whole chilli peppers ● Catch a falling oak leaf

Convulsions	• Children wearing a necklace of beads made from peony root are protected
Cramp	• Carry a hare's foot • Leave your shoes in the shape of a "T" at night • Wear a ring made from the hinge of a coffin • Keep a bowl of water under the bed • Keep a rusty iron sword under the bed
Deafness	• Wear amber
Disease in general	• Wear a chameleon charm • Hang a cut onion in the room
Dropsy	• Wear jacinth (zircon)
Drunkenness	• Eat large quantities of lettuce • Drink an infusion of orange peel • Wear amethyst • Carry a piece of hazel cut at midnight on Halloween
Epilepsy	• Carry the right hoof of a donkey • Wear the body of a dried frog about your neck in a silk bag

	• Wear powdered frog livers about you neck in a silk bag • Eat owl egg broth • Wear coral or jet
Eye diseases	• Wear an emerald
Faintness	• Wear an emerald
Fever	• Carry a snake's tooth • Wear blue threads around your neck • Look into marigold for a long time first thing in the morning • Wear agate, carnelian or jacinth (zircon)
Hay fever	• Wear amber on your throat
Headache	• Wear a castoff snakeskin inside your hat • Wear agate or turquoise
Indigestion	• Wear amber or carnelian
Infection	• Keep an orange stuck with cloves • Hold a piece of amber in your mouth to stop infection spreading • Wear carbuncle
Inflammations	• Wear a necklace of blue beads

	● Wear garnet
Insomnia	● Use an infusion of primrose heads ● Drink tea made from violet leaves
Memory loss	● Wear emerald
Nausea	● Carry dried parsley ● Use rosemary wood
Nerve pain	● Wear white carnelian
Oversleeping	● Eat hare's brains in wine
Plague	● Wear a spider in a walnut shell around your neck ● Wear amber, carbuncle, diamond jacinth (zircon), or sardonyx
Pleurisy	● Wear rabbit-skin socks
Rheumatism	● Wear a castoff skin of a snake around your leg ● Carry a hare's foot ● Have two turtle doves nest near your house ● Carry the knucklebone of a sheep ● Carry a shrew in your pocket ● Leave your shoes in the shape of a "T" at night

	• Wear white carnelian or malachite • Wear a sprig of rowan (mountain ash)
Saddle sores	• Carry some elder wood when riding
Sciatica	• Carry the knucklebone of a sheep
Stomach trouble	• Wear aquamarine, carbuncle, jacinth (zircon) or ruby
Teething in children	• Children wearing a necklace made from the root of a peony are protected
Throat disease	• Wear carbuncle or cat's-eye
Toothache	• Wear the tooth taken from the skull of a dead man • Always put your left shoe on first • Bite a piece of iron before Easter
Whooping cough	• Wear coral

SPELLS OF EMPOWERMENT

Spells used to dispel anger

For this spell the witch needed to be outside, near flowing water, in a quiet place where he or she wouldn't be disturbed.

1 Get into the right frame of mind, perhaps by meditating.
2 Find a black stone.
3 Cast your magic circle.
4 Pick up the black stone and touch it to your forehead. Focus on sending all your anger into the black stone until you feel you have no more anger to send.
5 Throw the stone into the water, if possible, where no one will find it. You may want to say something as you do this, such as

> *Anger in this stone*
> *Now is gone*
> *Where none shall find it*
> *Water bind it*

6 Place both palms on the ground and envisage your magic circle fading.

Spell used to understand the language of animals included the following:

1 On October 27th, enter a forest with two friends.
2 Catch an animal.
3 Take it home and eat it along with the heart of a fox.

Spells used to improve life included

1 Create the right environment, a place where you won't be disturbed.
2 Read the information about the four elements in the section on Correspondences. Decide which of the four elements best represents your current needs.
3 Assemble your equipment (candles in appropriate colors, incense, etc.) and a small knife or toothpick.
4 Get into the right frame of mind, perhaps by meditating.
5 Ritually cleanse your working area.
6 Cast your magic circle.
7 Turn to the north and imagine all things associated with it, then to the east, south and west. Each time, try to imagine those things associated with each element.
8 Raise a candle to the element that best represents your needs. Mark your initial into the candle using the toothpick or knife. Repeat an affirmation like the one here, three times.

Candle burn, candle burn So I turn
Candle bright, candle bright
Turn me now towards the light

9 Thank each of the four elements, snuff out your candle and imagine your magic circle fading.
10 Ground yourself once more, perhaps by eating or drinking something.
11 Each day light your special candle, each time repeating your chant three times. Allow the candle to burn down completely.

Spells used to ensure any favor was granted for you included the following:

Mix up some of the powder described here and sprinkle it at your feet.

1 Pick some sage when the sun is passing through the sign of Leo.
2 Grind the sage into a powder.
3 Place the powder in a pot and bury the pot in a dung heap for 30 days.
4 After 30 days, dig up the pot. The powder will have turned to worms.
5 Burn the worms between two red hot bricks and crumble into powder.

Spells used to double your money included

1 Take a hair from the vulva of a mare in heat saying "Drigne, Dragne, Dragne"
2 Fill an earthenware pot with water from a spring.
3 Put the hair into the pot, put the lid on, and bury the pot for nine days.
4 On opening the pot you will find a small snake. When the snake rears up at you, say, "I accept the pact."
5 Put the snake in a box made from new pine and feed it each day on wheat husks.

Whenever you want gold or silver, simply put some coins in the box and fix the lid closed for three hours. On opening the box you will find your money has doubled. You will never be able to obtain more than 100 coins at any one time (unless the snake appears with a human face, in which case you may get up to a thousand coins.)

Methods to gain the power of prophecy included

- Eating an eel heart
- Swallowing a mole's heart
- Placing a moonstone in your mouth during a waning moon
- Placing mimosa under your pillow for prophetic dreams

Gain the power to open locks by magic by

- Using vervain or moonwort
- Placing the root of a lotus reed beneath your tongue and saying, "Ssgn, Arggis" at the door. It would be magically unlocked.

Methods to become more intelligent included

Drawing the following charm on a brass plate, using saffron paste as ink. Lick it every morning for seven days.

٦٣	٩١	٣٨	٣٩
٦	٣	٣٠	٩٤
٩٠	٦٣	٩	١
٣	٤	٦٥	٦٩

Gain the power to see in the dark by

- Washing your face in bat's blood
- Eating carrots

Be unbeatable at gambling games by

- Carrying a badger's tooth

Methods to give you courage

- Eating a bear's heart
- Using thyme

Method to give you strength was

- Rubbing leeks over your body

Way to endow you with magic powersincluded

- Carrying the bones of a frog that has been ritually killed

Way to be charming and persuasive included

- Kissing the Blarney Stone in Ireland

Method to enable you to walk on water included

- Creating an amulet by writing the letters "XD" on a piece of lead plate, then placing it on your belt and you would be able to walk on water.

Methods to increase your vocal skills included

- Eating three lark's eggs before church on Sunday morning.

- Eating nightingale's tongues
- Drinking liquid made from crushed crickets

Success in battle could be had by

- Carrying an owl's heart
- Binding a diamond to your left side.

Ways to conjure rain included

- Using jasper
- Holding a cockerel in the flames of a brazier

Way to get supernatural assistance

- Tossing a stone with a hole in it into a churchyard.

Method to insure a good crop included

- Burying a copy of this charm (*below*) in a field or garden where the crop was planted.

٢	٢٠	٣	٨
٢	٢	٨٢	٢٢
٢٤	٤٢	٩	١
٢	٧	٢٢	٢٥

GEMSTONES USED FOR EMPOWERMENT

Quality	Gemstone	Quality	Gemstone
Athleticism	agate	Long life	agate
Cheerfulness	garnet		pearl
	emerald	Modesty	white coral
Compassion	amber	Poise	crystal
Confidence	carnelian	Prosperity	aquamarine
Contentment	amethyst	Serenity	amethyst
	jacinth		crystal
	(zircon)	Sincerity	amethyst
	ruby	Strength	emerald
Courage	bloodstone		lodestone
	diamond	Success	aquamarine
	ruby		carbuncle
Eloquence	agate		emerald
	emerald	Wealth	pearl
	sardonyx		sapphire
Energy	sapphire	Wisdom	amber
Fertility	agate		aquamarine
Fortitude	black coral		coral
	diamond		emerald
	emerald		lodestone
Health	agate		sapphire
	lodestone	Wit	emerald
	malachite		
	pearl		
	sapphire		
Honesty	emerald		
Hope	opal		
Insight	ruby		
Inspiration	chrysolite		
Intuition	lodestone		

EVIL SPELLS

Methods to turn someone into stone included

1 Writing the name "HUGH" on a laurel leaf followed
  by the person the witch wished to enchant.
2 Buryingit in the victim's garden.

Methods to deprive someone of wealth included

1 Gathering dust from an anthill at night
2 Saying "ANVH", throwing it in the victim's face.

Methods to cause discord included

1 Scratching the following charm onto a piece of
  lead using an iron point., and then wearing it in a
  pouch around the neck.

> H D H D H
> I D I D I
> D H D H D
> D I D I D

2 Two people would start fighting if the words
  "ROUDMO" and "PHARRHUA" were shouted
  seven times to the four quarters of the globe.
3 Saying the victim's names under your breath, and
  repeating the words "Fight, fight, Roudmo."

To stop the fight, the witch said, "Omdor."

Method to send a plague to attack someone by

1 Putting nail clippings from more than one person into a pot.
2 Burying the pot in a cemetary saying, "ASHUTI KKTHUS."
3 Digging up the pot and burying it in a place the witch was sure had never been trodden on by horses, and leaving it there for three days.
4 After three days the nail parings would have turned to dust. By scattering them to the wind, it was believed that they would carry a plague to the victim.

Force people to reveal their secrets to you by

Placing the tongue of a frog on them while they are sleeping.

Ways to make someone the object of ridicule

1 Obtaining the bone of a rhinoceros.
2 Repeating this mantra over the bone, 1000 times:

ONG, MUNG, MUNG, MUNG, OATKUNG, THATHA

3 Burying the bone either at a crossroads or at the house of the witch's victim.

The victims were meant to lose the power of speech and only be able to make the noise of a ram, causing them to be riduculed wherever they went. The spell was broken by digging up the bone.

Methods to ward off evil spells included

Washing your hands with urine in the morning.

DEATH SPELLS

Examples of death spells

- One of the most simple death spells was to take something from the intended victim and bury it in an existing grave.
- Another spell involved making a wax image of the person intended to die and inflicting wounds on it. These wounds were believed to be reproduced at a distance, by occult transmission, causing the victim the same agonies. Two examples are shown *below, right*.
- Another method was to pierce a human heart with pins.
- Another method involved drawing a charm like the example (*below*). In each of the triangles the witch wrote the name of the enemy he or she wished to kill.

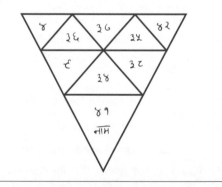

Voodoo method for casting a death spell

1 Using incantation, the voodoo sorcerer produced an image of his victim in a bucket of water.
2 The sorcerer stabbed the reflection of his victim, using a knife.

If the spell was successful, the water in the bucket became red, as if with blood.

Using a wax image to cast a death spell

Method one
1 A wax image was made.
2 On the head, the name of the person was written.
3 On the ribs, the words "ailif, casyl, zaze, hit, mel, meltat" were written.
4 The image was buried.

Method two
1 Nail parings, saliva or hair from the victim was taken and mixed with wax from a honeycomb.
2 An image was made of the victim.
3 The image was slowly roasted over a flame each night for a week while saying,"I am not burning wax; I am burning the heart, the liver, the body of (name of the victim)."
4 On the seventh night, the figure was completely melted.

GLOSSARY OF MAGIC

Abracadabra A magic word perhaps derived from the name of the demon Abraxas. In numerology, the letters in the name Abraxas add up to 365, the number of days of the year.

Air signs The *zodiac* signs Gemini, Libra and Aquarius, all of which are associated with the *element* Air.

Alchemy The practice of turning base metals into gold but also of attaining spiritual perfection.

Amulet A *charm* with magic power, made from a substance that protects against evil, such as wood, stone or metal and inscribed with magical characters or figures. They may be used to invoke the help of *spirits* and divert evil from the wearer but do not necessarily attract luck to the wearer or endow them with magical qualities.

Angel A form of good *spirit* residing in heaven.

Anima Female spirituality.

Animus Male spirituality.

Asson A rattle used by *voodoo priests* and *priestesses* to summon the *loa*, one of many vodoun gods.

Athame A black-handled knife used by *witches* in magic ceremonies.

Augur Aristocrat living in ancient Rome, divining the future for government officials.

Babalawo A priest of the highest order belonging to the Santería religion, similar to vodoun, with magic powers, including the ability to heal the sick, divine the future and punish wrongdoers.

Bakor Also known as a *boko*, this is a *houngan* involved in *black magic*.

Besom Also called a *broomstick*, this is a tool used by *witches* to help them fly. Modern witches use a besom for ritual cleaning.

Birth number An unchangeable number which, according to numerologists, reveals the influence of numbers at the time of birth.

Black Book Book kept by the master of a *coven* into which the names of newly-initiated *witches* were written during the medieval *sabbat*.

Black Books Also called *grimoires*, these are handbooks of magic in which the names of *demons* are often set out, with instructions for their invocation and *exorcism*.

Black cakes Cakes made from black millet and the flesh of unbaptized infants, believed to be presented to *the Devil* by *witches* during a medieval *sabbat*.

Black Magic Magic used for evil purposes.

Black magician A *magician* who practices magic for the purposes of evil. In medieval times such a person may have been called a *sorcerer*.

Black Mass A *Black Magic* ceremony in which a perversion of the Roman Catholic Mass is used.

Black witch A *witch* who practices magic for the purposes of evil. In medieval times such a person may have been called a *sorcerer*. In the Santería religion a black witch (also known as a *mayombero*) is a *santero* who specializes in *necromancy*, revenge and the destruction of human life.

Blasting rod Also called a *rod* or *wand*, this is a tool used by *witches* and *magicians* for conjuring and directing energy.

Boko Also known as a *bakor*, this is a *houngan* involved in *Black Magic*.

Bokor A voodoo *sorcerer*.

Book of Shadows Also known as the *Book of Spells,* this is a book used by modern *witches* for recording *spells* and rituals, magic diagrams, recipes and anything associated with their art.

Book of Spells Also known as the *Book of Shadows,* this is a book used by modern *witches* for recording *spells* and rituals, magic diagrams, recipes and anything associated with their art.

Broomstick Also called a *besom,* this is a tool used by *witches* to help them fly. Modern witches use a broomstick for ritual cleaning.

Cabala Also known as the kabala, *kabbalah* and *qabalah,* this is an ancient Hebrew mystical doctrine, elements of which are sometimes used in *witchcraft*.

Cardinal signs Signs of the *zodiac* Aries, Cancer, Libra and Capricorn which, according to astrologers, are believed to use their abilities to achieve ambitions.

Cauldron Associated with medieval *witches,* this is a large iron pot into which poisons, ointments and *philtres* were brewed.

Celtic Tree Alphabet Also known as *Ogham staves* or Ogam staves, this is an ancient alphabet consisting of 25 symbols, described by Robert Graves in *The White Goddess* and used by modern *druids* for *divination*.

Censer Used by *witches* and *magicians,* this is a small container used to burn incense, herbs, chemicals, wood, etc.

Chalice Used in modern *witchcraft,* this is a cup or goblet often associated with the *element* Water.

Charm Anything that protects against evil.

Charm wand A glass rod resembling a walking stick, filled with seeds, used to protect a house from evil *spirits*.

Circle of Being The name used by some modern *witches* to describe a *magic circle*.

Cone of power Also known as *raising the power,* this is a heightening of awareness brought about in modern *witch* ceremonies by chanting and dancing.

Conjure man Also called a *witch doctor*, *jujuman, root* *doctor*, *obeahaman* and *leaf doctor,* this is a priest and physician called upon by African tribal members and followers of religions such as vodoun, Santería and macumba. Conjure men practitioners who use their powers only for good are known as *ngangas*.

Cord A ceremonial cord made from silk, other natural material or nylon, used by some modern *witches*.

Correspondences A system used by *magicians* for relating things—especially, planets, *elements*, signs of the *zodiac* and numbers—to each other.

Coven A group of *witches*.

Cunning folk Also known as *white witches,* these were medieval witches believed to practice magic for the purposes of good rather than evil.

Dedication A term used by some *witches* for initiation.

Demon An evil *spirit* that may take many different forms. In Western tradition they are sometimes referred to as *infernal spirits* and have been said to exist in hundreds of thousands. In other traditions they are thought to exist in billions.

Demonic possession Possession by a *demon,* sometimes resulting in strange behaviour such as the vomiting of strange objects.

Deosil Clockwise.

Devas Water *elementals* who live in streams, rivers, clouds and mists.

Devil's grease Also known as *unguentum sabbati* or *witches' salve,* this is a lotion believed to have been used by medieval *witches* to enable them to fly. The principal ingredient was thought to be infant flesh.

Devil's mark A mark given to *witches* by *the Devil* during their initiation. (Note, this is different from a *witch's mark*).

Devil, the God's adversary, also called *Satan Lucifer* (the name he was given before he was thrown out of heaven for opposing God), *Satan* or *Lucifer*. The worst of all *demons,* he is portrayed in many different forms, often as a black goat, or with three horns, the taloned feet of a bird of prey, the claws of an alligator and a second face where his genitals would be.

Dianus Also known as the *Horned God* or *Janu,* this is a fertility god worshiped by some modern *witches* who claim there is no relationship between this deity and *the Devil*.

Divination Ascertaining future events by magical means.

Drawing down the Moon A term used by some modern *witches* for the casting of a *magic circle*.

Druids Celtic people who, in Europe in ancient times, acted as judges, lawmakers and priests and practiced *divination*. Druids today use the *Ogham script* as a means of divination.

Dukkerin Also known as *dukkering,* this is the term used by Romany peoples for *divination*.

Earth Mother Also known as the *Great Mother,* this is a deity worshiped by some modern *witches*.

Earth signs The *zodiac* signs Taurus, Virgo and Capricorn, all of which are associated with the *element* Earth.

Ebbos In the Santería religion this is a counter *spell* cast by a *santero*.

Effigy Also called a *fith-fath*, this is a doll-like image of a person made using material such as wax, clay or straw and used by *witches* and *magicians* for inflicting injury or death or for healing purposes. They are particularly important in love an death *spells*.

Element One of four elements, Earth, Air, Fire or Water, believed to be particularly significant to magic ritual, for hundreds of years linked to other things (such as the planets and the signs of the *zodiac*), using a system of *correspondences*.

Elementals Disembodied beings that have no *spirit* and

consist mainly of etheric forces. They are also sometimes called *sprites*. Elementals are unpredictable and may be cruel. Short-lived artificial elementals may be created by magicians from emotions such as lust, hate and vengeance. Such elementals appear as half-humans or animals and are used to accomplish evil. Incubi and succubi are the spirit elementals of sex.

Elixir of Life Also known as the *Philosopher's Stone*, this was a substance alchemists attempted to make in order to restore youth, prolong life and turn metals into gold.

Esbat One of thirteen modern *witch* rituals carried out during a full-moon.

Evil Eye Also known as *overlooking* or *fascinating* this is a woldwide belief in the ability of some people (especially *witches*) and animals to bring about harm by looking at someone.

Exorcism A ritual performed to expel an evil *spirit*.

Familiar A low-ranking *demon* given to a *witch* by *the Devil* for the purpose of strengthening the witch's power. In medieval times familiars were commonly thought to be animals such as cats, dogs, rabbits and toads. In shamanism, a familiar is a *spirit* who protects a *shaman* from illness and unfriendly forces and is also known as a *totemic animal*, *guardian spirit*, *power animal*, or *tutelary spirit*.

Fairies Air *elementals* who live in light and thought.

Fascinating Also known as having the *Evil Eye* or *overlooking*, this is a woldwide belief in the ability of some people (especially *witches*) and animals to bring about harm by looking at someone.

Fates Air *elementals* who live in light and thought.

Fire signs The *zodiac* signs Aries, Leo and Sagittarius, all of which are associated with the *element* Fire.

Fith-fath Also called an *effigy*, this is a doll-like image of a person made of material such as wax, clay or straw and used by *witches* and *magicians* for inflicting injury or death or for healing purposes. They are particularly important in love an death *spells*.

Fixed signs Signs of the *zodiac* Taurus, Leo, Scorpio and Aquarius, which, according to astrologers, are believed to hold on to what they have and resist change.

Flying ointment Known as *Devil's grease, unguentum sabbati* or *witches' salve,* this is a lotion believed to have been used by medieval *witches* to enable them to fly. The principal ingredient was thought to be infant flesh.

Ring of gyges A magic ring believed to make the wearer invisible.

Gematria A magico-philosophical science of numbers found in the *Kabala* and based on the 22 letters of the Hebrew alphabet.

Gibbous Moon Also called a *humped* Moon this is when the Moon appears between half and full.

Gnomes Earth *elementals* who live in stones and trees.

Great Mother Also known as the *Earth Mother,* this is a deity worshiped by some modern *witches*.

Gremlin A mythical creature believed to tamper with all kinds of machinery.

Grimoires Also called *Black Books*, these are handbooks of magic in which the names of *demons* are often set out, with instructions for their invocation and *exorcism*.

Guardian spirit Also known as a *power animal*, *tutelary spirit*, *totemic animal* or *familiar,* this is a *spirit* who protects a *shaman* from illness and unfriendly forces.

Gypsy wise women Gypsy women with the power of *divination*.

Hakata Bones, dice, seeds or shells which, in religions such as vodoun, are used by a *witch doctor* for *divination*.

Hand of Glory The hand of a hanged man which, when dried according to specific ritual, can be used to cast a *spell* on others in which they fall into a death-like trance.

Hedgewitch A *witch* who practices alone rather than in a *coven*.

Hex Another word for *witchcraft*, sometimes used to mean a *spell* or the sign of a star within a circle often painted on barn doors, perhaps as a means of warding off the *Evil Eye*.

Hexagram A six-pointed star, also known as the *Star of David*, used in magic (especially *Black Magic*), representing the balance between masculine and feminine.

Horned God Also known by some as *Dianus* or *Janu* this is a fertility god worshiped by some modern *witches* who claim there is no relationship between this deity and *the Devil*.

Houngan Also known as a *voodoo priest*, *papa* or *papa-loa*, in the vodoun religion this is a man who summons vodoun gods in order to divine the future or heal. A houngan involved in *Black Magic* is known as a *bakor* or *boko*.

Humped Moon Also known as a *gibbous Moon*, this is when the Moon appears between half and full.

Incubus A *demon* sent by *the Devil* to have sexual intercourse with sleeping women. Incubi are sex *elementals* and may be half human, half animal.

Infernal hierarchy A proposed hierarchy for the *demons* in Hell.

Infernal spirit Another name for a *demon*, an evil *spirit* residing in Hell and which may take many different forms.

Instruments of the Art Tools used by *witches* and *magicians*.

Italeros A *babalawo* who practices *divination* using seashells.

Janu Also known as the *Horned God* or *Dianus,* this is a fertility god worshiped by some modern *witches* who claim there is no relationship between this deity and *the Devil*.

Jujuman Also called a *witch doctor*, *obeahman*, *root doctor*, *conjure man* and *leaf doctor,* this is a priest and physician called upon by African tribal members and followers of religions such as vodoun, Santería and macumba. Jujumen practitioners who use their powers only for good are known as *ngangas*.

Jinn Arab name for a *spirit*.

Kabbala Also known as the *cabala*, kabalah and *qabalah* this is an ancient Hebrew mystical doctrine, elements of which are sometimes used in *witchcraft*.

King's Evil Another name for scrofula, a disease of the glands of the neck, which, during the Middle Ages was believed to be cured by the touch of a monarch.

Kisengue A scepter (a human tibia bone wrapped in black cloth) given to a *mayombero* during his initiation ceremony.

Kiss of shame Also known as *osculum infame*, the "*obscene kiss*," the practice of kissing *the Devil's* buttocks during a medieval *sabbat*.

Leaf doctor Also called a *witch doctor*, *jujuman*, *root doctor*, *conjure man* and *obeahaman,* this is a priest and physician called upon by African tribal members and followers of religions such as vodoun, Santerîa and macumba. Leaf doctor practitioners who use their powers only for good are known as *ngangas*.

Loa The voodoo name for a god.

Lucifer Another name for *the Devil*, God's adversary, the worst of all *demons*. He is portrayed in many different forms, often as a black goat, or with three horns, the taloned feet of a bird of prey, the claws of an alligator and a second face where his genitals would be.

Lycanthrope Creatures that are half human, half animal, the most well-known of which is the werewolf.

Magic circle A circle used by *witches* and *magicians* to concentrate their powers and protect against psychic entities. Witches may call the circle the *Circle of Being*.

Magic square A square made up of smaller squares each containing a number, popular with *magicians* for making *talismans*.

Magician A man who practices magic, perhaps using the *kabbalah*.

Mam Also known as a *manman*, *mambo* or *voodoo priestess*, in the vodoun religion this is a woman who summons vodoun gods in order to divine the future or heal.

Mambo Also known as a *voodoo priestess*, *manman* or *mam*, in the vodoun religion this is a woman who summons vodoun gods in order to divine the future or heal.

Mandrake A plant with a human-shaped root believed to have particularly magical qualities.

Manman Also known as a *voodoo priestess*, *mambo* or *mam*, in the vodoun religion this is a woman who summons vodoun gods in order to divine the future or heal.

Medicine man Also called a *shaman*, this is someone with magic powers resulting from contact with the supernatural. Common in the religion of the Eskimos, Maoris, Mongolians, Polynesians and American Indians.

Mutable signs The *zodiac* signs Gemini, Virgo, Sagittarius and Pisces which, according to astrologers, are believed to be always searching and often changing.

Mayombero Also known as a *black witch*, this is a *santero* who specializes in *necromancy*, revenge and the destruction of human life.

Name number A changeable number which, according to numerologists, shows acquired or developed personality traits.

Necromancy Summoning the dead for the purposes of

divination.

Nganga A special *cauldron* which holds the magical powers and potions of a *mayombero*.

Ngangas *Witch doctors* who use their powers only for good.

Ngozi A grudge-bearing spirit in vodoun religion.

Numerology A form of *divination* in which numbers exert an influence on every facet of our lives and personality.

Nymphs Water *elementals* who live in streams, rivers, clouds and mists.

Obeahman Also called a *witch doctor*, *jujuman*, *root doctor*, *conjure man* and *leaf doctor*, this is a priest and physician called upon by African tribal members and followers of religions such as vodoun, Santería and macumba. Obeahman practitioners who use their powers only for good are known as *ngangas*.

Obscene kiss Also known as *osculum infame*, the "*kiss of shame*," the practice of kissing *the Devil's* buttocks during a medieval *sabbat*.

Ogham staves Also known as Ogam staves or the *Celtic Tree Alphabet* this is an ancient alphabet consisting of 25 symbols, described by Robert Graves in *The White Goddess* and used by modern *druids* for *divination*.

Olympic spirit One of seven *spirits* (Aratron, Bethor, Hagith, Och, Ophiel, Phalec, and Phul) closely related to the seven planets.

Oracle Priest or priestess of ancient Greece with the power of prophecy.

Osculum infame Meaning the "*kiss of shame*" or the "*obscene kiss*," the practice of kissing *the Devil's* buttocks during a medieval *sabbat*.

Overlooking Also known as *fascinating* or having the *Evil Eye*, this is a woldwide belief in the ability of some people (especially *witches*) and animals to bring about harm by looking at someone.

Pact with the Devil An agreement made by an individual with *the Devil* in which a person agrees to carry out evil deeds in return for wealth or power.

Papa Also known as a *voodoo priest*, *houngan* or *papa-loa*, in the vodoun religion this is a man who summons vodoun gods in order to divine the future or heal.

Papa-loa Also known as a *voodoo priest*, *houngan* or *papa*, in the vodoun religion this is a man who summons vodoun gods in order to divine the future or heal.

Palindromes These are words or phrases that read the same backward or forward. They were often made into magic squares and were believed to have powerful magic properties.

Pentacle A five-pointed star within a circle, used as a means of protection by *witches* and *magicians*.

Pentagram A five-pointed star used in many magic rituals including the invoking or banishing of spirits. In some positions it represents *the Devil*.

Phases of the Moon Changes in the appearance of the Moon as seen from earth.

Philosopher's mercury According to alchemists this is mercury from which earth, air, fire and water have been removed. It is associated with *prima materia*, the substance from which all other matter is composed.

Philosopher's Stone Also known as the *Elixir of Life* this was a substance alchemists attempted to make in order to restore youth, prolong life and turn metals into gold.

Philtre A love potion originally made by combining wine, herbs and drugs.

Power animal Also known as a *guardian spirit*, *tutelary spirit*, *totemic animal* or *familiar*, this is a *spirit* who protects a *shaman* from illness and unfriendly forces.

Prima materia According to alchemists this is the substance from which all other matter is composed. It was associated with *philosopher's mercury*, mercury from which Earth, Air, Fire and Water have been removed.

Puffer Alchemists who concentrated solely on turning base metals into gold. The term later came to be used to describe any kind of alchemist.

Qabalah Also known as the *cabala*, kabala or *kabbalah,* this is an ancient Hebrew mystical doctrine, elements of which are sometimes used in *witchcraft*.

Raising the power Also known as the *cone of power* this is a heightening of awareness brought about in modern *witch* ceremonies by chanting and dancing.

Resguardo In the Santería religion this is a protective *talisman* made by a *santero*.

Rod Also called a *wand* or *blasting rod*, this is a tool used by *witches* and *magicians* for conjuring and directing energy.

Root doctor Also called a *witch doctor*, *jujuman*, *conjure man*, *obeahaman* or *leaf doctor,* this is a priest and physician called upon by African tribal members and followers of religions such as vodoun, Santería and macumba. Root doctor practitioners who use their powers only for good are known as *ngangas*.

Runes Ancient symbols of Nordic and Germanic origin, used for divination.

Sabbat A seasonal festival celebrated by *witches*.

Salamanders Fire *elementals* who live in flames.

Santero A priest or priestess belonging to the Santería religion, similar to vodoun, with magic powers, including the ability to heal the sick, divine the future and punish wrongdoers. The highest order of priest is the *babalawo*.

Satan Another name for *the Devil*, God's adversary, the worst of all *demons*. He is portrayed in many different forms, often as a black goat, or with three horns, the taloned feet of a bird of prey, the claws of an alligator and a second face where his genitals would be.

Satan Lucifer Name of *the Devil* before he was thrown out of heaven for opposing God.

Seal of Solomon Also known as the *Star of Solomon*, this is a *hexagram* within a circle, used by *witches* and *magicians* to help protect against *demons*.

Shaman Sometimes called a *medicine man*, these are people who have magic powers resulting from contact with the supernatural. Common in the religion of the Eskimos, Maoris, Mongolians, Polynesians and American Indians. In some cases they may be female.

Sigil A symbol representing a *spirit*.

Sky clad Term used by modern *witches* to describe being naked.

Snakestone A naturally-occurring stone with glass-like qualities believed by some to be the hardened saliva of adders and used to protect against evil.

Sorcerer In medieval times this term was used to describe almost anyone who practiced science or set up a laboratory. Some use the term to describe a *black witch* or *black magician*.

Spell Words which when written or spoken have magic power. Some spells are cast without the use of words but usually rely on the use of special signs and rituals.

Spirit A term used to mean different things in different cultures. It may mean the independent part of a person that survives after death; in magic it tends to refer to a supernatural being without a body.

Spirits of Solomon Seventy-two *spirits* which, according to legend, were shut up in a brass vessel by King Solomon of Israel and later released by the Babylonians.

Sprite A name sometimes used for an *elemental*.

Square of Jupiter A *magic square* consisting of 16 smaller squares, which when added up horizontally, vertically or diagonally total 34. It is often used as a *talisman* where the qualities of the planet Jupiter are required.

Square of Mars A *magic square* consisting of 25 smaller squares, which when added up horizontally, vertically or diagonally total 65. It is often used as a *talisman* where the qualities of the planet Mars are required.

Square of Mercury A *magic square* consisting of 64 smaller squares, which when added up horizontally, vertically or diagonally total 260. It is often used as a *talisman* where the qualities of the planet Mercury are required.

Square of Saturn A *magic square* consisting of 9 smaller squares, which when added up horizontally, vertically or diagonally total 15. It is often used as a *talisman* where the qualities of the planet Saturn are required.

Square of Venus A *magic square* consisting of 49 smaller squares, which when added up horizontally, vertically or diagonally total 175. It is often used as a *talisman* where the qualities of the planet Venus are required.

Square of the Moon A *magic square* consisting of 81 smaller squares, which when added up horizontally, vertically or diagonally total 369. It is often used as a *talisman* where the qualities of the Moon are required.

Square of the Sun A *magic square* consisting of 36 smaller squares, which when added up horizontally, vertically or diagonally total 111. It is often used as a *talisman* where the qualities of the sun are required.

Star of David A six-pointed star (*hexagram*) used in magic (especially *Black Magic*) and representing the balance between masculine and feminine.

Star of Solomon Also known as the *Seal of Solomon*, this is a *hexagram* within a circle, used by *witches* and *magicians* to help protect against *demons*.

Succubus *Demon* sent by *the Devil* to have sexual intercourse with sleeping men, Succubi are sex *elementals* and may be half human, half animal.

Superior spirits of Hell Six of the most important *demons* of Hell (Lucifuge, Satanachia, Fleuretty, Sargatanas, Nebiros and Agaliarept) who between them are thought to command many thousands of lesser demons.

Sylphs Air *elementals* who live in light and thought.

Talisman An *amulet* engraved with characters that attract occult influences, often used to perform a specific act, such as healing. They bring good luck and avert danger. Unlike an amulet (which is passive) a talisman must be waved, kissed, touched or used in some similar way.

Totemic animal Also known as a *guardian spirit*, *power animal*, *tutelary spirit*, or *familiar* This is a *spirit* who protects a *shaman* from illness and unfriendly forces.

Tutelary spirit Also known as a *guardian spirit*, *power animal*, *totemic animal* or *familiar.* This is a *spirit* who protects a *shaman* from illness and unfriendly forces.

Undines Water *elementals* who live in streams, rivers, clouds and mists.

Unguentum sabbati Also known as *Devil's grease* or *witches' salve,* this is a lotion believed to have been used by medieval *witches* to enable them to fly. The principal ingredient was thought to be infant flesh.

Vampire Corpse that returns to life at night in order to suck people's blood.

Vévé In voodoo this is a symbol representing a god (*loa*).

Voodoo priest Also known as a *houngan*, *papa* or papa-*loa*, in the vodoun religion, this is a man who summons vodoun gods in order to divine the future or heal.

Voodoo priestess Also known as a *mambo*, *manman* or *mam* in the vodoun religion, this is a woman who summons vodoun gods in order to divine the future or heal.

Wand Also called a *rod* or *blasting rod,* this is a tool used by *witches* and *magicians* for conjuring and directing energy.

Waning Moon When the Moon is becoming increasingly less visible.

Warlock A Scottish term meaning *demon*, *wizard* or *magician* and used in medieval times to describe male *witches* but rarely used by male witches themselves today.

Water signs The *zodiac* signs Cancer, Scorpio and Pisces, all of which are associated with the *element* Water.

Waxing Moon When the Moon is becoming increasingly visible.

White Magic Magic that is performed for the purposes of good rather than evil.

White magician A *magician* who practices magic for the purposes of good.

White witch Also known as *cunning folk,* these were medieval *witches* believed to practice magic for the purposes of good rather than evil. The term is also used by some to describe a modern *witch*.

Wicca A term used by some modern *witches* to describe their cult.

Wiccecraft An Anglo-Saxon term meaning "craft of the wise."

Widdershins Counter-clockwise.

Witch From the Anglo-Saxon *wicca*, meaning "the wise one;" a person who practices *witchcraft*.

Wizard A man who practices magic.

Witchcraft From the Anglo-Saxon *wiccecraft* meaning "craft of the wise."

Witch doctor Also called an *obeahman*, *jujuman*, *root doctor*, *conjure man* and *leaf doctor,* this is a priest and physician called upon by African tribal members and followers of religions such as vodoun, Santería and macumba. Witch doctors who use their powers only for good are known as *ngangas*.

Witch's mark A place on a *witch's* body from where his or her *familiar* feeds.

Witches' salve Also known as *Devil's grease* or *unguentum sabbati,* this is a lotion believed to have been used by medieval *witches* to enable them to fly. The principle ingredient was thought to be infant flesh.

Witches' tools Items used by *witches,* including the *athame, censer, chalice, cord, pentacle* and *wand*.

Zodiac Twelve groups of stars (Aries, Taurus, Gemini, Cancer, Leo, Virgo, Libra, Scorpio, Sagittarius, Capricorn, Aquarius and Pisces) distinguished with traditional symbols.

Zombie Corpse brought back to life by a voodoo *sorcerer* (*bokor*).

GLOSSARY OF SPIRITS

This section provides a glossary of all the spirits mentioned in this book, principally those most commonly associated with Western magic. It does not include mythical creatures or any of the hundreds of spirits inherant to religion worldwide.

'Agîêl The kabbalistic spirit of the planet Saturn.

Aauoush The English name for an Arab jinn whose attribute is enmity.

Agaliarept One of the six superior spirits of Hell. A General who discerns secrets and unveils mysteries.

Agares One of the 72 spirits of Solomon who teaches all languages, causes earthquakes, brings back runaways and destroys dignities.

Aini Also known as Aym or Haborym, this is one of the 72 spirits of Solomon who gives true answers to questions, teaches cunning, and spreads destruction.

Allocen Also known as Alloien and Allocer, this is one of the 72 spirits of Solomon who provides good familiars and teaches astronomy and the liberal sciences.

Allocer Also known as Alloien and Allocen, this is one of the 72 spirits of Solomon who provides good familiars and teaches astronomy and the liberal sciences.

Alloien Also known as Allocen and Allocer, this is one of the 72 spirits of Solomon who provides good familiars and teaches astronomy and the liberal sciences.

Amduscias One of the 72 spirits of Solomon who provides good familiars, fells trees and makes musical instruments heard but not seen.

Amon One of the 72 spirits of Solomon who discerns the

past, foretells the future, reconciles friends and foes and procures love.

Amy One of the 72 spirits of Solomon who provides good familiars, teaches astronomy and the liberal sciences and who can discern treasures hidden by other spirits.

Anael An angel ruling Friday, Anael instills a passion for luxury, procures love, cures disease and provides silver.

Andras One of the 72 spirits of Solomon who is highly dangerous and may kill a magician and any of his assistants.

Andrealphus One of the 72 spirits of Solomon who teaches astronomy and geometry and everything concerning measurement. He can also transform men into birds.

Andromalius One of the 72 spirits of Solomon who locates hidden treasure, reveals thieves, returns stolen goods and discovers all wickedness.

Aratron One of the seven Olympic spirits. Aratron is ruled by the planet Saturn and confers invisibility, bestows long life, converts things to stone, provides familiars, teaches alchemy, magic and medicine, and can transform coal into treasure or treasure into coal.

Asmoday Also known as Sydonay, this is one of the 72 spirits of Solomon who must be invoked bareheaded. He confers invisibility, locates hidden treasure, guards hidden treasure and teaches arithmetic, geomancy and handicrafts.

Astaroth One of the 72 spirits of Solomon who discerns the past and present, foretells the future, discovers secrets and teaches liberal sciences. He has stinking breath which you must shield yourself from by using a magic ring.

Aym Also known as Aini or Haborym, this is one of the 72 spirits of Solomon who gives true answers to questions, teaches cunning, and spreads destruction.

Aypeos Also known as Ipes, Ayporos or Ipos, this is one of the 72 spirits of Solomon who discerns the past, present and future and confers wit and courage.

Ayporos Also known as Ipes, Ipos or Aypeos, this is one of the 72 spirits of Solomon who discerns the past, present and future and confers wit and courage.

Baal One of the 72 spirits of Solomon who confers invisibility and wisdom.

Badyoush The English name for an Arab jinn whose attribute is love.

Balam One of the 72 spirits of Solomon who discerns the past and present, foretells the future, confers invisibility and teaches wit.

Barbas Also known as Marbas, this is one of the 72 spirits of Solomon who causes and cures disease,teaches mechanics, changes men into different shapes and imparts knowledge about things that are hidden or secret.

Barbatos One of the 72 spirits of Solomon who discerns the past, foretells the future, reveals treasure that has been hidden by enchantment, reconciles friends and teaches all sciences.

Barsâbêl The kabbalistic demon of the planet Mars.

Bathin Also known as Bathym or Marthim, this is one of the 72 spirits of Solomon who reveals the value of herbs and precious stones and can transport men between countries.

Bathym Also known as Bathin or Marthim, this is one of the 72 spirits of Solomon who reveals the value of herbs and precious stones and can transport men between countries.

Beal Also known as Berith, Bofi or Bolfry, this is one of the 72 spirits of Solomon who discerns the past and present, foretells the future and turns metal into gold. However, he is a liar and must not be trusted.

Beleth Also known as Byleth, this is one of the 72 spirits of Solomon who procures love. Furious when first summoned, Beleth must be commanded into a magic triangle using a hazel wand.

Belial One of the 72 spirits of Solomon who provides good familiars causes favors of friends and foes. Belial must be made offerings and sacrifices.

Berith Also known as Beal, Bofi or Bolfry, this is one of the 72 spirits of Solomon who discerns the past and present, foretells the future and turns metal into gold. However, he is a liar and must not be trusted.

Bethor One of the seven Olympic spirits. Bethor is ruled by the planet Jupiter and obtains treasure, prolongs life to 700 years and reconciles other spirits.

Bifrons One of the 72 spirits of Solomon who teaches astrology, geometry and mathematics, and reveals the value of herbs and precious stones.

Bofi Also known as Beal, Berith or Bolfry, this is one of the 72 spirits of Solomon who discerns the past and present, foretells the future and turns metal into gold. However, he is a liar and must not be trusted.

Bolfry Also known as Beal, Bofi or Berith, this is one of the 72 spirits of Solomon who discerns the past and present, foretells the future and turns metal into gold. However, he is a liar and must not be trusted.

Botis One of the 72 spirits of Solomon who discerns the past and present and reconciles friends and foes.

Buer One of the 72 spirits of Solomon who provides good familiars, heals all diseases, teaches philosophy and logic and reveals the value of herbs.

Bune One of the 72 spirits of Solomon who answers questions, confers eloquence and wisdom and gives riches.

Byleth Also known as Beleth, this is one of the 72 spirits of Solomon who procures love. Furious when first summoned, Byleth must be commanded into a magic triangle using a hazel wand.

Caacrinolas Also known as Glasvalabolas and Caassimola, this is one of the 72 spirits of Solomon who discerns the past, present and future, confers invisibility, incites bloodshed and teaches all the arts and sciences.

Caassimola Also known as Caacrinolaas and Glasvalabolas this is one of the 72 spirits of Solomon who discerns the past, present and future, confers invisibility, incites bloodshed and teaches all the arts and sciences.

Caim One of the 72 spirits of Solomon who foretells the future and reveals the language of animals including the meaning of birdsong and the lowing of cattle.

Cassiel An angel ruling Saturday, Cassiel procures hatred and deceit, arguments and causes evil thoughts.

Cerberus Also known as Naberius, this is one of the 72 spirits of Solomon who restores lost dignities and honors and teaches arts and sciences.

Chax Also known as Shax or Scox, this is one of the 72 spirits of Solomon who provides good familiars, discovers hidden things, steals money and who will transport anything. However, he is deceptive and must be commanded into a magic triangle.

Cimeries One of the 72 spirits of Solomon who discovers buried treasure, reveals lost or hidden things, teaches grammar, logic and rhetoric, and can make men appear as soldiers.

Curson Also known as Purson, this is one of the 72 spirits of Solomon who provides good familiars, discerns the past, present and future and can conceal or reveal hidden treasure.

Danoush The English name for an Arab jinn whose attribute is passion.

Dantalian One of the 72 spirits of Solomon who knows all human thoughts and can change them at will, procures love and teaches all arts and sciences.

Decarabia One of the 72 spirits of Solomon who provides birds as familiars, discovers the virtues of herbs and precious stones.

Devil, the God's adversary, the worst of all demons. He is portrayed in many different forms, often as a black goat, or with three horns, the taloned feet of a bird of prey, the claws of an alligator and a second face where his genitals would be.

Eligor One of the 72 spirits of Solomon who causes war, discovers hidden things and procures love.

Flauros One of the 72 spirits of Solomon who discerns the past, present and future and destroys and burns enemies of the person by whom he is invoked. He is, however, deceptive, and must be commanded into a magic triangle.

Fleuretty One of the six superior spirits of Hell. A Lieutenant-general able to perform any deed during the night.

Focalor One of the 72 spirits of Solomon who has power over the winds and sea, drowns men and sinks warships.

Foraii Also known as Morax or Forfax, this is one of the 72 spirits of Solomon who provides good familiars, knows the value of herbs and gemstones, and teaches astronomy and the liberal sciences.

Foras Also known as Forcas, this is one of the 72 spirits of Solomon who confers invisibility, wit, wisdom and eloquence, reveals the value of herbs and precious stones and discovers hidden treasure and lost things.

Forcas Also known as Foras, this is one of the 72 spirits of Solomon who confers invisibility, wit, wisdom and eloquence, reveals the value of herbs and precious stones and discovers hidden treasure and lost things.

Forfax Also known as Foraii or Morax, this is one of the 72 spirits of Solomon who provides good familiars, knows the value of herbs and gemstones and teaches astronomy and the liberal sciences.

Forneus One of the 72 spirits of Solomon who procures love between enemies, teaches all arts, sciences and languages and confers a good reputation.

Furcas One of the 72 spirits of Solomon who teaches astronomy, logic, philosophy, rhetoric, chiromancy (divination by palm reading) and pyromancy (divination by fire).

Furfur One of the 72 spirits of Solomon who raises thunder, lightning and wind and procures love between and man and wife. Furfur will not open his mouth until commanded into a magic triangle.

Gaap Also known as Tap or Goap, this is one of the 72 spirits of Solomon who discerns the past, present and future, delivers familiars from the custody of other magicians, and transports men between places.

Gabriel An angel ruling Monday, Gabriel transports things, procures silver and discloses secrets.

Gamygyn One of the 72 spirits of Solomon who reveals information about those who have died in sin and teaches the liberal sciences.

Glasyalabolas Also known as Caacrinolaas and Caassimola this is one of the 72 spirits of Solomon who discerns the past, present and future, confers invisibility, incites bloodshed and teaches all the arts and sciences.

Goap Also known as Tap or Gaap this is one of the 72 spirits of Solomon who discerns the past, present and future, delivers familiars from the custody of other magicians, and transports men between places.

Gomory One of the 72 spirits of Solomon who discerns the past, present and future, discovers hidden treasure and procures the love of women.

Graphîêl The kabbalistic spirit of the planet Mars.

Gusayn Also known as Gusion, this is one of the 72 spirits of Solomon who discerns the past, present and future, answers all questions and reconciles enemies.

Gusion Also known as Gusayn, this is one of the 72 spirits of Solomon who discerns the past, present and future, answers all questions and reconciles enemies.

Haborym Also known as Aini or Aym, this is one of the 72 spirits of Solomon who gives true answers to questions, teaches cunning, and spreads destruction.

Hagenti One of the 72 spirits of Solomon who turns metal into gold and wine into water and confers wisdom.

Hagîêl The kabbalistic spirit of the planet Venus.

Hagith One of the seven Olympic spirits. Hagith is ruled by the planet Venus and converts copper into gold or gold into copper and provides a magician with other spirits.

Halpas One of the 72 spirits of Solomon who transports men to war or other places and burns towns.

Ipos Also known as Ipes, Ayporos or Aypeos this is one of the 72 spirits of Solomon who discerns the past, present and future and confers wit and courage.

Hasmâêl The kabbalistic demon of the planet Jupiter.

Hasmôdây The kabbalistic demon of the Moon.

Housh The English name for an Arab jinn whose attribute is benevolence.

Ipes Also known as Ipos, Ayporos or Aypeos, this is one of the 72 spirits of Solomon who discerns the past, present and future and confers wit and courage.

Ipos Also known as Ipes, Ayporos or Aypeos, this is one of the 72 spirits of Solomon who discerns the past, present and future and confers wit and courage.

Kapoush The English name for an Arab jinn whose attribute is neutrality.

Kedemèl The kabbalistic demon of the planet Venus.

Lerajie One of the 72 spirits of Solomon who causes wounds to putrefy and brings about battles.

Lucifer Another name for the Devil, God's adversary, the worst of all demons. He is portrayed in many different forms, often as a black goat, or with three horns, the taloned feet of a bird of prey, the claws of an alligator and a second face where his genitals would be.

Lucifuge One of the six superior spirits of Hell. A Prime Minister with power over all treasures on earth.

Malaphar Also known as Valefor, this is one of the 72 spirits of Solomon who is a thief.

Malka Betharshesîm The kabbalistic spirit of the Moon.

Malpas One of the 72 spirits of Solomon who provides good familiars and destroys the thoughts and desires of enemies.

Marbas Also known as Barbas, this is one of the 72 spirits of Solomon who causes and cures disease,teaches mechanics, changes men into different shapes and imparts knowledge about things that are hidden or secret.

Marchosias One of the 72 spirits of Solomon who gives true answers to all questions.

Marthim Also known as Bathym or Bathin, this is one of the 72 spirits of Solomon who reveals the value of herbs and precious stones and can transport men between countries.

Michael An angel governing Sunday, Michael procures wealth, makes people the recipients of favors and confers honors.

Morax Also known as Foraii or Forfax this is one of the 72 spirits of Solomon who provides good familiars, knows the value of herbs and gemstones and teaches astronomy and the liberal sciences.

Murmur One of the 72 spirits of Solomon who facilitates evocation of the dead and teaches philosophy.

Naberius Also known as Cerberus, this is one of the 72 spirits of Solomon who restores lost dignities and honors and teaches arts and sciences.

Nakîêl The kabbalistic spirit of the Sun.

Nebiros One of the six superior spirits of Hell. A Field-marshall and Inspector General who teaches the properties of metals, minerals, vegetables and animals; who discerns the location of the Hand of Glory; a necromancer who can do evil to anyone.

Nuloush The English name for an Arab jinn whose attribute is love.

Och One of the seven Olympic spirits. Och is ruled by the Sun and converts anything into gold or precious stones, provides 600 years of perfect health, bestows wisdom, teaches medicine and provides familiars or gold.

Ophiel One of the seven Olympic spirits. Ophiel is ruled by the planet Mercury and provides spirits as well as teaching all arts and alchemy.

Orias One of the 72 spirits of Solomon who transforms men and teaches about the planets.

Orobas One of the 72 spirits of Solomon who discerns the past, present and future and protects against temptation from other spirits.

Ose One of the 72 spirits of Solomon who changes men into any shape, makes men insane for about an hour, teaches liberal sciences and gives true answers to questions.

Paimon One of the 72 spirits of Solomon who provides good familiars, gives the magician power over other men and teaches the arts and sciences.

Phaleg One of the seven Olympic spirits. Phalec is ruled by the planet Mars and confers honor in war affairs.

Phoenix One of the 72 spirits of Solomon who is an excellent poet and understands all sciences.

Phul One of the seven Olympic spirits. Phul is ruled by the Moon and prolongs life to 300 years, converts all metals into silver, provides spirits and heals dropsy.

Procel Also known as Pucel, this is one of the 72 spirits of Solomon who can cause great commotion, can warm water and teaches geometry and the liberal sciences.

Pucel Also known as Procel, this is one of the 72 spirits of Solomon who can cause great commotion, can warm water and teaches geometry and the liberal sciences.

Purson Also known as Curson, this is one of the 72 spirits of Solomon who provides good familiars, discerns the past, present and future and can conceal or reveal hidden treasure.

Puyoush The English name for an Arab jinn whose attribute is goodness.

Qapush The English name for an Arab jinn whose attribute is amity.

Raphael An angel ruling Wednesday, Raphael reveals the past, present and future, pacifies judges, gives victory in war, teaches experiments and opens all locks.

Raum One of the 72 spirits of Solomon who discerns the past, present and future, procures love between friends and foes, destroys cities and steals treasure.

Roneve Also known as Ronobe or Ronove, this is one of the 72 spirits of Solomon who teaches the arts, rhetoric and languages.

Ronobe Also known as Roneve or Ronove, this is one of the 72 spirits of Solomon who teaches the arts, rhetoric and languages.

Ronove Also known as Roneve or Ronobe, this is one of the 72 spirits of Solomon who teaches the arts, rhetoric and languages.

Sabnack Also known as Saburac, this is one of the 72 spirits of Solomon who provides good familiars, inflicts wounds and sores and builds cities and buildings.

Saburac Also known as Sabnack, this is one of the 72 spirits of Solomon who provides good familiars, inflicts wounds and sores and builds cities and buildings.

Sachiel An angel governing Thursday, Sachiel procures the love of women, makes people joyful, pacifies arguments and heals the sick.

Saleos Also known as Zaleos, this is one of the 72 spirits of Solomon who procures love.

Samael An angel ruling Tuesday, Samael causes infirmity, death, war and combustion.

Sargatanas One of the six superior spirits of Hell. A Brigadier who can confer invisibility, open locks, transport anything anywhere and teach lovemaking.

Satan Another name for the Devil, God's adversary, the worst of all demons. He is portrayed in many different forms, often as a black goat, or with three horns, the taloned feet of a bird of prey, the claws of an alligator and a second face where his genitals would be.

Satan Lucifer The name of the Devil before he was thrown out of Heaven for opposing God.

Satanachia One of the six superior spirits of Hell. A Commanding-general with power over women and girls.

Scox Also known as Chax or Shax, this is one of the 72 spirits of Solomon who provides good familiars, discovers hidden things, steals money and who will transport anything. However, he is deceptive and must be commanded into a magic triangle.

Seere One of the 72 spirits of Solomon who discovers thefts and transports goods.

Shax Also known as Chax or Scox, this is one of the 72 spirits of Solomon who provides good familiars, discovers hidden things, steals money and who will transport anything.

However, he is deceptive and must be commanded into a magic triangle.

Separ Also known as Vepar, this is one of the 72 spirits of Solomon who causes storms at sea, guides battleships and causes death from infected wounds.

Shaboush The English name for an Arab jinn whose attribute is friendship.

Shêdbarshemoth Sharthathan The kabbalistic demon of the Moon.

Solas Also known as Stomas, this is one of the 72 spirits of Solomon who teaches astronomy, the virtues of herbs and the virtues of gemstones.

Sôrath The kabbalistic demon of the Sun.

Stomas Also known as Solas, this is one of the 72 spirits of Solomon who teaches astronomy, the virtues of herbs and the virtues of gemstones.

Sydonay Also known as Asmoday, this is one of the 72 spirits of Solomon who must be invoked bareheaded. He confers invisibility, locates hidden treasure, guards hidden treasure and teaches arithmetic, geomancy and handicrafts.

Sytry One of the 72 spirits of Solomon who procures love and causes women to reveal themselves naked.

Tap Also known as Gaap or Goap, this is one of the 72 spirits of Solomon who discerns the past, present and future, delivers familiars from the custody of other magicians, and transports men between places.

Taphthartharath The kabbalistic demon of the planet Mercury.

Tawayush The English name for an Arab jinn whose attribute is hatred.

Valac One of the 72 spirits of Solomon who reveals hidden treasure and delivers serpents to the magician.

Valefor Also known as Malaphar. this is one of the 72 spirits of Solomon who is a thief.

Vapula One of the 72 spirits of Solomon who teaches philosophy and science and confers skill in manual professions.

Vassago One of the 72 spirits of Solomon who discerns the past, present and future and discovers things lost or hidden.

Vepar Also known as Separ, this is one of the 72 spirits of Solomon who causes storms at sea, guides battleships and causes death from infected wounds.

Vine One of the 72 spirits of Solomon who discerns the past, present and future, reveals witches and hidden things, destroys walls and builds towers.

Vual One of the 72 spirits of Solomon who discerns the past, present and future, procures the love of women and procures friendship between foes.

Yôphîêl The kabbalistic spirit of the planet Jupiter.

Zagan One of the 72 spirits of Solomon who turns water into wine, blood into oil, oil into water, metals into coins and who confers wit.

Zaleos Also known as Saleos, this is one of the 72 spirits of Solomon who procures love.

Zâzêl The kabbalistic demon of the planet Saturn.

Zepar One of the 72 spirits of Solomon who inflames women with love for men and who can make women barren.

INDEX

Because of the large number described in this book, the names of individual spirits are not included in this index. Most can be found in chapter 2, Magic Beings.

If you liked this book, you'll love this series:

Little Giant Book of Optical Illusions • Little Giant Book of "True" Ghost Stories • Little Giant Book of Whodunits • Little Giant Encyclopedia of Aromatherapy • Little Giant Encyclopedia of Baseball Quizzes • Little Giant Encyclopedia of Card & Magic Tricks • Little Giant Encyclopedia of Card Games • Little Giant Encyclopedia of Card Games Gift Set • Little Giant Encyclopedia of Dream Symbols • Little Giant Encyclopedia of Fortune Telling • Little Giant Encyclopedia of Gambling Games • Little Giant Encyclopedia of Games for One or Two• Little Giant Encyclopedia of Handwriting Analysis • Little Giant Encyclopedia of Magic • Little Giant Encyclopedia of Mazes • Little Giant Encyclopedia of Names • Little Giant Encyclopedia of Natural Healing • Little Giant Encyclopedia of One-Liners • Little Giant Encyclopedia of Palmistry • Little Giant Encyclopedia of Spells & Magic • Little Giant Encyclopedia of Puzzles • Little Giant Encyclopedia of Superstitions • Little Giant Encyclopedia of Toasts & Quotes • Little Giant Encyclopedia of Travel & Holiday Games • Little Giant Encyclopedia of Word Puzzles • Little Giant Encyclopedia of the Zodiac

Available at fine stores everywhere.